INTERNATIONAL TRADE IN SERVICES

The American Enterprise Institute
Trade in Services Series

COMPETING IN A CHANGING WORLD ECONOMY PROJECT

Deregulation and Globalization: Liberalizing International Trade in Air Services – *Daniel M. Kasper*

Global Competition in Financial Services: Market Structure, Protection, and Trade Liberalization – *Ingo Walter*

International Trade in Business Services: Accounting, Advertising, Law, and Management Consulting – *Thierry J. Noyelle and Anna B. Dutka*

International Trade in Construction, Design, and Engineering Services – *James R. Lee and David Walters*

International Trade in Films and Television Programs – *Steven S. Wildman and Stephen E. Siwek*

International Trade in Ocean Shipping Services: The United States and the World – *Lawrence J. White*

When Countries Talk: International Trade in Telecommunications Services – *Jonathan David Aronson and Peter F. Cowhey*

International Trade in Services: An Overview and Blueprint for Negotiations – *Geza Feketekuty*

International Trade in Services

An Overview and Blueprint for Negotiations

Geza Feketekuty

An American Enterprise Institute/Ballinger Publication

Ballinger Publishing Company, Cambridge, Massachusetts
A Subsidiary of Harper & Row, Publishers, Inc.

© 1988 by the American Enterprise Institute for Public Policy Research, Washington, D.C. All rights reserved. No part of this publication may be used or reproduced in any manner whatsoever without permission in writing from the American Enterprise Institute except in the case of brief quotations embodied in news articles, critical articles, or reviews. The views expressed in the publications of the American Enterprise Institute are those of the authors and do not necessarily reflect the views of the staff, advisory panels, officers, or trustees of AEI, nor do they necessarily represent the official positions of the Office of the U.S. Trade Representative, or the U.S. Government.

"American Enterprise Institute" and ⃝ are registered service marks of the American Enterprise Institute for Public Policy Research.

International Standard Book Number: 0-88730-241-6

Library of Congress Catalog Card Number: 88-11974

Printed in the United States of America.

Library of Congress Cataloging-in-Publication Data

Feketekuty, Geza
　International trade in services: an overview and blueprint for negotiations / Geza Feketekuty.
　p. cm. — (American Enterprise Institute series on trade in services)
　Includes bibliographies and index.
　ISBN 0-88730-241-6
　1. Service Industries.　2. Service Industries—United States.　3. International trade.
I. Title.　II. Series
HD9980.5.F45　1988
658.8'48—dc19　　　　　　　　　　　　　　　　　　　　　　　　88-11974
　　　　　　　　　　　　　　　　　　　　　　　　　　　　　　　　　　CIP

CONTENTS

List of Tables — xi

Editor's Foreword — Claude E. Barfield — xiii

Foreword — William E. Brock — xvii

Chapter 1 Overview — 1

Some Examples of Trade in Services — 3
Who Buys Imported Services? — 5
How Exporters Sell Services to Foreign Customers — 12
A Buyer's Calculus: Buying Services Abroad — 16
International Trade in Services and the World
 Economy — 18
Conclusions — 23
Notes — 24

Chapter 2 The Invisibility of Trade in Services — 27

A Descriptive Model of International Trade in
 Services — 28
Consequences of the Invisibility of Trade in
 Services — 30
Conclusions — 34
Notes — 35

CONTENTS

Chapter 3   Services in the World Economy   37

A Historical Perspective   38
Global Economic Integration   39
The Information Revolution   41
Centralization of Business Services   48
Internationalization of Business Services   52
Consumer Services and International Trade   55
Conclusions   56
Notes   58

Chapter 4   The Changing Perception of Services   59

Why Services Have Been Considered Unproductive   60
The Postindustrial Services Economy   62
Why Trade in Services Was Considered an
   Oxymoron   67
Growing International Recognition of Trade in
   Services   70
Conclusions   72
Note   73

Chapter 5   Concepts, Issues, and Definitions   75

Alternative Definitions of Trade in Services   75
The Substantive Policy Debate over the Definition
   of Trade in Services   80
Conclusions   88
Notes   88

**Chapter 6   Does International Trade Theory Apply
                to Trade in Services?**   91

Normative and Descriptive Theories of
   International Trade   96
Does the Theory of Comparative Advantage Apply
   to Trade in Services?   100

Dynamic Gains and Losses from Trade in Services	115
Economic Development	119
Empirical Investigations	122
Conclusions	123
Notes	124

Chapter 7   Barriers to International Trade in Services   129

What Is a Barrier to Trade in Services?	131
Where to Expect Barriers to Trade in Services	135
What Surveys Show about Barriers	137
Reflections on the Nature of Barriers	141
Conclusions	144
Note	145

Chapter 8   Applying the Trade Policy Framework to Services   147

The Goals and Tools of Trade Policy	149
Extending the Framework to Trade in Services	160
The Relationship between Trade Policy and Regulatory Policy	169
Conclusions	174
Notes	174

Chapter 9   Bilateral Agreements with Israel and Canada: Models for a Framework Agreement   175

U.S./Israeli Agreement on Trade in Services	176
U.S./Canadian Agreement on Trade in Services	183
Conclusions	187
Notes	187

CONTENTS

Chapter 10 A General Agreement on Trade in Services 191

The Uruguay Declaration 193
The Goal of Multilateral Negotiations 200
The Basic Framework of a General Agreement on Trade in Services 205
Relationship between the GATT and the GATS 236
Conclusions 238
Notes 239

Chapter 11 Elaborating the General Agreement on Trade in Services for the Individual Sectors 241

Sectoral Annotations of a General Agreement on Trade in Services 243
Illustrative Sectoral Annotations 249
Conclusions 273
Notes 273

Chapter 12 Negotiating Strategies for Binding and Reducing Barriers to Trade in Services 275

Review of the Basic Framework 275
Negotiating Substantive Commitments on an MFN Basis 277
Negotiating Regulatory Commitments on a Conditional MFN Basis 283
Alternative Scenarios for Negotiating Barriers to Trade in Services 286
Criteria for Evaluating Alternative Negotiating Scenarios 288
Basic Ground Rules for Organizing the Negotiations 290
Conclusions 292
Notes 292

Appendix	**The History of a Campaign: How Services Became a Trade Issue**	295
	The Birth of a Concept	296
	The Effort to Negotiate on Trade in Services in the Tokyo Round	301
	Development of a Strategy to Build Support for Negotiation	305
	The OECD Study of Trade in Services	314
	The GATT Debate	318
	Notes	321
References		323
Name Index		339
Subject Index		341
About the Author		357

LIST OF TABLES

3–1	U.S. Employment, by Sector	43
3–2	Percentage Distribution of Gross National Product, by Industry, 1974–1977	45

EDITOR'S FOREWORD

The American Enterprise Institute's *Trade in Services Series* represents an important step toward creating the policy alternatives necessary to enhance the international competitiveness of American services.

The series is part of a larger, continuing AEI project, *Competing in a Changing World Economy*. Launched in 1983, this project has produced a wealth of publications, seminars, and conferences, analyzing the most significant policy challenges confronting U.S. policymakers in the areas of international trade and finance, science and technology policy, and human capital development.

Early in the project, we concluded that the United States would be successful in its drive to initiate a new round of trade negotiations with the other major trading nations, under the auspices of the General Agreement on Tariffs and Trade (GATT). We also chose to concentrate our resources on the new issues that would be placed on the table in that round: trade in services, intellectual property, and trade-related investment. In September 1986, at Punta del Este, Uruguay, the United States and the other members of GATT did indeed reach an agreement to launch a new multilateral round of trade negotiations, the Uruguay Round. Trade in services, along with intellectual property and investment issues, was included on the agenda. Hence, over the next several years negotiators in Geneva and top policy officials in all the major trading nations will face the formidable task of forging trading rules for these new issues.

In the area of services, a number of countries, including the United States, have produced individual, national studies of service trade liberalization. Yet government and private-sector officials agree that these studies are only a first step, and that substantial research remains to be done in key service sectors before major policy questions can be answered regarding a new service trade regime.

Designed to fill this policy gap, *Trade in Services* brings together eleven outstanding writers who have committed their expertise to analyzing the seven key service sector industries:

- Aviation—Daniel M. Kasper, Harbridge House

- Banking—Ingo Walter, Graduate School of Business Administration, New York University

- Construction—James R. Lee, American University, and David Walters, Staff Economist, Office of the U.S. Trade Representative

- Professional services—Thierry J. Noyelle and Anna B. Dutka, Conservation of Human Resources, Columbia University

- Shipping—Lawrence J. White, Member, Federal Home Loan Bank Board, on leave from the Graduate School of Business Administration, New York University

- Telecommunications: Information and Data Processing— Jonathan David Aronson, School of International Relations, University of Southern California, and Peter F. Cowhey, Department of Political Science, University of California at San Diego

- Telecommunications: Motion Pictures, Television, and Prerecorded Entertainment—Steven S. Wildman and Stephen E. Siwek, Economists Incorporated

In addition, Geza Feketekuty, of the Office of the U.S. Trade Representative, has written this overview volume for the series.

All of the books in the series embody two main goals: first, to analyze the dynamics of international competition for each of the seven industries, identifying existing and potential barriers to

EDITOR'S FOREWORD

trade; and second, to formulate and assess policy approaches for opening service markets through an umbrella service agreement and subsequent individual sector agreements in GATT.

A related goal is to disseminate the results of our research through conferences and seminars, televised forums, and a variety of publication formats. We aim to make our findings known to government officials, trade experts, the business and financial communities, and concerned members of the public. To that end, during 1987 we convened major conferences in London, Geneva, and Washington, and in early 1988 the team of authors traveled to Tokyo and Singapore. Thus, as with all AEI projects, we have sought to ensure that the studies not only make a significant contribution to scholarship but also become an important factor in the decision-making and negotiating processes.

In addition to the authors, who have produced outstanding books, we would like to thank John H. Jackson, Hessel E. Yntema Professor of Law at the University of Michigan, and Gardner Patterson, who for many years served in the GATT Secretariat. Both of these men provided invaluable help and guidance as advisers to the project.

—Claude E. Barfield
Coordinator
Competing in a Changing World Economy

FOREWORD

Some historians suggest that the turning of a millenium has always been an unsettled, confusing, even tumultuous time. As we approach the year 2000, the historical precedents appear to be increasingly valid as forecasts.

We are already in the midst of the most radical work force shift in our economic history. Like the industrial revolution experienced by our forebearers, this reshaping of our economic lives has substantial human consequences. Economic lives have become less predictable, less understandable, less controllable than in the past. Workers and managers alike, caught in a changing industrial system, are beset by uncertainty and a vague sense of powerlessness in the face of economic shifts beyond their ken or command.

For decades our manufacturing employment has remained relatively stable while services jobs have virtually exploded in number. It is an oft ignored fact that many of those "services" exist primarily in order to make our manufacturing firms more productive. Informatics, computer services, satellite communications, education and training, financial services, transportation, engineering, accounting—all are available as enormous assets for the U.S. industrial base to an extent equalled by no other nation in the world. Many, in fact, are specialized spin-offs from manufacturing firms of a few years ago.

It is misleading, and even dangerous, to ignore these developments or to mischaracterize them as an attack on manufacturing. Our memories cannot be so short that we forget earlier years in this century when one of every three or four citizens worked on the farm. Today one out of thirty Americans feeds not only all of our own people, but much of the rest of the world.

Similarly, we produce far more manufactured goods than did the preceding generation, and we do so more efficiently and with less "people per pound" of production. That trend will continue. We need to understand how to make it work to our benefit and how to seize the new trading and employment growth opportunity paved by a healthy services and manufacturing economy.

This book, then, is important on more than one level. In it Geza Feketekuty seeks to explain the negotiations on international trade in services currently under way in the Uruguay Round of Multilateral Trade Negotiations. In the process of examining the underlying rationale for these negotiations, however, he provides a much broader insight into the role of services in economic activity.

As United States Trade Representative from 1981 to 1985, I was deeply involved in efforts of the United States to put trade in services on the world agenda, and as Secretary of Labor more recently, I became equally involved in helping U.S. workers adjust to the new economy. I am convinced that a profound understanding of the role of services in both our economy and the world economy is required to deal intelligently with the crucial policy issues in areas such as trade, manpower retraining, labor laws, education, taxation, and regulatory reform.

Before U.S. trade officials began talking about trade in services in the early 1980s, very little was known about either the international flow of services or the new role of services as a major driving force in the domestic economy. As we began discussing trade in services, we increased public awareness of this forgotten element of the world economy and of the crucial role it plays in generating economic growth. Insights gained from an analysis of the trade dimension yielded new insights into the role of services at home.

This process, whereby international discussion of trade in services has lead to increasing public awareness of the role of services in the economy, has been fascinating to observe in many countries, including developing countries. While developing countries, for example, initially made opposition to international negotiations on trade in services a doctrinal issue, more and more of them came to see that not only could trade play an important role in their economic growth, but that their traditional neglect of the service sector created a major domestic bottleneck to economic growth.

My first effort to place trade in services on the world trade agenda in the 1982 GATT Multilateral generated considerable controversy, and the compromise we hammered out in the predawn hours—after several days of nonstop negotiations—was widely reported by the press at the time as a failure. Wrong. It set in motion a process of inquiry into the GATT that led to a decision by trade ministers four years later to include trade in services as a major negotiating item in the Uruguay Round of Multilateral Trade Negotiations. The account of how a process of intellectual inquiry and U.S. political leadership led to a collective judgment that the liberalization of trade in services was in the interest of individual countries around the globe, itself a fascinating story, is described in the appendix of this book.

Geza Feketekuty has played an important leadership role throughout the process of taking an idea and a glimmer in the eyes of a few farsighted business leaders to a negotiation on the world stage. *International Trade in Services: An Overview and Blueprint for Negotiations*—is well worth reading, both for the background it provides to the negotiations on trade in services in the Uruguay Round and the insight it offers on the issues we must confront at home in coming to terms with the new services based economy. The American Enterprise Institute is to be congratulated for its sponsorship of this book, as well as of the other books in the American Enterprise Institute Trade in Services Series.

—*William E. Brock*

1
OVERVIEW

On a recent flight from London to Hong Kong, I met a law professor from London who 1) taught English common law to French law students attending the University of London under a joint degree program with the Sorbonne, 2) was on her way to Hong Kong to teach a six-week course on international commercial law at one of the Hong Kong universities, and 3) was working on a book on international commercial law for international distribution. In the course of our conversation, after I told her about my own activities, she asked, "What is trade in services?" I pointed out to her that every one of her three activities involves trade in services.

This was not a unique incident, but revealing. Long-standing perceptions about the nature of services and their role in the world economy make it difficult even for those most intimately involved in international trade in services to perceive what they are doing in terms of trade. Most people struggle with the concept of trade in services because their mental image of trade and their mental image of services are incompatible.

The word *trade* connotes getting something from here to there. The word *services*, interpreted through the prism of daily life, evokes an image of an activity that is bound by the here and now, an activity that requires producers and consumers to be at the same place at the same time. The service that seems to come to mind most often is haircutting. If a person in need of a haircut and the barber are not in the same place at the same time, the haircut cannot be performed. In fact, most services consumed by individuals require a close proximity between the producer and the consumer, and this does seem incompatible with trade that takes place between producers and consumers in different countries. The term *trade in services* thus seems an oxymoron, a term that contains an internal contradiction. The impression that trade in services is not really possible, and if possible could not be very large, is not merely an opinion of uninformed people. Until recently, this was the opinion of most government officials, professors of economics, and business executives, even those who were making a living selling services to foreigners.

The conceptual problem disappears once we recognize that there are various ways of preserving the proximity required between producers and consumers of services. The English law professor cited above used different means for delivering services to the three user groups. The French law students crossed the English channel so they could attend her law courses (buyer travels to seller). In contrast, her students in Hong Kong remained in place, and she flew to Hong Kong to teach them (seller travels to buyer). In her third activity involving trade in services, neither she nor the readers of her book on international commercial law had to travel, since the necessary proximity was created through the intermediation of an information medium, namely the book (the product "travels" from seller to buyer).

The example illustrates another important point about trade in services: Most services that are produced in close proximity to consumers also have close substitutes that are supplied indirectly. The substitutes may be not exactly like the real thing, but a workable alternative that can fulfill many of the same needs. Listening to a record in one's home may not be the same thing as attending a live concert, but it can be a satisfactory alternative. Reading a book may not be the same thing as talking with the author, but it may be almost as informative. Lugging a television set to the shop or shipping it back to the factory may be far less convenient than having a repairman come to one's home, but it will ultimately accomplish what is needed, which is to get the TV to work. Alternatives are available even for more personal services, including haircuts.

The issue of haircuts seems to come up in most discussions of trade in services, even in the deliberations of seasoned officials on the subject. On one occasion, the Swiss delegate to the Trade Committee of the Organization for Economic Cooperation and

Development dismissed trade in services by pointing out how impossible it was for him to have his hair cut by a barber in another country. The chairman of the committee, who happened to be a woman delegate from Germany, replied that every woman in Germany had benefited enormously from French exports of hairdressing services, and she was confident that the delegate's wife would confirm the same was true in Switzerland.

What the chairman of the Trade Committee meant was that hairdressing services in Germany benefited enormously from French exports of information about hairdressing techniques and hairstyles. Haircutting services involve not only the physical activity of cutting hair, but also the application of information about hairstyles, and to a woman the information available to her hairdresser on hairstyles is as critical as the physical act of cutting her hair.

SOME EXAMPLES OF TRADE IN SERVICES

A discussion of trade in services is best started with a large number of examples.

The following people are all exporting services:

1. An advertising executive developing a TV commercial for a foreign client
2. A secretary at a law firm answering a call from a foreign client
3. A cabby who drives a foreign businessman from the airport to the hotel
4. The cast of a television show that will be broadcast abroad
5. A doctor operating on a foreign patient
6. The doorman and the bartender at a posh hotel serving foreign guests

7. An accountant unraveling the financial affairs of a foreign corporation
8. An engineer designing a bridge to be built in another country
9. A caterer preparing a meal to be served at a foreign embassy
10. A management consultant advising a foreign client

The following persons or companies are all importing services:

1. Every reader of this book who has taken a foreign vacation
2. An auto company that asks a foreign firm to design a new model
3. Someone who buys a ticket to a performance by a foreign orchestra
4. A student attending a foreign university
5. A businessman who extracts information from a foreign data base
6. A housewife who goes to "Jean Pierre" for the latest French hair styling
7. A consumer who has a camera repaired abroad
8. An investor who buys securities at a foreign stock exchange
9. The actress who has her legs insured in London with a Lloyd's broker
10. A traveler who uses a credit card issued by a foreign bank

Obviously, the range of activities that lead to international trade in services is wide. In many cases the persons involved are likely to be only dimly aware that they are exporting or importing services and that their economic interests are tied to policies and events that influence trade in services.

Undoubtedly, a number of the examples will raise a question in the reader's mind, "Is this really trade?" Chapter 5 is devoted to the definition of trade in services and the ragged edges around that definition. For this initial discussion, we will adopt a simple convention: Services bought from or sold to foreigners constitute trade in services.

WHO BUYS IMPORTED SERVICES?

Most services produced in an economy are purchased by individual consumers, while most imported services are purchased by business. The services most commonly purchased by consumers from foreigners—tourism, education, and entertainment—usually involve international travel, since consumption of these services requires close proximity to producers. In contrast, many of the services purchased by business can be produced at a distance and this opens up greater opportunities for trade. The large corporations that buy services around the world operate in an environment that is very difficult for an individual to comprehend on the basis of personal experience.

In order to understand trade in services and why it is so important, one needs to understand how commercial enterprises use imported services to supply the goods and services we buy as final consumers. At the same time, most people buy many more imported services than they realize.

Purchases of Imported Services by Consumers

Consider the following list of services consumed by the average person: the daily commute by bus or train, a haircut or shoeshine, a doctor's visit, a church service, a call to a travel agent for information on airline schedules, a theater performance or ballet, the radio news, a television program, a movie, insurance on life, health, home, and the family car, a bank check, a course in horticulture or judo wrestling, dinner at a restaurant, a football game. On the face of it this list does not seem to offer extensive possibilities for trade. Yet, the judo instructor could have learned his skills in Japan, the restaurant's cook could have been trained in China, the dance company could be from Russia, the hairdresser could be using hair styles shown in a French trade magazine, the movie could be from Italy, the television program could be from England, and the discussion with the travel agent could involve a vacation in Tahiti.

The average consumer is most likely to purchase imported services in connection with international travel. A foreign vacation constitutes a bundle of imported services, including air transport on a foreign airline and hotel, restaurant, entertainment, tour guide, financial, car rental, insurance, air reservation, communication, taxicab, and film processing services.

Entertainment represents another major category of imported services purchased by individual consumers. French TV viewers watching an American program such as *Dallas* or American TV viewers watching a British program such as *Upstairs, Downstairs* are consuming imported entertainment services. Every New Yorker who attends a performance by the Bolshoi Ballet, or a performance by a Nepalese dance group, or a soccer match between Brazil and Britain, or an international beauty contest is consuming imported services.

Education is another imported service that is frequently purchased by individual consumers. Since time immemorial, young people have gone abroad to attend a foreign university, to study with world famous artists, musicians, and scientists, or to learn by seeing the world. Nearly one of every five American university students attends a foreign university at one point in his or her education. Forty percent of all graduate students and 60 percent of all graduate engineering students in American universities are from other countries.

Other imported services purchased by individual consumers include medical services such as a heart transplant operation performed in a foreign hospital, financial services such as those associated with a secret account in a foreign bank or a credit card issued by a foreign company, and legal services provided in connection with the purchase of a vacation property in a foreign resort or in connection with the settlement of the last will and testament of a foreign relative.

Most international trade in services that are purchased directly by individual consumers involves international travel by either the consumer or the producer. Tourists who visit a foreign country, students who attend a foreign university, and patients who go abroad for treatment in foreign hospitals import services by traveling to another country to be in close proximity to the producers of desired services.

Producers of services to be traded internationally often have to go abroad to render the service—doctors to treat famous patients or to teach, an orchestra to play guest performances, a beauty queen to participate in a beauty contest, or a sports team to play a game. Someone who wants to open a secret Swiss bank account might succeed in doing so by mail, but probably only if well known in banking circles; the average person will have to make a personal appointment with a Swiss banker.

This raises a question: Is there real trade if either the producer or the consumer travels to another country? The answer is that transactions between people who normally live in different countries are usually considered trade. As long as Joe Smith normally lives in France, any money he spends outside France for either goods or services is counted as French imports, and any money he earns from selling either goods or services outside France is counted as French exports, even if he is an American citizen. Services purchased abroad result in an expenditure of foreign exchange just like imports of goods, and income derived from services delivered abroad results in foreign exchange earnings just like exports of goods.

Another way to explain the basic idea is that purchases made abroad by tourists, students, or patients have to be paid out of funds earned in the country where they normally live, and income earned abroad by musicians, professionals, or workers who remain abroad only a short time will be available to be spent in the country where they normally live. Statisticians who compile the national income accounts therefore treat all income earned by residents as part of national income, even if the work was performed abroad (see Chapter 4).

Purchases of Imported Services by Business Enterprises

Every commercial enterprise, whatever it produces, needs a large number of service inputs in running the business. It needs the services of accountants, tax advisers, management experts, market analysts, personnel managers, lawyers, economists, computer programmers, system analysts, salesmen, statistical analysts, and financial experts. Those enterprises that build their own physical facilities need the services of architects, engineers, interior decorators, landscape designers, electricians, and those who repair, maintain, and clean the facilities.

A company that produces services as outputs also needs a wide variety of services as inputs, some of which require specialized knowledge. A beauty parlor, for example, needs service inputs from experts on the latest trends in hair styles. A bank needs service inputs from experts in every type of financial transaction desired by customers, from foreign exchange trading and export financing to mortgage financing.

A manufacturing company needs the service inputs of research scientists, engineers, and industrial designers to develop new products and the service inputs of many different kinds of engineers to design the machinery and production process. The trend in recent years has been toward increased demand for service inputs by business enterprises and toward a greater variety of specialized service inputs.

In many manufacturing enterprises, the cost of service inputs now exceeds the cost of production workers by a considerable margin. A number of manufacturing companies now employ more white-collar workers than blue-collar workers, while ten to fifteen years ago the inverse was true.[1] Moreover, among blue-collar workers, an increasing proportion are engaged in repair, maintenance, and other support functions normally categorized as services jobs, rather than assembly line work.

In a small enterprise such as a local store or a local dental practice, there may be only limited specialization in the broad range of service tasks that need to be performed. The store owner, the dentist, or the insurance broker could well perform most general administrative and managerial tasks associated with running their businesses, including tasks such as bookkeeping, hiring employees, developing a marketing plan. Even the most self-sufficient professional or businessman, however, is likely to buy service inputs that require specialized training in law, architecture, or plumbing from firms that specialize in such services.

    In large service enterprises, such as large money center banks, major insurance companies, or large department stores, there is usually a high degree of specialization, and each of the tasks listed above is often subdivided into dozens of subtasks and is performed by experts in a narrow area of specialization. Even large firms often find it cheaper and more efficient to buy specialized services from outside suppliers who can afford to develop the necessary skills. Advances in technology and management techniques have made it necessary to develop a high degree of specialization among producers of sophisticated services.

    Most of the service inputs used by a business enterprise can be either purchased from outside suppliers or produced within the firm itself. The choice depends partly on whether it is cheaper and more efficient to hire the person who can supply the desired expertise or to buy that expertise from an outside vendor. It also depends on operational considerations such as the degree of interaction required between the managers of the firm and the person supplying the service input, the need to protect the confidentiality of the firm's activities, and the organizational philosophy of the firm. The trend has been toward producing fewer service inputs within the firm and buying more of the service inputs from outside vendors.

    Retail businesses have to purchase many service inputs from other firms. The local insurance agent and the local travel agent merely represent the firms that actually produce the insurance or the travel services.

A local bank may turn to a larger bank for such specialized services as foreign exchange transactions, export financing, or traveler's checks. A local bank may also resell some of the mortgages it has acquired to other financial institutions. An insurance company may reinsure a risky policy or an unbalanced portfolio with other insurance companies. An architect may ask a colleague to design the foundation of a building being constructed on a difficult geological site.

Many of the more specialized service inputs purchased by businesses selling services are also produced locally. Often, however, the local firm has to turn to firms that are located in distant cities or even other countries. This is possible because most of the services purchased by businesses can be transmitted from the supplier to the user in the form of information. The producer and the business user therefore often do not have to be in the same place. In this respect services purchased by businesses tend to be fundamentally different from services normally purchased by consumers.[2]

Modern communications, data processing, and transportation facilities have dramatically reduced the cost and time required to acquire services from more distant suppliers, and this has expanded the geographic area within which service inputs are bought and sold. The advantages of centralizing the production of service inputs over a large geographic area is demonstrated by the existence of large regional, national, and international chains of service establishments providing hotel, fast food, car rental, banking, real estate, temporary labor, and retail services. These chains have evolved because there is an economic advantage in centralizing the production of service inputs over large geographic areas.

Centralized production of service inputs on an international scale results in international trade in services, both when the service inputs are produced and consumed within the same firm and when they are purchased from independent suppliers outside the firm. Engineering, computer programming, and research and development services provided centrally by a multinational corporation to its subsidiaries in other countries thus constitute exports of services from the home country. This is the case whether the company is primarily a manufacturing or a service business. Hilton Hotels and General Electric are thus both major exporters of U.S. engineering, computer programming, and management consulting services, and Sony and Nomura Securities are major exporters of Japanese research and development services.

International trade in business service inputs is important in businesses that experience intense international competition. The quality and cost of the engineering, design, and marketing services can mean the difference between success or failure in the marketplace. This has been well demonstrated with respect to the global competitiveness of firms producing manufactured goods such as cars, textiles, clothing, footwear, kitchen appliances, and consumer electronics. Companies that want to compete on a global scale must acquire world-class design, engineering, and marketing services or fail in the marketplace. If services of that caliber are not available at home, or if they can be acquired at home only at a significantly higher cost, then they must be purchased from suppliers in other countries.

Both American and Japanese auto manufacturers have found it advantageous to commission Italian industrial artists to design new sport models and to commission design studios in California to develop yuppie models. Designers in different parts of the world thus tend to develop a reputation for a certain look, and, depending on current fashions and public tastes, even the most successful companies find that they must turn to outside designers to expand the appeal of their products. Many textile manufacturers have thus turned to Finnish designers for designs used in industrial fabrics, while French designers have retained their reputation in the design of clothing apparel.

Similarly, some countries have developed a reputation for professional excellence in certain areas of engineering, software design, accounting, management consulting, architecture, economic analysis and forecasting, printing, data processing, and advertising. In some cases, the competitive edge of one country over another in some area of services has nothing to do with the national environment, but is the result of the professional excellence or artistic flair of an individual. The fact that a person with a particular set of skills or expertise lives in a particular country could be pure chance. In most cases, however, the strength of a country in various services is the result of the unique blending of national culture, education, local role models, and individual talent.

HOW EXPORTERS SELL SERVICES TO FOREIGN CUSTOMERS

Service firms can use four different approaches to reach and serve foreign clients. They can establish local production and distribution facilities in the importing country, use local businessmen to market and distribute services in the importing country, establish partnership or other cooperative arrangements with local firms in the importing country, or serve foreign customers out of the home office, or regional offices in third countries. Each of these approaches has its advantages and disadvantages and is more widely used in some industries than in others.

Establishment of Local Production and Distribution Facilities

Most services purchased by consumers have to be produced on the spot where sold. With respect to services purchased by businesses, there is usually greater flexibility in locating production facilities at some distance from the buyer, but even businesses often find it most practical and convenient to buy from vendors with local facilities. Most large service firms that are serious about selling to foreign customers therefore find it advantageous to establish a local business in the market they want to serve. A foreign producer can thus locate all the activities that require close proximity to the customer in the foreign market, while locating other activities that can benefit from economies of scale in the home country or in third countries.

In some industries the proportion of service inputs that are ideally produced locally is quite high (medical services, for example) while in other industries only a small proportion of the service inputs need be produced locally (motion pictures). Of course, the validity of the distinction depends on the definition of medical services and motion picture services. If the definition of medical services were to cover not only the diagnosis provided by the local doctor, but also the specialists who might be consulted, and the medical research that supports the doctor, we might reach a different conclusion.

Using Local Agents, Contractors, and Licensees

A foreign supplier could decide to forgo the advantages of a local production facility in a targeted market for any number of reasons, including resource constraints and restraints imposed by the host government. In such case, the foreign supplier could take the alternative route of engaging local persons or businesses to serve as agents or licensees. Under such an arrangement, the local agent establishes a locally owned firm to carry out the local activities necessary to sell, market, and support the services in question, while the foreign services company supplies the service inputs that can be produced abroad, and perhaps even the equipment and supplies needed to carry out the local activities.

In some service industries, a whole chain of agents, brokers, wholesalers, and retailers gets involved in marketing and selling services offered by foreign suppliers. A tourism or transportation company, for example, can use travel agents throughout the country to market its tour packages. An insurance company can use local insurance brokers to market its insurance policies. The one service industry where this kind of arrangement is not used is retail banking, though banks often establish corresponding banking relationships with local banks in other countries to attract business from foreign clients.

In order to manage the relationship with local agents, contractors, or licensees, the foreign companies usually find it useful to establish a national sales office in the importing country, and in some cases even regional sales offices. In some industries, a foreign supplier may also have to establish itself as a separate legal entity in the importing country in order to satisfy local fiduciary regulations. The foreign firm may be required to maintain deposits in local banks or to invest in local assets. In many cases, a government might even require a foreign producer to perform certain production activities inside the country as a precondition to the right to sell services.

Forming Partnerships or Cooperative Arrangements with Local Businesses

Another approach to international trade in services is to establish an international association or partnership among independently owned service firms.[3] Such an association or partnership can be no more than a mutual referral service, or it can establish common standards and offer common administrative services to its members. Many international professional firms in law, accounting, consulting, executive recruiting, and real estate are legally international associations of national partnerships. Each national partnership in such an arrangement is an independent business but agrees to maintain agreed standards and share certain common costs. Some international hotel chains such as the Relais and Chateaux chain headquartered in France are in reality international associations of independently owned hotels.

International franchising companies in consumer-oriented services such as fast food, car rental, and retail stores are frequently international associations of locally owned businesses that use the common name, technology, support services, and standards supplied by the franchising company. All of these arrangements allow small, consumer-oriented businesses to take advantage of the economies of scale made possible by a large international business while maintaining the incentives and regulatory advantages of local ownership.

Selling Services to Foreign Clients in the Home Country of the Supplier

As a fourth option, a foreign supplier could decide to serve foreign customers out of the home market. The cost of establishing even an indirect presence in the import market in the form of a sales office and local agents may be too high in relationship to the potential business, or it may be much too difficult to overcome restrictive and burdensome regulations imposed by the importing country government. By forgoing the local production and the local distribution of services in the importing country, a foreign producer often can escape these costs or limitations and still be able to export services to such a country. Since the actual production of the service takes place in the producer's home country or a third country, however, both the buyer and the seller may incur high travel and communication costs.

A service company that intends to sell services to foreign customers from its home office could still open a representative office in the importing country and place advertisements in local papers and magazines. The presence of a local office can save the customer many of the costs of doing business in another country. Any deals that might come out of local contacts between a representative office and a client have to be concluded in the exporting country or in third countries, however. As soon as a local office or a local agent assumes responsibility for the sale of services, the official point of sale is transferred from the producer's country to the buyer's country, and such sales become subject to local laws and regulations.

In order to illustrate how a deal is arranged through a representative office, let us assume that the Bank of America has a representative office in Sweden, which is contacted by a Swedish construction company that wants to borrow money. The representative office could supply the construction company with an application blank and pass the completed form to the nearest branch, which could be located in London. If the bank indicates a sufficient interest to pursue the loan, an executive of the Swedish firm would be expected to fly to London to meet with the loan officer of the bank and conclude the deal.

Representative offices are commonly used in banking, transportation, consulting, data processing, tourism, engineering, and construction. One bank in New York, for example, does business with firms in about sixty countries, has no foreign branches or subsidiaries, but has representative offices in about fifteen of those countries.

A BUYER'S CALCULUS: BUYING SERVICES ABROAD

In order to decide whether to buy at home or abroad, a buyer must weigh the cost and inconvenience of buying abroad, as against the advantages of buying abroad. A buyer must consider the cost of travel and the ongoing communications costs. A buyer must also consider the inconvenience and aggravation of not being able to meet the supplier on short notice when something goes wrong. Advances in technology have reduced the cost and enhanced the quality and speed of international transportation and communications, but the fact remains that it is more costly and less convenient to meet someone in another country than to meet someone who works in the same city.

On the other side, the buyer must consider the cost savings associated with a lower price or the higher quality of the services that can be obtained abroad. Where the home market is highly protected, both the price and quality differentials could be quite large. Finally, the buyer must also consider whether government regulations restrict the use of services obtained abroad. Plans drawn by a foreign architect, for example, might not be eligible for a building permit, or an audit performed abroad might not fulfill an audit requirement, or a foreign insurance policy might not satisfy compulsory insurance regulations.

Buying services abroad is a practical option only in certain situations: First, buying abroad makes sense if a large business needs to buy a relatively homogeneous service that does not require frequent contacts between the customer and the producer. The amount of money involved has to be large enough to justify the added costs and inconvenience. Production of the service must not require extensive knowledge of the local environment. Services that meet these criteria include data processing, data entry, large loans, insurance of large liabilities such as supertankers, reinsurance, printing, large consulting projects, economic forecasting, and preparation of advertising copy.

Second, buying services abroad also makes sense when the required services pertain to international transactions. Examples of such transactions are export financing, export insurance, hiring an executive to work in a third country, advertising in an airline magazine, setting up a global communications system for a company, providing security for an international credit card company, and putting together a multinational project.

Third, buying abroad is a practical option where any buyer, large or small, needs a highly specialized service that can only be purchased abroad. A gourmet, for example, may go to Paris twice a year just to eat. Other examples include seeking medical treatment for a rare disease, studying with a world expert on some subject, or visiting a foreign shrine.

Businesses that operate in a global market are likely to find that they frequently need expertise that is available only in certain countries. A Texas company, for example, may be known for its skill in extinguishing fires in oil wells or for its data on international oil movements. In other cases, the scale of the proposed project may be so large that only a handful of services firms in a few key cities may be large enough to provide the necessary services. A company that wants to float a billion-dollar bond issue may be able to do so only in New York and London. Only a handful of architectural firms may be able to take on a hundred-story building. Only Lloyd's of London may be able to provide liability insurance on a megatanker.

INTERNATIONAL TRADE IN SERVICES AND THE WORLD ECONOMY

International business would not be possible without extensive international trade in services. Every aspect of international business—international trade in goods, finance, travel, and the operation of multinational enterprises—requires international trade in services. The service industries provide the transportation, the communications, the financing, the insurance, the know-how, and all the other support systems that are needed for world commerce.

International Trade in Services and Trade in Goods

Internationally traded goods have to be transported, whether by ship, truck, train, or airplane. International trade also requires the services of intermediaries such as traders, merchants, and wholesalers. Goods in transit need to be financed and insured. In order to develop a market abroad, exported goods have to be advertised. The services of lawyers are required to deal with the many different health, safety, and other regulatory requirements abroad, and to settle the disputes that can so easily arise when people involved come from different countries with conflicting cultures, customs, and laws. The services of translators and interpreters are needed. Finally, in order to keep track of everything, and to calculate the profits, international trade needs to be supported by accountants, data clerks, and data processing experts.

International trade in technologically complex goods also has to be supported by a wide range of customer support services. A computer, for example, requires not only software that can cost more than the computer itself, but also the support of systems engineers, documentation and training specialists, and repair personnel. Similarly, the export of industrial robots, complete factories, and power plants may require the assistance of experts in a dozen different areas of expertise to install the machinery, to get it running, to train local managers to keep it running, and to assist in subsequent maintenance and improvements.

Sometimes these support services are purchased in the exporting country, and sometimes they are purchased in the importing country; sometimes they are provided as part of the export price quoted by exporters to foreign importers, and sometimes they are billed separately. Statisticians and economists have therefore never been sure whether to count such services as part of the value of internationally traded goods or to identify them separately as international trade in services.

International Trade in Services and International Finance

Banks engage in international trade in services whenever they supply financial services to someone who lives in another country—when they accept deposits from foreign clients, when they lend money to firms located in other countries, when they sell foreign bonds, when they provide cash management services to foreign clients, and when they transfer funds for foreign clients.

In carrying out their international activities, banks are also large users of communications services, data processing services, legal services, accounting services, economic information services, data entry services, computer programming services, and advertising services. The fees charged by banks for their services (in the form of a spread between deposit rates and loan rates, or between buying and selling rates for foreign exchange) in effect cover the cost of a bundle of business services that go into the production of international banking services.

When a bank uses service inputs produced at home to support a foreign client, it is indirectly exporting a large number of different services. Banks also export services more directly when they sell such services to their foreign branches and subsidiaries, or when they sell such services to foreign clients for a separate fee. Banks also import services whenever they use services produced by one of their foreign branches or by a foreign vendor in offices at home.

International Trade in Services and International Travel

International travel generates trade in a wide variety of services. Expenditures by Americans while traveling abroad constitute U.S. imports of services, while expenditures of foreign tourists while traveling in the United States constitute exports of services. Travelers have many different needs. First of all, travelers need transportation. Travelers need places to eat and sleep. They may also need the services of travel agents, credit card companies, insurance companies, and tour guides.

International travel has increased rapidly in the past few decades as it has become cheaper and easier to travel, even to faraway places like Tibet, North Borneo, or Mauritius that until recently were inaccessible. A steady increase in the standard of living has also meant that more people could afford to take their vacations abroad. The needs of a high-tech world and the needs of a more highly integrated and interdependent world have also made it necessary for an increasing number of scientists, sports officials, business executives, engineers, and government officials to travel to other countries on a regular basis.

Many people thus spend a considerable amount of time and money traveling to other countries both on business and for pleasure. By expanding the amenities available in otherwise inhospitable or underdeveloped regions of the world, international trade in travel services can substantially improve the quality of travel and reduce the psychological and physical stress of travel.

International Trade in Services and International Business

The operation and management of multinational enterprises has to be supported by extensive international trade in services. To a considerable extent, international trade in supportive business services takes place within the company itself. The head of international operations in the home office exports managerial services to all the countries in which the company has facilities; so do the central data processing department, the accounting department, the legal office, the central office design staff, the advertising staff, the government relations office, and the economics department whenever they do work related to the operation of a factory, a warehouse, a maintenance facility, or a sales office located abroad.

On the other hand, research carried out in one of the company's laboratories abroad, or support services supplied by a foreign subsidiary to the home office, constitute imports of services.

Multinational companies also regularly buy services from outside vendors on an international scale. Advertising, management consulting, investment banking, accounting, data processing, and other business services are regularly purchased from large firms located in key commercial centers such as New York, London, Paris, Tokyo, Hong Kong, and Singapore.

Most international trade in services is organized and carried out by large corporations. Only large enterprises can afford to pay the overhead transportation and communications costs of maintaining frequent and extensive contacts between producers and users of services that are separated by long distances. While communications and transportation costs have declined significantly in recent years, they remain a barrier for smaller enterprises.

The large enterprises that are the principal actors in international trade in services, however, do not buy exclusively from each other. Their wide reach enables them to find and to develop relationships with small suppliers of services in many different places around the world. In fact, that ability to tap into small centers of professional excellence gives these large organizations one of their distinct advantages.

Large organizations inevitably have their limits, however, particularly when they are spread over wide distances. Centralization of management control over large geographic areas can lead to decisions that are out of touch with local conditions. Centralization also tends to discourage innovation by local managers. Large department stores have thus given way in many areas to shopping centers filled with dozens or even hundreds of boutiques. In fact, the very dynamism of the American economy in recent years has been the result of an explosion of small businesses, largely in services.

The same shifts that have been observed in retailing have also taken place in banking, insurance, real estate, and stock brokering. Over the years, small local service establishments have been absorbed by larger firms covering wide geographic areas that are better able to improve quality and reduce costs through greater specialization in managerial and professional support functions. The growth of these large service firms, however, has now created a new movement to smaller, specialized service firms that retain the advantages of specialization without sacrificing the expanded possibilities for innovation and entrepreneurship in a small firm. Wall Street has therefore seen the emergence of so-called financial boutiques that occupy specialty niches in the financial market.

The inherent advantages of local enterprises in services—familiarity with local conditions, the opportunity to innovate in a small organization, and the ability to cultivate relationships with local clients—limit the expansion of trade in services. Trade in services is thus unlikely to reach the same level of penetration in local markets as trade in goods.

It is easy to underestimate, however, the potential international scope of smaller enterprises and even individuals. Small businesses that produce high-quality services and individuals who achieve professional excellence inevitably get to know each other, even across national frontiers. Such contacts lead to a flow of ideas, knowledge, and skills. These informal networks also serve as channels of trade, as leads on potential clients and suppliers are passed from person to person.

It is interesting to speculate whether cheaper international telecommunications will enhance the role of such informal networks in international trade in services. In the United States, the rapid growth of electronic bulletin boards and interest sections within such electronic bulletin boards is creating a new system for the dissemination of information among individuals with similar interests, and electronic banking is gradually transforming the organization of the banking industry. Only the future will tell to what extent these new channels of communications will alter the production and distribution of services globally.

CONCLUSIONS

At the level of individual consumers, international trade in services depends largely on international travel by either the consumer or the supplier of services such as education, entertainment, or tourism. Most international trade in services, however, is carried out by large international business enterprises, which use advanced data processing and communications, technologies to export and import services that can be transferred from one place to another through a flow of information. By organizing their work on a global basis, these large corporations have been able to make previously nontradeable services into tradeable products.

Since services are absorbing an increasing proportion of national resources, the cost of services is becoming an important economic issue, with major implications for the standard of living. In fact, lagging productivity gains in the service sector are slowing economic growth in most countries today, and this is putting the spotlight on policies that affect the cost of services.[4] Government regulation of services has thus become a major public policy issue in many countries. Similarly, government policies that restrict imports of cheaper and better services are bound to become an equally important public policy issue.

Tradeable services constitute an increasingly important input into the production of manufactured goods, and the quality of such inputs is therefore often crucial to the global competitiveness of a country's manufacturing industry. To the extent a country is able to produce high-quality service inputs into advanced manufacturing processes and products, it will be able to strengthen its manufacturing industries and expand services exports. To the extent that a country lacks critical service inputs into manufacturing, it must import such services if it wants to preserve the competitiveness of its industries. Some critics have argued that the growing public policy focus on services is a threat to a country's manufacturing sector. They could not be more wrong.

While the most important public policy issues in services concern services purchased by businesses, increased trade in services consumed by individuals can also add considerably to the quality of life. The services most frequently imported by consumers are tourism, education, and entertainment services. Expenditures on these items constitute a significant portion of the consumer budget, and the increase in value provided by imports of services in these categories can significantly enhance an individual's sense of economic well-being. Policies that affect the expansion of trade in services will play an increasingly important role in stimulating domestic economic growth and raising the national standard of living.

NOTES

1. Personal communications.
2. The geographic distribution is well treated in the book by Stanback et al. (1981) entitled *Services: The New Economy*. See especially ch. 2. The pioneering work in this area was done by George Stigler. Two key publications are an article published in the *Journal of Political Economy* in June 1951, "The Division of Labor Is Limited by the Extent of the Market," and a book published in 1956, *Trends in Employment in the Service Indus-*

tries. The most lively treatment has been provided by John Naisbitt (1982) in *Megatrends*.
3. For an excellent discussion of the role international partnerships play in accounting, see the article by Frank Rossi (1986). Also see the book by Thierry Noyelle (1988) on trade in professional services.
4. The low productivity gains in services are in part the result of difficulties faced by statisticians in measuring real output in services. (This is explained more fully in Chapter 4.) Most experts would agree, however, that statistical measurement problems do not account for the difference between productivity data for the manufacturing sector and producivity data for the services sector. In other words, productivity gains in services are in fact lower than they are in manufacturing. Government regulations and import barriers that shield services from competition have undoubtedly contributed to this phenomenon.

2
THE INVISIBILITY OF TRADE IN SERVICES

People have such a hard time believing that trade in services is important because they cannot see it and it is very difficult to measure. Trade in services has justifiably been called trade in invisibles.

Because the act of selling services is more visible than the flow of services across the border, governments have been more inclined to control sales of services through the domestic regulatory process, rather than through explicit controls on cross-border flows of services, as is the case with goods. Barriers to trade in services are thus intermingled with domestic regulatory measures, and often difficult to distinguish from such measures. Barriers to trade in services therefore tend to be as invisible to the average person as trade in services itself, and this only compounds the skepticism that there is anything to talk about with respect to trade in services.

The purpose of this chapter is to identify some of the key characteristics of trade in services and to develop a descriptive model of services that focuses on the means for storing and transporting services. Such a model helps to overcome the difficulty of visualizing trade in services.

A DESCRIPTIVE MODEL OF INTERNATIONAL TRADE IN SERVICES

International trade in services purchased by consumers—tourism, education, live entertainment—usually requires international travel. These services are transferred from one country to another when either the consumer of imported services or the producer of exported services travels from one country to another.

Services are exported and imported through information flows, including architectural drawings, advertising copy, computer software, credit card transactions, legal opinions, medical information, insurance, and sporting events.

A third category of services consists of those exported through transfer of money from one nation to another. This is the case with banking and other financial services.

Finally, some services become tradeable through an international shipment of goods. Repair services, for example, are exported and imported by transporting the object in need of repair from one country to another.

We can summarize these observations in the following single statement: *All international trade in services is linked to an international movement of people, information, money, or goods.*[1]

In order to become tradeable, services either have to be applied to people, information, money, or goods that provide the means for transferring the services to another country, or have to be used to move people, information, money, or goods from one country to another. We might call the first category of international trade in services "trade in value-enhancing services" and the second category "trade in transfer services."

The easiest way to conceptualize trade in services is to think of it in terms of an application of "value-enhancing services" to goods, people, money, or information in the exporting country and a transfer of the enhanced goods, people, money, or information to the importing country with the help of internationally traded support services. Another way to look at trade in services is as trade in economic benefits created by the application of services.

Services can be stored for later consumption somewhere else only when they are incorporated in goods, money, people, or an information medium. A repaired machine incorporates repair services. A check from the stockbroker incorporates investment services. A student returning from a foreign university incorporates educational services, and a tourist returning home from a foreign vacation incorporates tourism services. A computer tape from an auditing firm incorporates accounting services, and a television signal bounced off an international communications satellite incorporates entertainment services.

Internationally traded services have to be carried across the border in the form of goods, people, money, or information that have been made more valuable in economic terms through the application of services. A repaired machine that crosses the border carries with it imported repair services.[2] A happy tourist crossing the border on the way home is importing tourism services, or a New York lawyer crossing the border to advise a French businessman on the intricacies of American law is exporting American legal services.[3]

Ten thousand dollars crossing the border into Switzerland on the way to a secret bank account provides the means for importing Swiss banking services. A blueprint that crosses the border on the way to a foreign construction site or a computer tape that crosses the border on the way to a foreign computer center incorporates exports of professional services. Most elusive of all, electronic signals bounced off communications satellites or conducted through a buried copper cable could be transferring exports of insurance services, banking services, legal services, accounting services, engineering services, software services, advertising services, medical services, or any other service that can be communicated in the form of electronic information.

All international movements of goods, people, money, and information are in turn facilitated by international trade in transportation, communications, and services. International trade in goods is facilitated by international trade in related services such as shipping, export financing, transport insurance, and trade law, to name just a few. International travel is supported by travel agents, airlines, hotels, restaurants, and taxi drivers. The international flow of money is supported by a wide range of banking, communications, and information services. Similarly, the international flow of information is facilitated by trade in international transport and communications services.

We can summarize this discussion with the following proposition: All international trade in services either requires the application of value-enhancing services to goods, people, money, or information that are subsequently moved from one country to another, or requires the application of services that will help move goods, people, money, or information from one country to another.[4]

International movements of goods, people, money, and information provide the means for transporting services from one country to another. The international movement of goods, people, information, and money in turn is facilitated by international trade in services such as transportation services, travel services, transport insurance services, communications services, and financial services.[5]

CONSEQUENCES OF THE INVISIBILITY OF TRADE IN SERVICES

An observer who is at the right spot at the right time might see the goods, money, people, or an information medium crossing the border, but such an observer would find it extremely difficult to see the services that are being exported or imported.

A person crossing the border could be visiting an aunt, giving a speech, coming to repair a machine, seeing the world, attending an official conference, marketing shoes, or providing consulting services. Without extensive probing, a border official has no way to know what services, if any, a person is exporting or importing.

Similarly, a piece of information contained in an electronic signal could be accounting information, a personal message, an order for books, a state secret, information processed in a foreign computer, or the latest news wire story. Without an ability to decode the signal and to read its content, a government official charged with monitoring imports or exports of services would have no way of knowing whether services were being imported or exported.

Money that crosses an international border could be a payment for smuggled goods, a deposit headed for a Panamanian bank account, or the inheritance of Aunt Nellie. As officials charged with administering foreign exchange controls well know, it is difficult to determine why money is being transferred without extensive probing into the affairs of all the people and institutions involved in the transaction.

The difficulty in visually observing imports and exports of services has a number of important implications. Governments cannot measure the services actually crossing the border. Instead, data on international trade in services has to be collected in one of two ways: 1) by asking domestic producers and consumers of services to report all exports and imports of services or 2) by maintaining a comprehensive foreign exchange control system that allows the government to keep track of all foreign exchange earned or spent by its citizens.

Collecting information from individual producers or consumers of services is difficult because the government first has to identify the producers of services who might have sold services to foreigners and the consumers of services who might have purchased services from foreigners. The government then has to persuade all firms and individuals that buy services from foreigners or sell services to foreigners to maintain detailed records of the transactions.

Governments that maintain foreign exchange control systems could theoretically use data collected on sales and purchases of foreign exchange for developing detailed data on trade in services, but few developed countries still impose comprehensive foreign exchange controls and developing countries often lack the technology for compiling the data they collect. Most countries therefore have only the foggiest notion about the magnitude, composition, and direction of trade in services and the lack of data reinforces the mystery surrounding international trade in services.

All existing data on international trade in services are extremely poor.[6] Most governments have managed to capture data on only the most obvious forms of trade in services such as international shipping, air transport, insurance, banking, and tourism, and even most of those data provide little detail on specialized services within these broad categories or the countries with whom such trade took place. Data on international trade in professional services, data processing, and information services are virtually nonexistent.

Efforts are now under way in the United States and in many other countries to collect more data,[7] but it has become obvious that governments will never be able to collect data of the same detail and quality as the existing data on trade in goods. Not only are services much more difficult to define with great precision, but there is tremendous public resistance to the detailed reporting that would be necessary. It is likely, therefore, that many of our most important insights into trade in services will come not from aggregate data collected by governments but from case studies carried out by individual economists.

The difficulty of visually observing exports and imports of services also makes it difficult to control the international flow of services. In order to assert control over services that cross the border in the form of goods, people, money, or information, a government can adopt one of two strategies: it can extract more information about the people, money, goods, and information crossing the border and use that information to control the flow of services, or it can control all goods, people, money, and information crossing the border. This creates a major dilemma for democratic governments. How deeply should they pry into the affairs of their citizens and to what extent should they control the free flow of information, people, and money just in order to control the flow of services?

To a significant degree, control over the movement of services and maintenance of democratic freedoms are incompatible. Virtually every government has had to wrestle with this basic problem, and no government has been able to avoid major controversy when it has tried either to establish more detailed monitoring of people, information, and money crossing the border or to assert greater control over such movements. When professionals crossing the border between the United States and Canada are thoroughly grilled by customs inspectors or immigration officials as to the purpose of their trip, they complain vociferously.

The French government at one point made a proposal to inspect all information transmitted or carried across its border, and thereby triggered a major outcry in the international business community. And, of course, there is not a democratic government with a foreign exchange control system that has not managed to generate controversy by trying to increase the effectiveness of such controls through more extensive reporting.

Most democratic governments of advanced countries respect the rights of the individual and recognize the need to limit the amount of information that individuals should be required to report to the government. Democratic governments are therefore usually unable to develop detailed information about the data, money, and people crossing the border, and without such information they are usually in a poor position to control the flow of services. This means that such governments find it far more difficult to limit imports of services purchased abroad than to limit domestic sales of imported services. Most barriers to trade in services are therefore embedded in domestic regulations that control the sale of services.

A government can try to control purchases of services by its citizens in foreign countries by establishing restrictions on such purchases, but it can enforce such restrictions only through a comprehensive foreign exchange control system or a comprehensive system for regulating the consumption of particular services. For example, the government can refuse to allocate foreign exchange to the purchase of foreign architectural services or it can insist that only architectural plans signed by a domestically registered architect be used to construct buildings. A government can also refuse to allocate foreign exchange for the purchase of insurance abroad, or it can insist that only insurance sold by an approved insurance company can satisfy the requirement for compulsory auto insurance, or that only a will signed by a local lawyer is recognized by the courts.

Where a transaction occurs, therefore, turns out to be crucial for trade in services. If the sale takes place in the home country of the producer, the laws and regulation of the exporting country will apply to the sale, and the government of the importing country may not have any effective means for controlling the resulting imports. If the sale takes place in the home country of the customer, the laws and regulations of the importing country will fully apply to the sale. This difference in the degree of control that the importing country government can exercise over imports purchased abroad versus imports purchased at home has had a major impact on the structure of the world market in services, the evolution of national policies regarding trade in services, and efforts to develop rules for trade in services.

For some time, the Eurodollar market has been the fastest growing financial market in the world because both people with money and people who wanted money could escape the controls of their own governments. This basic fact of life has persuaded an increasing number of governments to establish offshore markets to attract more of the banking business. It has also persuaded a number of governments that it was futile and counterproductive to protect their own banking system by keeping out foreign banks. Sweden provides one example of this trend. Sweden has traditionally kept foreign banks out and has kept Swedish banks from going abroad. The result was that more and more Swedish companies did their banking in London, where money was cheaper and available in larger quantities. In face of the growing loss of customers, Swedish banks as well as the government came to recognize that it would be better to allow foreign banks to compete in Sweden, rather than to see the continued erosion of the volume of banking done in Sweden.

CONCLUSIONS

Since nobody can readily identify the services embodied in goods, money, people, or information crossing the border, it is difficult both to measure and to control the flow of services across national borders without considerable government intrusion into the affairs of its citizens. Governments find it much easier to control sales or purchases of imported services within their own territories. This explains why most barriers to trade in services are embedded in domestic regulations that control the production, sale, and comsumption of services.

NOTES

1. The term *money* is used here as a surrogate for financial assets. All future references to a movement of money as a vehicle for trade in services should similarly be interpreted as a shorthand reference to international movements of financial assets.
2. The application of services to goods is normally treated as manufacturing as long as the goods involved have not been sold to a final consumer. Any work performed by the same manufacturer after the goods have been sold to the final consumer is treated as a service. Once such products are sold back to a manufacturer for reconditioning, any reconditioning work is treated once again as manufacturing. The same production activity will therefore be counted as trade in goods in one case and trade in services in the other case, depending on who owns the goods.
3. Services carried across the border by people, however, are counted as exports only if the person involved intends to stay abroad only a short period. Thus services provided by an American lawyer or acrobat while in another country are counted as American exports only if the individuals involved remain residents of the United States. Similarly, services purchased by Americans while traveling abroad are counted as American imports only if such travelers remain residents of the United States. Services produced or consumed by individuals who intend to live and work abroad for a prolonged period (defined as a period in excess of three to six months) are not counted as trade (see Chapter 5).
4. Jagdish Bhagwati (1984a, pp. 134–135) has described the process of trade in services that do not require international travel by either the producer or the consumer in terms of the "disembodiment" of services from the producers of services, a process that sometimes involves the splintering of goods from services, and services from goods. International trade in a videotape of a

performance of Mozart's *Magic Flute* at La Scala in Milan thus involves the "disembodiment" of the performance from the opera singers by splintering a videotape from the singing and set design services provided by the opera company.
5. Sampson and Snape (1985, pp. 172–173) have classified trade in services on the basis of four categories: 1) transactions that occur without the movement of factors of production or of the receiver of the service; these transactions include what Jagdish Bhagwati (1985) has called long-distance services and what Sampson and Snape called "separated services" (separated from the producer); 2) transactions that occur as a consequence of the movement of the factors of production but not of the receiver of the service; 3) transactions that occur with the movement of the receiver of the service but not the provider; 4) transactions that occur with the movement of both factors of production and the receiver of the service.
6. For detailed analyses of the difficulties in collecting data on trade in services, and the shortcomings of U.S. government data on trade in services see Lederer, Lederer, and Sammons (1982), Economic Consulting Services (1981), and Ascher and Whichard (1987).
7. For a description of the plan developed by the U.S. government to develop better data see U.S. Department of Commerce (1984b).

3
SERVICES IN THE WORLD ECONOMY

After an arduous journey of four years from Venice to Shang-Tu near modern Peking, Marco Polo arrived in 1275 at the court of Kublai Khan, the mongol emperor of China. He brought the emperor glass and jewelry produced by Venetian craftsmen and letters from the Doge of Venice and from Pope Gregory VIII in Rome. He also brought along something even more important to Kublai Khan, knowledge and professional skills, and for the next seventeen years Marco Polo worked for Kublai Khan as an adviser and emissary before returning to Venice in 1292.

The story of Marco Polo illustrates the close relationship that has existed between trade in goods and trade in services throughout history. We could find similar reports in the clay tablets that have been unearthed from the ruins of the ancient cities of Sumer and Babylon. They have left us reports on the comings and goings of the merchants, craftsmen, storytellers, and ambassadors who carried out trade in goods and services between one city-state and another.

In some ways not much has changed. Businessmen still travel from Europe to China bringing goods, messages, knowledge, and information as in the days of Marco Polo. What has changed is that modern technology has made it possible to transport goods and people from Europe to China in a matter of hours rather than years, in relative comfort rather than at great personal risk and discomfort, and at a fraction of the cost. Communication satellites and computers have made it possible to send long messages and large sums of money to remote parts of the world in seconds.

Because it is so much easier and cheaper to move goods, money, people, and information from one country to another, the minuscule international flow of goods and services of Marco Polo's time has become so large that most people are affected by it either as consumers or as producers and the companies that supply the transportation, communications, and other international services have become large business enterprises employing hundreds of thousands of people. Increased economic importance has also brought growing influence on policy, and it has become increasingly difficult to treat international services as peripheral activities not worthy of the attention of trade policy officials. They deserve attention both because they are crucial for all international economic activity and because they are an important source of income and jobs.

The same technological advances that have made it easier to move information from one country to another have also made the creation, processing, and distribution of information the source of new economic growth in the industrialized countries. The development of increasingly powerful computers has led to an economic revolution as profound as the industrial revolution of the eighteenth century. Increasingly automated factories require fewer blue-collar workers on the production line, but more white-collar workers to program the computers, to design new products, and to process performance data.

A growing demand for information-based business services and a new capability to transmit large amounts of information without a time lag has thus created a new area of international trade. Labor-intensive processing of information can take place almost anywhere—across the street or at the other end of the world—and an increasing number of business enterprises are taking advantage of this possibility.

A HISTORICAL PERSPECTIVE

International trade in services has existed for as long as neighboring tribes, villages, or cities have traded with each other, visited each other, financed each other, or done business with each other. As people traveled, they carried skills, knowledge, information, and artistic talent from one country to another.

Scientists, engineers, astronomers, and experts on many other subjects have traveled to other countries since time immemorial, offering their advice to foreign kings and merchant princes.

Some of the earliest literature is based on an oral tradition preserved by wandering bards, who mesmerized their audiences with tales of foreign lands, spreading the fame of great heroes and kings. Artists, musicians, and actors have traveled far and wide in search of inspiration and patrons. Students traveled to attend foreign universities, to apprentice themselves to master craftsmen abroad, and to learn by seeing the world.

The earliest traders had to provide their own transportation, find their own shelter, and cook their own food. As the international flow of goods, people, money, and information increased, more and more of the services that support international travel could be purchased from enterprises along the way.

Further reductions in the real cost of travel have come as a result of new technologies—steamships, railroads, and jet aircraft, which made travel not only cheaper and faster but also easier.

The growth in the market for services has created both very large companies that are able to take advantage of large economies of scale and many small companies that are better suited to meet the needs of narrow segments of the market. In both cases, specialization has added to the reduction in the cost of support services brought about by advances in technology. This in turn has stimulated a further expansion of international trade, international travel, international finance, and international information flows.

GLOBAL ECONOMIC INTEGRATION

Today, most countries export a larger percentage of their total output and import a larger portion of what they consume than ever before. Travel to other countries has become commonplace. Vast sums of money move from one country to another in a matter of hours or even minutes. Information sometimes moves faster from Washington to London and back than from one street to another within a city. Foreign markets have thus become more closely linked to local markets, and jobs and business profits are now tied much more closely to competition in the global marketplace.

As international competition in the context of a global market has become more of a reality, corporate users have become much more sensitive to the cost of service inputs. In a world where expanded international competition has reduced margins and businesses succeed or fail on the basis of relatively small differences in costs, the cost and quality of available services can affect the profitability of a firm. Firms with large international operations have become far more vocal than in the past about the effect of foreign government policies on the availability and cost of services such as communications and transportation. This has led to a user-oriented focus to international trade discussions of such services as telecommunications, a somewhat startling concept to officials accustomed to a world of national telecommunications monopolies.

International trade in services has also become big business. In the United States, many companies that supply international services—American Express (travel services), Citibank (financial services), Pan American (air transport services), Sea Land (ocean and land transport services), AIG (insurance), AT&T (communications), and EDS (data processing)—are among the largest companies in the country. These firms have become far more conscious than in the past of the advantage of influencing government policies that affect their ability to deliver services worldwide, and their rapid growth in recent years has given them the clout to get attention from the government. Both business executives and government officials are thus more inclined than in the past to look at barriers in services as key commercial issues.

The rapid increase in international economic activity and the resulting growth of services made it inevitable that government officials responsible for trade policy would sooner or later pay more attention to policies that affect the delivery of services.

THE INFORMATION REVOLUTION

The crucial role of information-based business services to economic growth today and the tradeability of these services through modern communication and data processing facilities has convinced many governments that they should pay more attention to trade in services sooner rather than later.

Services are at the heart of an economic revolution equivalent in influence to the industrial revolution that displaced artisans with factories in the eighteenth century. In the emerging economy the creation, processing, and distribution of information are displacing manufacturing as the primary economic activity of most workers. In fact, the creation, processing, and distribution of information are so central to the new economic revolution that it may well become known as the information revolution.[1]

The information revolution has fundamentally changed the scope, character, and significance of trade in services. Old ideas about the nature of services have become a hindrance to the efficiency of government policies affecting the organization of services activities in the world economy.

The Growth of Service Jobs

Computers, factory robots, and completely automated factories are rapidly reducing the need for physical labor in manufacturing. At the same time, sophisticated agricultural machinery, fertilizers, pesticides, and biogenetic engineering are reducing the need for physical labor in growing food. In the new economy, more and more people are earning their living by working in services.

The new service jobs fall into two categories: services directly provided to consumers and services provided to business. The people who hold jobs in the first category support our daily life: the legendary short-order cook at the local McDonald's, waiters at the local restaurant, taxicab drivers, the salesclerk at the corner store, the nurses and doctors at the local hospital, the teacher at your child's school, the plumber and the electrician, the TV repairman, the circus clown, and the preacher.

The second category of service jobs are being created in response to the increasing demand by business enterprises for service inputs. A wide range of services are required to develop, program, install, operate, and maintain computers and factory robots. Increasingly complex products have to be planned, designed, engineered, tested, and advertised. At the same time, the growing complexity of the economy has substantially increased the demand for financial, legal, accounting, general managerial, and, of course, government services.

Table 3–1 breaks down employment in the U.S. economy for the years 1975, 1980, and 1985. It shows the rapid growth of jobs in service industries in recent years. Table 3–2 shows the shift in the percentage distribution of gross national product in the United States from 1947 to 1977. The breakdown in this table is interesting because it highlights the distinction between services sold to consumers and services sold to business enterprises.

The Role of Information in the New Economy

In the new economy that is emerging from the widespread application of computers, more and more of the jobs will be based on the application of specialized knowledge and the manipulation of information with computers. Most people will be earning their living by working with information—creating it, manipulating it, delivering it, managing its flow, applying it, or communicating information to others. The jobs that fall into this category include most office workers and managers, scientists and engineers, computer programmers and data entry clerks, teachers and preachers, lawyers and accountants, government officials, poets and journalists, and architects and planners. It has been estimated that about half of U.S. workers in 1967

Table 3–1. U.S. Employment, by Sector.

	Annual average (thousands)		
	1975	1980	1985
Sector I, Agriculture and Mining	4,319	4,472	4,262
Sector II, Traditional Industries	18,500	21,121	19,540
Construction	3,457	4,469	4,662
Manufacturing excluding infomation machines (below) and printing/publishing equipment	15,043	16,652	14,879
Sector III, Knowledge-Intensive Manufacturing	2,225	2,927	3,126
Electrical, electronic, and communication equipment excluding household appliances and electric lighting	1,426	1,744	1,865
Instruments and related equipment	489	711	724
Office and computing machines	284	431	506
Printing/publishing equipment	26	41	31
Sector IV, Knowledge-Based Services	28,582	33,794	38,101
Education[a]	7,448	7,650	8,371
Health	5,393[b]	6,287	7,583
Communications media	1,434	1,687	1,877
Telecommunications (mainly telephone and postal service)	1,710	1,739	1,833
Business services	1,629	2,523	3,732
Computer and data processing services	143	293	1,819
Other business services	1,486	2,230	3,275
Professional services (legal, engineering, accounting, etc.)	743	1,353	1,819
Financial services (banking, insurance, real estate)	4,223	5,162	5,924
Government not included elsewhere	6,002	7,393	6,962
Sector V, Tertiary Services	27,257	32,407	36,042
Transportation and public utilities[c]	3,888	4,397	4,477
Wholesale trade	4,177	5,275	5,769
Retail trade	12,771	15,292	17,425
Lodging	979	1,071	1,368
Personal services	835	931	1,125
Auto and other repair services	656	889	1,066
Tertiary business services	477	615	836
Other tertiary services	3,474	3,937	3,976

Table 3–1. *(Continued)*

a. Federal education employment included under government.
b. OTA estimate.
c. State transportation employment included under government.

Note: Totals may not add because of rounding.

Sources: Office of Technology Assessment, U.S. Congress, *International Competition in Services* (Washington, D.C.: OTA, 1987), p. 229, table 32, for which data were obtained from *Supplement to Employment and Earnings* (Washington, D.C.: Department of Labor, Bureau of Labor Statistics, July 1983 and June 1986); *Employment and Earnings Bulletin*, 1979, pp. 1311–1312; except for farming, forestry, and fishing from "Projections to 1995," Bulletin No. 2253 D-2, April 1986, Department of Labor, Bureau of Labor Statistics.

were in jobs that were in one way or another related to the production, processing, or dissemination of information.[2]

In the service industries that produce service inputs for other businesses, most of the jobs involve work with information. In the service industries that produce services purchased by individual households, the percentage of jobs that involve work with information is smaller, but even in many of these industries more than half of the employees work in white-collar office jobs. The salesman in the local store, the doctor, the minister, the barber, the auto mechanic, the electrician, the plumber, and the mortician provide services that involve close interactions with consumers and their personal possessions.

The establishments that provide these services, however, also employ a large number of clerks, computer programmers, accountants, secretaries, lawyers, and managers who are not in direct contact with customers. In one local department store chain, about a third of all employees are sales personnel and over a half work behind a desk as manager, buyers, bookkeepers, secretaries, telephone operators, computer programmers, advertising copywriters and artists, and lawyers.[3] Many of these employees do not have to be at the same geographic location as the customer.

Table 3–2. **Percentage Distribution of Gross National Product, by Industry, 1947–1977 (billions, $ 1972).**

	1947		1969		1977	
Industry Classifications	$	%	$	%	$	%
Agriculture, extractive and transformative	175.1	37.38	388.3	35.99	437.4	32.81
Agriculture	26.1	5.57	33.0	3.06	38.3	2.87
Extractive and transformative	149.0	31.81	355.3	32.93	399.1	29.94
Manufacturing[a]	(114.9)	(24.53)	(276.2)	(25.60)	(322.3)	(24.18)
Services	293.6	62.68	690.9	64.03	881.1	66.09
Distributive services	62.6	13.36	161.8	15.00	220.1	16.51
Retail services	51.8	11.06	105.5	9.78	131.8	9.89
Nonprofit services	12.5	2.67	38.6	3.58	53.8	4.04
Producer services[b]	72.6	15.50	197.0	18.26	268.2	20.12
Mainly consumer services	25.6	5.47	36.2	3.35	41.5	3.11
Government and government enterprises	68.5	14.62	151.8	14.07	165.7	12.43
Residual and rest of the world	-0.3	-0.06	-0.2	-0.02	14.6	1.10
All Industries	468.4	100.0	1,079.0	100.00	1,333.1	100.00

a. Includes central administrative offices and auxiliary establishments.
b. Excludes central administrative offices and auxiliary establishments.

Sources: Thomas M. Stanback, Peter J. Bearse, Thierry J. Noyelle, and Robert A. Kersack, *Services: The New Economy* (Totowa, N.J.: Allanheld, Osmun, 1981), p. 16, table 1.4, for which data were obtained from U.S. Department of Commerce, Bureau of Economic Analysis, *The National Income and Product Accounts of the United States, 1929–74 Statistical Tables* (Washington, D.C.: USGPO, 1977), table 6.2; "Gross National Product by Major Industry. Workfile 1205-02-03." Unpublished material provided by BEA; and "U.S. National Income and Product Accounts: Revised Estimates, 1975–77," *Survey of Current Business*, July 1978, table 6.2, p. 52.

The Communications System as the Transport System of the World Information Economy

During the eighteenth and nineteenth centuries the building of roads, canals, and railroads made it possible to centralize the production of goods in factories by providing efficient means for delivering raw materials to factories and delivering manufactured goods to markets. In the last part of the twentieth century, computers, optical fiber networks, communications satellites, and microwave networks are making it possible to centralize more of the information-based services activities by providing efficient means for delivering information from those who supply information to those who use information.

Communications technology has progressed to the point where 1.5 billion bits of information can be transmitted through one circuit per second with complete reliability. In the very near future, computer-communication links are expected to operate at over 1.5 trillion bits per second. This tremendous increase in capacity has been accompanied by sharp decreases in the cost of transmission. The cost for a typical international voice or telex message was $3 per minute in 1970; today the cost is only a few cents. Moreover, a signal that is transmitted through a communications satellite can be sent to another location that is 3,000 miles away as cheaply as to a place that is a few hundred miles away.

How Trade in Business Services Has Altered the World Economy

By making it possible to move large amounts of information efficiently, cheaply, and reliably over long distances, the information revolution has made many more information-based services tradeable. The production of services based on the creation or processing of information can now benefit from the same kind of international specialization that led to the rapid growth of trade in goods in the past.

Take data processing services. Large computer centers in New York, North Dakota, and Amsterdam now often serve clients from many different parts of the world. Workers in Jamaica, Korea, and Taiwan code and convert information into machine-readable form for many multinational companies headquartered in the United States. Large American construction companies employ engineers in India for building projects in third countries.

At the same time, the information revolution is transforming the global organization of many manufacturing industries. Since it is now possible for managers in widely separated facilities to share the same information, there has been a sharp increase in international specialization in the production of the components and parts that go into finished products. The typical home computer contains parts manufactured in over a dozen countries.

Other manufactured products that are now produced on a global basis, with inputs from many different countries, include automobiles, airplanes, television sets, automated machine tools, and boats. These globally produced goods inevitably incorporate service inputs from a number of different countries. Many of these globally produced goods finally compete in global markets, as perhaps best illustrated by airport shops around the world that display the same electronic gadgets, fashion apparel, and liquor.

Overall, the information revolution is internationalizing markets to a far greater degree than before. Traders now have the ability to know the prices being charged at any one time in markets around the world, and they are able to determine with some precision the cost of shifting goods and services from one place to another. National markets are becoming much more closely linked to each other.

The foreign exchange market and the Eurodollar market were perhaps the first markets to become highly integrated on an international basis. As time passes, more stock exchanges are establishing direct linkages with each other, and traders in London can now buy and sell shares on the Singapore exchange after the London exchange has closed. Trading in any relatively homogeneous commodity now reflects price movement in other parts of the world. Needless to say, these global markets are supported by business services supplied on a global basis.

International trade in business services has been central to the internationalization of economic activity. Behind the goods and services purchased by consumers from local retail establishments is an increasingly complex web of networks that tie together producers of specialized goods and services in many different countries.

CENTRALIZATION OF BUSINESS SERVICES

In order to understand fully the emergence of international trade in services as a key issue, we have to understand the economic forces that have affected the production, delivery, and role of business services, and the requirements of an increasingly integrated world economy.

The Emergence of Business Services

In the past, most services required to operate a manufacturing business were produced within the firm itself. A typical firm employed bookkeepers, accountants, engineers, experts in finance, marketing, public relations, training, and personnel management, secretaries, clerks, industrial designers, security guards, a cleaning and maintenance crew, statistical analysts, computer programmers, and research scientists. Most of these services were produced in close proximity to the factory. Business enterprises producing services also require a broad range of service inputs, and these too were largely produced within the enterprise in close proximity to the local bank, store, hospital, or radio station.

A typical firm also purchased a limited number of services such as insurance, banking, transportation, legal, architectural, and auditing services from independent local suppliers who specialized in the production to these services. All these activities were carried out in close proximity to each other because each activity is closely related to every other activity and requires constant interactions and exchanges of information among those carrying out those activities.

Since most support services in the past were tied to the local factory or the local service establishment, the possibility for specialization was quite limited. Depending on the scale of the local factory or services business, those responsible for individual activities had only a limited opportunity to hone their skills and to deepen their knowledge in a subset of their area of responsibility.

Continuing improvements in communications and transportation facilities over the years gradually led to increased centralization and specialization in the production of business services. Manufacturing enterprises that had a number of factories at different locations or services firms with many retail outlets centralized the production of administrative services at corporate headquarters. This permitted functional specialists to develop greater skills and knowledge in narrower areas of activity. It also made it possible to take advantage of new economies of scale in processing data and to make better use of outside specialists.

The trend toward greater centralization and specialization in the production of business services was accelerated by a growing demand for more specialized service inputs. As both products and the machinery used to produce such products became technologically more complex, manufacturing companies needed not only more engineers and research scientists, but also engineers and scientists with more highly specialized skills. At the same time, the growing demand by consumers for greater variety in both goods and services created a greater need for industrial designers, marketing experts, planners, and development staffs.

The growing integration of both national and international markets has sharpened competition, and any firm that wants to survive has to acquire the best design, engineering, and marketing services available. High-quality service inputs, of course, are expensive, and the expense can be justified only if the scale of production is large enough.

The growing centralization and specialization in the production of service inputs within business enterprises have had the interesting result that some manufacturing companies have become major suppliers of business services. Manufacturing companies that were able to cut the cost of their own service inputs through a process of centralization often found that they could profitably supply the same service inputs to other businesses. Manufacturing giants like Boeing, McDonnell Douglas, General Motors, General Electric, Mead Paper Company, and Montedison, for example, became major suppliers of data processing and information services. So did financial institutions like Citibank and Merrill Lynch. Companies that made a major investment in developing computer programs to facilitate various management and engineering tasks have similarly found that they can profitably sell these computer programs to others in the industry and thereby recoup the development costs.

Of course, it does not make sense to centralize the production of all business services. Some business services require so many interactions and such a close working relationship with workers on the factory floor or with customers and sales personnel in retail outlets that it would not be practical to supply such services from a long distance. For example, detailed record-keeping of materials used, hours worked, and available inventory is best carried out at the local level. On the other hand, aggregation of such data and analysis of the data might well be carried out more efficiently at corporate headquarters.

Services that require extensive familiarity with the local environment are also best carried out at the local level, while services that require in-depth knowledge or services that can be produced much more cheaply in large volumes are best carried out on a centralized basis. The basic design of a factory producing paper or of a fast food outlet can be produced more efficiently at corporate headquarters, while the adaptation of the drawings to meet local building codes or zoning requirements might be done more efficiently by a local architect familiar with the regulations.

Advertising and marketing of brand names is usually done more efficiently at the national corporate level, while arrangements for placing advertisements in local newspapers are best left to the manager of a local store. George Stigler (1956), an eminent economist at the University of Chicago, was one of the first theorists to draw our attention to this transformation of business services. A recent study by the Office of Technology Assessment has pulled together some recent data on shifts in the organization of service industries (1987, ch. 8); also see Stanback et al. (1981, chs. 3 and 5).

Firms alter the distribution of service functions between the local level and regional, national, or international levels as the technology changes or as experience shows that a different distribution of functions leads to better results. How changes in technology can affect the distribution of functions is illustrated by developments in data processing departments. In the early days of mainframe computers, firms centralized a large number of data processing functions in one department. These centralized data processing departments, however, were often unresponsive to local needs, and the development of personal computers led to a new decentralization of many data processing functions in many companies.

The last few years have seen a strong trend in many companies to using external sources for many business services. Even large corporations often do not have sufficient internal demand for many services to justify the development of internal staff expertise at a required level of professional competence. Corporate headquarters staff also tend to become unresponsive to needs in the field and tend to spend too much time coordinating with each other. By hiring an outside expert, a business manager can use as much or as little of that expert's time as may be required to meet current needs. Outside experts also tend to be more responsive to management needs or wishes since it is easier and cheaper to change outside consultants than in-house staff.

Fortune magazine (February 2, 1987, pp. 47–50) predicted that over the next ten years most companies will significantly reduce the ranks of middle managers who provide most in-house services and replace them with independent suppliers of business services. Many companies have become too large to respond rapidly to shifts in markets and technology, and a reduction of corporate staff will tend to make such companies leaner and meaner and able to respond more decisively to changes in the environment.

The major changes that have taken place in the production of service inputs used by business have made it far more difficult to interpret data on manufacturing and services employment. A reduction in manufacturing employment does not necessarily mean that there has been a real displacement of jobs in manufacturing if companies in an industry decide to shift the production of service inputs to outside suppliers. On the other hand, a relatively stable employment figure in a manufacturing industry can hide a significant shift from production workers to office workers.

INTERNATIONALIZATION OF BUSINESS SERVICES

Many of the business services that can be produced in a corporate headquarters office—whether in a neighboring city or in a city across the country—can be produced just as efficiently in another country. Besides, any number of cities in Canada are closer to Portland, Maine, than Chicago or Los Angeles, and travel to and from a corporate headquarters in Montreal or Toronto would be less inconvenient than travel to and from Los Angeles. The same economic forces that lead to the growth of national firms and to the centralization of business services within countries have also led to the growth of international firms and to the centralization of some business services at an international level.

Of course, national borders do matter. Some business services such as marketing, for example, require an intuitive grasp of the national culture, and other business services may require an extensive knowledge of national laws and regulations. Government regulations may require that certain business services be performed within the country. In all such cases service inputs are produced within the same country where they are used.

Multinational services companies with local branches in many countries can take advantage of international economies of scale by centralizing activities that do not require close physical proximity to users, while maintaining a local market presence for all activities that require close physical proximity to customers.

A study carried out by the Organization for Economic Cooperation and Development (OECD, 1983, pp. 11–12) showed that multinational companies typically use centralized data processing services to carry out the following functions:

- Production control, illustrated by the growth in robotics and computer-assisted manufacturing
- Research, in particular the coordination of functions among research divisions or the improvement of information resources available to staff
- Design/engineering, as used with computer-aided design
- Marketing, especially for transmitting information about local conditions, enabling direct ordering, and arrangement of credit
- Distribution, including scheduling, routing, and producing required transport or export documentation
- Order processing, to tie together interdependent production facilities
- Maintenance, such as tracking after-sales defects and maintenance histories
- Financial reporting and consolidation, in particular to standardize the firm's financial reporting systems
- Financial management, such as the central management of currency exposure or monitoring of credit risks
- Administrative management, including the maintenance of centralized financial, personnel, and communication records

Many multinationals have also found it efficient to buy service inputs for their subsidiaries and branches abroad from vendors at home with whom they have had a long-standing relationship. Many banks, insurance companies, accounting firms, and consulting firms have thus developed an international business by following their major clients into foreign markets. This has promoted both the growth of trade in services and the development of multinational services enterprises.

Increased international competition among global manufacturing enterprises has also boosted international trade in business services. Much as greater competition within countries made it essential that producers of goods acquire the best service inputs that were available nationally, intensified competition at an international level has made it essential that producers acquire the best service inputs available internationally. A company that wants to gain a competitive edge in the world market for cars, television sets, videotape recorders, or kitchen appliances must have world-class design, engineering, and marketing services, and if the services available at home are not of world standard, it must procure such services abroad. The internationalization of markets and growth of trade in business services are closely related.

International trade in business services is a relatively recent phenomenon, at least in terms of volume. American banks, insurance companies, and consulting firms began expanding into international markets in the 1960s. It was not until the 1980s, however, that advances in information technology made it practical to centralize the production of such business services. The same advances in information technologies have now made it possible to centralize the in-house production of business services such as research and development, data processing, information systems, economic forecasting, marketing, advertising, accounting, personnel management, and planning. This does not mean that companies have universally centralized the production of all of these service inputs, but rather that they have centralized activities that require a high degree of specialization or activities that can be done much more cheaply in large volumes. Service inputs that require an extensive knowledge of the local environment or frequent interactions with local managers obviously are not good candidates for centralization at an international level.

CONSUMER SERVICES AND INTERNATIONAL TRADE

Consumer services such as food services, health services, entertainment services, educational services, household insurance services, and retail banking services are produced where they are consumed, and they are therefore not tradeable. Food served in restaurants has to be cooked and served where it will be eaten. The doctor and patient both have to be present at the same location for a medical examination or an operation. The loan officer at the bank undoubtedly wants to have a personal interview before providing a personal loan. The insurance company needs a local claims adjuster to assess damages claimed by policy holders.

Retail service establishments, like all other businesses, also need many service inputs that can be provided from a distance: accounting, data processing, finance, facilities design, planning, training, information services, and specialized professional advice. Many of these service inputs can be provided from a central corporate office in another city or in another country. Indeed, the advantages of economies of scale in retail services are demonstrated by the steady growth of multiestablishment firms in retail services, including the growth of international chains like Hertz, Baskin-Robbins, Kentucky Fried Chicken, Hospital Corporation of America, Berlitz, and Holiday Inns.

Unfortunately, we have very little aggregate data that would tell us to what extent business has centralized the production of business services. Evidence derived from individual companies leads one to believe that companies have centralized many activities such as data processing, engineering, research and development, training, design, finance, and personnel. It is impossible to judge, at this stage, how far the process has gone. Under these circumstances it is possible to have differences of opinion among analysts, and such differences are reflected among the authors of the different volumes produced for the American Enterprise Institute on trade in services.

It is highly probable that international trade in business services will continue to grow. Future advances in technology will continue to improve the quality and reduce the cost of communications. Individuals will become more comfortable with the use of personal computers, electronic mail, and teleconferencing in interacting with coworkers at more distant locations. Government regulations that now often impede the international flow of services will eventually break down in response to economic pressures and international negotiations.

It is interesting to speculate, though difficult to predict, to what extent true international trade might emerge in consumer services such as banking, insurance, retailing, information, and entertainment services. The development of the personal computer has created a new system for delivering consumer services to the individual household, and a market that is not strictly tied to geographic location. Many people now do their personal banking and investing through an electronic hookup between a personal computer and a bank that could be hundreds of miles away. Electronic shopping through computer terminals is spreading rapidly, tracking the earlier rapid growth of mail order shopping. Is there any reason why the same technology could not lead to electronic hookups with banks, mail order outlets, or data bases abroad?

CONCLUSIONS

International trade in services has become an important issue because international trade in services has become big business, and the enterprises that conduct this trade are counted among some of the largest corporations in the world. It has also become important because internationally traded business services are an increasingly strategic resource in the production of both goods and services.

A third reason why international trade has become a more important issue is that new technology and an expansion of the market have opened up new opportunities for competition in service industries previously dominated completely by monopolies. As some countries have moved to deregulate significant segments of the telecommunications and transportation industries, issues that were previously addressed by domestic and international regulation now have to be addressed in terms familiar to trade policy officials—rules for market competition, distortions introduced by government restrictions, and interactions between competitive markets and monopolies.

There are those who have attacked the proposition that services, and in particular trade in services, have become more significant to economic growth and welfare. They argue that manufacturing remains the core of the economy, and that the greater emphasis on trade in services will only serve to distract attention from improvements that need to be made in manufacturing and in trade rules affecting manufactured goods. These analysts, however, completely misunderstand or refuse to acknowledge the true nature of the economic revolution that is taking place. The issue is not services versus manufacturing, but the role of services in manufacturing.

The fundamental change that has occurred in the modern economy is how manufactured goods are produced. Manufacturing has come to depend more and more on service inputs, and the quality of manufacturing is increasingly a function of the quality of service inputs. Manufacturing has also become more globally competitive, and service inputs play an increasing role in that competitiveness.

Another important change that has occurred is in the way successful manufacturers look at the products they sell—namely, as products that are expected to generate a stream of services for buyers, rather than as physical assets that are purchased for their own sake. By looking at their output in terms of a capacity to produce a stream of services, these manufacturers have also come to appreciate the importance of complementary services to the competitive position of their products. IBM has understood this principle for some time, which has been an important source of its success.

A country that produces high-quality service inputs for its manufacturing industries also is in a good position to take advantage of its strengths in these services to expand its exports of services. Again, this should be seen not as a question of a choice between services and manufacturing, but as a mutually reinforcing relationship.

NOTES

1. The pioneering work in this area was done by Daniel Bell, who first coined the phrase *postindustrial society*. See, for example, Bell (1967). In terms of empirical work on the information economy, the best work has been done by Marc Porat (1977) at the U.S. Commerce Department. A 1987 study published by the Office of Technology Assessment also contains a great deal of useful information (see OTA, 1987, chs. 5 and 8). One of the more thought-provoking studies published recently on the new world information economy is the book by Albert Bressand and Catherine Distler, *Le Prochaine Monde*.
2. Porat (1977) showed that about 46 percent of GNP and 53 percent of national income in 1967 were produced by workers who were tied in one way or another to the production, processing, and distribution of information.
3. This number was obtained from a senior manager working at Hecht's, a major department store in the Washington, D.C., area.

4
THE CHANGING PERCEPTION OF SERVICES

In one of his more whimsical, yet nevertheless profound, moments, John Maynard Keynes (1935, p. 383) wrote:

> The ideas of economists and political philosphers, both when they are right and when they are wrong, are more powerful than is commonly understood. Indeed the world is ruled by little else. Practical men, who believe themselves to be quite exempt from any intellectual influences, are usually the slaves of some defunct economist. Madmen in authority, who hear voices in the air, are distilling their frenzy from some academic scribbler of a few years back. I am sure that the power of vested interests is vastly exaggerated compared with the gradual encroachment of ideas.

The power of ideas to shape public perceptions of policy issues and even to shape public perceptions of reality has been amply demonstrated with respect to services. Old ideas about services, distilled by economists and social theorists many years ago, have a powerful hold on public perceptions about both the productivity and the tradeability of services. Despite ample empirical evidence to the contrary, a large portion of the population continues to think that services are largely an unproductive activity and that services are not tradeable.

As we shall see, none other than Adam Smith, that venerable economist who wrote his pathbreaking book *The Wealth of Nations* at the dawn of the industrial revolution, thought that service workers were unproductive and a burden on society. Today, service work is still widely equated with low productivity, low wages, and marginal jobs for those unfortunate enough not to have real jobs producing goods. Yet, only a small proportion of the work force is actively engaged in producing goods, and most of those with blue-collar manufacturing jobs dream that their children will have higher status white-collar jobs in offices.

One of the factors that contributes to the continued hold that these ideas have on public perceptions is the inadequacy of statistical measuring tools. Real domestic output of services and trade in services are both difficult to measure, and the result has been that data on both productivity and trade have been consistently underreported. The data that have been published by governments have thus tended to reinforce traditional notions about the unproductive nature of services work and the unimportance of trade in services. Improvements in statistical collection efforts could produce better data, but one of the reasons that effort has lagged is that the data showed that services were not important.

WHY SERVICES HAVE BEEN CONSIDERED UNPRODUCTIVE

One of the ideas that has a dominant hold on thinking about services is that services are ancillary activities that are not in themselves productive and have no independent value. Consider the following quotation from Adam Smith (1776, p. 315).

> The labour of some of the most respectable orders in the society is, like that of menial servants, unproductive of any value, and does not fix or realize itself in any permanent subject, or vendible commodity, which endures after that labour is past, and for which an equal quantity of labour could afterwards be procured. . . . In the same class must be ranked, some both of the gravest and most important, and some of the most frivolous professions: churchmen, lawyers, physicians, men of letters of all kinds; players, buffoons, musicians, opera singers, opera dancers. . . . Like the declamation of the actor, the harangue of the orator, or the tune of the musician, the work of all of them perishes in the very instant of its production. . . . Both productive and unproductive labourers,

and those who do not labour at all, are all equally maintained by the annual produce of the land and labour of the country. This produce, how great soever, can never be infinite, but must have certain limits. According, therefore, as a smaller or greater proportion of it is in any one year employed in maintaining unproductive hands, the more in the one case and the less in the other will remain for the productive, and the next year's produce will be greater or smaller accordingly.

Adam Smith wrote his famous treatise when English factories began to produce the goods that energized British trade. Free trade in corn made a great deal of sense to the new industrialists, who wanted cheap food for their workers because that would enable them to keep wages low. By the same token, workers producing services limited the number of workers available for factory work, and the production of services therefore was something the new industrial class wanted to discourage.

To put the issue in more objective terms, the factories turning out industrial goods were the key source of economic power and national wealth in eighteenth-century England. It was therefore natural to conclude that workers producing services rather than industrial goods were not productive, in the sense that they did not contribute to the industrial output that defined national power and wealth. Echoes of this eighteenth-century view are still heard today.

At an earlier time in world history, anyone who did not grow food was viewed as unproductive and a burden on society. This view was natural at a time when the availability of agricultural workers limited the amount of extra food that was available to support the army and the craftsmen who produced the weapons and the other implements that defined national wealth and economic power. Today 4 percent of the U.S. population is able to raise all the food that the country can consume and that it can export. Nevertheless, farming is still regarded by many as a more desirable economic activity than other types of work and farmers are still accorded special economic and political privileges.

Old ideas thus maintain their hold on people long after they are no longer relevant, and the old idea in this case is that workers producing services perform a less desirable form of work. The surprising thing about these attitudes today is that a large majority of the population continues to believe that service work is less desirable even though more than half of the work force have service jobs and virtually every factory worker hopes that his or her offspring will have a higher status professional job in an office rather than on the factory floor. The attitude toward services is perhaps best symbolized by the fear that in the future everyone will be employed serving hamburgers in a fast food restaurant. One might call this the McDonald's syndrome.

THE POSTINDUSTRIAL SERVICES ECONOMY

The intellectual foundations for a change in the interpretation of the nature and role of services in the economy were laid by Daniel Bell (1967), who coined the phrase *postindustrial society*. In a number of articles and books, Bell has described the increasing role of information in the modern economy and the growing importance of work associated with the production, processing, analysis, and distribution of information.

Bell's theoretical work was followed ten years later by the empirical work done by Marc Porat (1977) in a study for the Department of Commerce. Porat's study demonstrated that 46 percent of GNP and 53 percent of national income in 1967 was produced by workers tied in one way or another to the production, processing, and distribution of information.[1]

A number of writers have popularized the concepts pioneered by Bell and Porat. The best known of these books is *Megatrends* by John Naisbitt (1982). At the same time, a number of economists have analyzed the changing structure of the economy and the new role of services in the economy. Two books, in particular, provide a good overview of this work. *Services: The New Economy* (1981) is a comprehensive study of services written by Thomas M. Stanback, Peter J. Bearse, Thierry

J. Noyelle, and Robert A. Karasek, four economists associated with the Conservation of Human Resources Project at Columbia University. The other book, *Managing the Services Economy: Prospects and Problems*, edited by Robert Inman (1985), includes a selection of thought-provoking articles by a number of economists, political scientists, and business executives who have analyzed the role of services in the economy. Old perceptions, however, are difficult to eradicate, and there is a general public impression that the work done by many of the authors cited above is futuristic—that it presents an unrealistic projection of the future rather than a hardheaded analysis of the present.

Data Problems in Services Perpetuate Old Shibboleths

One of the reasons why many people remain convinced that jobs in services are less productive than jobs in manufacturing is that data published by the government tend to show lower productivity gains in services than in manufacturing. One has to approach these numbers with a great deal of caution, however. Data on productivity growth in services are notoriously bad because it is very difficult to develop an objective measure of output in services, and this tends to result in a consistent understatement of gains in the real value of services produced in the economy.

Services do not come in discrete units like goods, and services are subject to large variations in quality that are difficult to measure in a consistent and objective manner. Statisticians thus generally find it very difficult to develop accurate measures of real output in services, independent of the monetary value assigned by the market. The task of measuring real value is particularly difficult insofar as the gain in real output takes the form of improvements in the quality of services. Indeed, the quality of services that require direct contacts between the consumer and the supplier is often a function of the number of sales clerks available to meet consumer needs, but how can statisticians measure the real value of personal attention? Since they cannot measure it very well, improvements in the quality of services through increased personal attention show up as a major deterioration in the productivity of the service industry involved. Data on investment show that service industries consistently invest large amounts of money in new capital equipment, something they would not do if it did not result in real gains in productivity.

Misinterpretations of the Postindustrial Economy

One reason for the resistance to the message about the productive contribution of the service sector is that the analysis of the postindustrial, information-centered economy has been misinterpreted by many who have used the term, creating the impression that in the new economy services and information would be displacing the production of hard goods. What many people who casually use this term have missed is that it does not imply that services are displacing the production of goods, but rather that services in general, and information-based services in particular, are a growing input into the production of hard goods, and that such service inputs make it possible to produce *more* and *higher quality* goods for consumption. In other words, the nature of work related to manufacturing is changing, and this is reducing employment in the traditional manufacturing sector but not the physical output of the manufacturing sector.

Another reason why many analysts miss or play down the growing input of services into manufacturing is that a much larger number of new service workers are employed in producing services consumed by individuals in the course of their daily life. In effect, the fundamental change in the pattern of employment associated with manufacturing is overshadowed by employment data on personal services.

As more consumers are able to satisfy their needs for the basic goods associated with the average life-style, consumer demand has shifted toward buying more services such as health, education, tourism, and entertainment. There should be no reason why anyone should feel that producing these services is less productive than growing food or producing manufactured goods. As long as the economy also generates the tangible goods that people and the government want to buy, the production of consumer services adds as much to national well-being as the production of goods.

The U.S. Trade Deficit and the Growth of Services Employment—A Source of Confusion

The debate over the changing role of services in the United States has been clouded in recent years by an argument that has been used by some official spokesmen that there was no need to worry about the impact of the trade deficit on the manufacturing sector since employment in the services sector has been growing rapidly, offsetting any loss of employment in manufacturing. This line of argument has led to a number of books arguing that manufacturing does matter, and that the productive role of services has been overblown. This debate has totally confused the analysis of the underlying, longer term changes taking place in the economy.

Recent macroeconomic policies in the United States have created a large gap between the total output of goods and services in the United States and the demand for goods and services by consumers, businesses, and the government. A gap between domestic production and domestic consumption is possible as long as the difference is made up by imported goods and services. Most services purchased by consumers are not tradeable, however, and an increased demand for such services can be met only by shifting resources from the production of manufactured goods, which are tradeable, to the production of nontradeable services. In other words, the rapid growth of services employment can be traced, in part, to the same macroeconomic policies that created the trade deficit. This does not explain all of the growth in services employment, however. In addition to the short-term shift in resources from the manufacturing sector to the services sector, there has been a long-term shift toward increased use of service inputs in manufacturing and increased consumer purchases of services.

All Economic Activity Utilizes a Stream of Services to Produce a Stream of Services

By far the largest input into production is human labor, all of which can be classified as service inputs. Whether labor services are supplied by full-time employees, contract employees, or other businesses that sell services, the basic ingredient is still labor services. Moreover, while the nature of the work performed by white-collar workers and blue-collar workers is somewhat different, the basic ingredient in both cases is still labor service. By looking at labor inputs as service inputs, both government policymakers and managers of enterprises might be able to get a clearer understanding about the changing nature of work in the modern economy and the implications of that change for the management of enterprises and for public policy in areas such as education.

Machines are increasingly displacing human workers in the advanced economies in performing repetitive and boring tasks, both because the machines are cheaper and because they are more reliable in carrying out such tasks. Human workers, on the other hand, provide the inputs that require thought, creativity, special skills, or an ability to interact and communicate with other human beings. This change in the nature of work is taking place not only in the high-technology industries but also in the traditional mass production industries such as consumer electronics, steel, automobiles, and textiles.

The companies that have recognized this trend and have taken steps to make it possible for their employees to develop and use these human qualities have generally outperformed competitors that still see their workers as unthinking automatons. The countries that recognize this trend and the implications for public education will outperform countries that do not. Looking at all economic activity in terms of service inputs thus will help to focus attention on the quality of labor input generally.

The ultimate purpose of all production activity is to generate a stream of services. Most people do not buy an automobile to own an object, but to produce a stream of transportation services. An automobile company that understands that it is in the business of producing a stream of transportation services will tend to be more successful than one that does not focus on the stream of services that its cars will generate. Many manufacturers have failed to produce what consumers want because they thought they were producing objects that people wanted to own, rather than objects that were merely the means for generating a stream of services. Even some service companies tend to lose sight of this basic concept.

WHY TRADE IN SERVICES WAS CONSIDERED AN OXYMORON

Until a few years ago, it was generally assumed that services were not tradeable because services had to be produced where they were consumed. One obvious way to overcome the contradiction between the requirement of proximity in services and international trade is travel. Travel to another country to buy services, however, was assumed to be impractical. We saw in the last chapter that international travel remained relatively difficult until the last few decades, and that anyone who traveled to another country was expected to stay for a prolonged period. It was therefore generally thought that anyone who traveled to another country became attached to that country, and that it could be assumed that purchases of services could be treated as internal domestic transactions in the country in which they were performed. What American would be crazy enough to travel to another country for a haircut?

In effect, international travel was considered a one-way street. Anyone who traveled to another country became a part of that country, and any services produced or consumed in another country were treated as internal transactions of that country. This was not an unreasonable assumption in the days of Marco Polo. Marco Polo did not return from his trip to China for eighteen years, and it was reported that his relations failed to recognize him on his return.

Over the years economic theorists reinforced the view that international travel did not have anything to do with international trade. In his theory of comparative advantage, David Ricardo (1817) showed that international trade could be explained in terms of each country's relative supply of factors of production such as labor and natural endowments such as land and climate. It followed from David Ricardo's theory that an international movement of labor was quite different from international trade.

In more recent years, two economists, Heckscher (1919) and Ohlin (1933), showed that international trade tends to reduce wage differentials among countries in the same way that the international movement of labor tends to reduce such differentials. They concluded that trade will therefore reduce the economic incentive for international labor movements. Conversely, they argued that international movements of labor tend to reduce the volume of profitable trade.

An international flow of money, like an international flow of people, has been treated as a one-way flow. It has traditionally been assumed that anyone who went through the difficult and risky process of transferring money from one country to another would want to leave it there. Money invested abroad thus became part of the foreign economy, and any investment service provided by a foreign financial institution was viewed as an internal domestic transaction.

Economists have thus looked at money that is invested in another country in the same way they have looked at people who travel to another country. It has been treated as an international movement of a factor of production that reduces the scope for international trade in goods, and therefore is something that is quite different from trade.

In the traditional view of the world, information and knowledge have been treated not as either tradeable items or factors of production, but as part of the economic environment like mountains, air, and water. In fact, there has been a tendency to view the international flow of information as a phenomenon that had more in common with natural laws and moral principles than with mundane economic considerations.

Governments have recognized, of course, that information about market opportunities or trade secrets could be extremely valuable, particularly if no one else had access to it. They have recognized the value of exclusive information, for example, by granting inventors exclusive rights to patents and authors exclusive rights to manuscripts for fixed periods of time. Nathan Meyer Rothschild made a fortune in the London commodity market by obtaining advance information on the outcome of the battle of Waterloo through his own carrier pigeons. None of these considerations, however, have been tied in the past to international trade in something quite so ephemeral as services. Like international movements of people and money, international movement of information has ultimately been viewed as a one-way flow out of the country.

This brings us to international shipping and communications services. Under the long-standing cash, insurance, and freight (CIF) method of valuing international trade in goods, exports of services related to trade in goods were incorporated in the value of international merchandise trade. This method of valuation reinforced the assumption that trade in transportation and other services was so closely tied to trade in goods that it was not necessary to pursue a separate analysis of trade in services.

Another convention frequently used by statisticians fully removed trade in transportation and communication services as a subject for analysis. It assumed that each country's ships or airplanes carry only its own people to other countries, and that each country's communications companies transmit only messages from its own people to other countries. The key point here is that under some long-standing statistical conventions international trade in support services was defined as something else.

Economists thus built a model of the world economy that did not have to account for trade in services. This model was a workable model for many years because international trade in services remained quite limited in practice. As international trade in services grew in volume and economic importance, the model of a world economy without trade in services became less and less credible.

GROWING INTERNATIONAL RECOGNITION OF TRADE IN SERVICES

A model of the world economy that does not accommodate trade in services has become increasingly unacceptable to enterprises selling services. These enterprises do not see a fundamental distinction between the sale of services and the sale of manufactured goods to customers in other countries; yet they see governments spending a great deal of effort in reducing foreign barriers to the sale of manufactured products and very little effort in reducing foreign barriers to the sale of services. The only obvious difference is that the sale of manufactured products to foreigners has been called trade and the sale of services to foreigners has not been called trade. It is therefore natural for them to ask why the sale of services to foreigners should not be considered a form of trade and given equal treatment by governments.

The appendix to this book describes how a group of business executives from American companies producing services persuaded the U.S. Congress to extend legislative provisions dealing with international trade to foreign sales of services, and how U.S. trade officials ultimately persuaded other countries to initiate multilateral negotiations to liberalize trade in services.

As governments began to give serious consideration to trade in services and the rules that might be devised for such trade, economists began to reexamine old assumptions about the nontradeability of services and to extend international trade theory to services. (The outcome of the resulting theoretical and empirical work is described in considerable detail in Chapter 6.)

Out of the debates and studies has come a growing awareness that advances in transportation and communication technologies have made it economically feasible to trade services, and that such trade is growing rapidly. There is now a much broader realization that trade in services can take place through international travel by either consumers or producers of services and, more important, through international flows of information and money. There is now also a greater awareness that international communication and transportation policies can have a major impact on the competitive position of firms competing in world markets.

The evolution of opinion is perhaps best illustrated by excerpts from a statement released in 1981 by the International Chamber of Commerce in Paris, with members in over 100 countries in both the developed and developing world:

> A vigorous and comprehensive liberalization of international trade in services is now urgently necessary. The International Chamber of Commerce therefore urges all governments to enter into reciprocal and mutually advantageous undertakings to reduce impediments to international trade in services in as far-reaching manner as possible. . . . The ICC believes that the inclusion of trade in the international market economy system is the best guarantee for the continued growth of international trade in both visibles and invisibles. In calling on governments to liberalize trade in services, the ICC recognizes that, as in the case of trade in goods, free trade in services is the standard against which the liberalization process should be measured.

The ICC was ahead of the governments of its member countries. It took another five years for trade ministers to agree on the launching of multilateral negotiations on trade in services.

The debate over trade in services has also led to a growing recognition in many countries that their domestic policies in services were badly in need of rethinking and reform. Work is now underway in many countries to gain a better understanding of the role of services as well as trade in services in economic growth and development.

CONCLUSIONS

Profound changes in the technology underlying the production of both goods and services have fundamentally altered the role of services in the world economy over the past few years. They have accelerated the international flow of services and increased the importance of service inputs in the production of goods.

Old ideas about the nature of service and its role in international trade have thus become less and less useful, and indeed a major hindrance, to managing the policies affecting the organization of service activities in the world economy. Old ideas, however, tend to have a tenacious hold on us and shape our perception of the world around us long after the world has changed. Long-standing assumptions about the nature of things affect how all of us—average citizens, senior government officials, scholars, and in particular statisticians—see the world. Since trade in services has not been considered a viable activity, little effort has gone into measuring it. Thus even as the world was changing, people clung to the idea that it was not possible to trade services.

A revolution in human thought was required in order to develop both the means and the will to identify and measure the growing trade in services. That revolution in thinking has only begun, and it may be some time before public perceptions have adjusted themselves to the new economic realities.

Just as outdated assumptions about trade in services have camouflaged the growing importance of trade in services to the world economy and to the economic interests of many countries, even older assumptions and prejudices about the unproductive nature of services have distorted public perceptions of the role of services in the domestic economy. These perceptions have led to a general neglect of the services sector in many areas of policy such as taxation and regulatory reform.

The growing international debate over trade in services has now led to a growing interest in the role of services in domestic economic growth. Trade negotiations in services thus could prove to be an important catalyst in facilitating long overdue reforms in domestic policies on services.

NOTE

1. Porat's numbers on information workers includes workers employed in producing machines used by information workers. The value of national output generated by service workers associated with the production, processing, and distribution of information would be somewhat smaller.

5
CONCEPTS, ISSUES, AND DEFINITIONS

Any concept that has been as little explored as trade in services lacks precision in language, and there is therefore a certain fuzziness in communications when people talk about the subject. As discussed in previous chapters, most people have only a vague notion about trade in services, and those who do know what the phrase means are likely to find few who agree with them on that meaning. This chapter is therefore devoted to an effort to clarify some of the differences in the concepts that are associated with trade in services, and to set out a consistent definition.

Now that serious negotiations have been launched on trade in services, the debate over the definition of trade in services has increasingly become a debate over the scope of the negotiations. Those who want to include certain activities within the scope of the negotiations are putting forward expansive definitions that would cover the desired activities. Those who are opposed to the inclusion of certain activities in the negotiations are putting forward restrictive definitions that would exclude such activities from the negotiations.

ALTERNATIVE DEFINITIONS OF TRADE IN SERVICES

The precise definition of a word inevitably depends on context. When the phrase *trade in services* is used as a label for an observable category of economic activities measured by statisticians for the national income accounts, it has a definition that is determined by the needs of national income accounting and the use of national income data for the management of macroeconomic policies. When the term is used by economists to describe a concept in economic theory, the definition is determined by the logical structure of such theories. When businessmen talk about trade in services they often talk about it in terms of the competitive position of the firm vis-à-vis its foreign competitors. And when lawmakers and policymakers talk about it they inevitably seek to fit the definition to broader political and policy requirements.

The Statistician's Definition of Trade in Services

The statisticians who are responsible for maintaining the national income and balance of payments accounts define exports of services as services that are sold to residents of another country, and imports of services as services that are purchased from residents of another country. A resident is anyone who has decided to live in a country for more than a temporary period.[1] Trade is the sale of something valuable to someone living in another country. A service is any economic activity that does not result in the manufacture of a product.

Alternatively, services can be defined as the output of a list of industries, professions, and establishments—shipping, banking, insurance, hotels, restaurants, barbershops, education, engineering, architecture, research, entertainment, massage parlors, travel agencies, computer software, information, communications, couriers, medical care, printing, advertising, executive recruiting, leasing, and car rental services. International trade in services can therefore be defined as the sale of products produced by these industries to people living in other countries.

A few examples might help to illustrate how a range of transactions would be classified in calculating exports and imports of services for national income and balance of payments accounts. An American employee of an American bank in France who helps an American tourist traveling in France is exporting French services to the United States, even though he is American and works for an American firm. The ownership of the bank and the nationality of the employee are irrelevant for the calculation of official trade statistics. Services supplied by a resident of France are counted as French services, even though the banker is a U.S. citizen.

Services provided by an American travel company in Italy to German tourists result in Italian exports of services to Germany. If the travel company processes the invoices in the United Kingdom and handles legal claims in New York, the sale of services by the American company in Italy will also result in British and American exports of services to Italy.

Definitions always have many gray areas and many of the dividing lines seem rather arbitrary. Why should the repair of a piece of equipment fall into the category of services, while the assembly of that equipment is called manufacturing?[2] Where do you draw the line between a resident and a temporary visitor? Is a computer tape full of information a manufactured product or a service, or is it both?[3] How do you distinguish between the residence of an individual producing services and the legal status of the company that employs that individual?[4]

International trade statistics collected by the government for the purposes of calculating national income and balance of payments are primarily designed to answer a number of questions related to the functioning of a nation's economy, and the management of macroeconomic policy. For example, the government wants to know how much domestic output of goods and services and how much domestic employment were generated by sales of goods and services to other countries. The government also wants to know to what extent domestic consumption of goods and services is satisfied by goods and services produced abroad. Third, the government wants to know to what extent the country's supply of foreign exchange was increased by exports and reduced by imports of goods and services.

A secondary purpose of government trade statistics is to shed light on the competitive position of producers located inside the country vis-á-vis producers in other countries. Data on exports and imports of a particular service such as advertising thus also provide information on how well a country's advertising industry is doing in competition with industries in other countries.

For all of these purposes the government needs a definition of trade in services that is based on territory. Anything that happens inside a country's borders is considered a domestic activity, and any sales to anyone living and working in another country's territory is therefore treated as trade.[5]

The Businessman's Definition of Trade in Services

Businessmen frequently have in mind a broader concept of trade in services based on the nationality of the firm producing the services. What counts for an individual firm is not whether a service was produced by a facility in the United States, but whether it was produced in a facility owned by the firm. In a world where global firms compete with each other head to head in a global market, this broader concept comes much closer to commercial reality, because a firm will ultimately succeed or fail in areas dominated by global competition on the basis of its ability to build up its share of the global market with all of its global facilities, not on the basis of its exports from the home country.

The U.S. government recognizes that the broad economic interests of the country are advanced when American firms do well in the global competition. Policy officials responsible for international commerce are therefore interested not only in transactions between U.S. territory and foreign territories, but also in the total volume of sales made by firms owned by U.S. citizens. As a reflection of this interest, the U.S. government collects data on all international sales and purchases of services by American-owned firms, encompassing both exports and imports of services from facilities in the United States, and all sales and purchases made from U.S.-owned facilities abroad. These data are collected not every three months as the data on trade based on a territorial definition are, but once every five years.[6]

For some purposes it might also be useful to have data on services produced abroad by a country's citizens living and working abroad. After all, as long as someone has decided to retain home country citizenship, this must be an indication of an intention to return. Many expatriates living abroad also send back regular remittances to family members who have stayed at home. Income earned abroad by citizens can thus be viewed as an addition to national economic wealth. Indeed, some countries, including the United States, tax their citizens residing and working abroad. Few countries, however, collect useful detailed statistics about the services produced by their citizens residing abroad.

With so many different concepts of trade in services it is easy to get confused. To avoid fuzzy thinking we will use the phrase *trade in services* only for transactions that fit the statistical definition based on the residence of the producer, and we will use the phrase *international transactions in services* or *international commerce in services* for transactions that fall into the broader definition based on the nationality of the firm.

The Policymaker's Definition of Trade in Services

The definition of trade in services has become a hot topic of debate because it can determine which policies are subject to international trade negotiations. To label an activity trade can be tantamount to saying that it should be covered by a country's trade laws and international trade agreements, and that can affect both profits and bureaucratic turf. As commercial interests line up behind one bureaucratic faction or another, a debate over definition begins to look more like a gladiatorial contest.

The definition of trade in services can affect the profits of particular enterprises and their owners since the application of domestic trade laws and international trade agreements to an activity carried out by an enterprise could either help or hurt an individual enterprise. An activity that falls within the definition of trade could benefit from government programs designed to assist exports or from international trade negotiations designed to relax foreign regulations that restrict exports. An activity that falls within the definition of trade could also be hurt if the home government agrees in the context of international trade negotiations to relax regulations that now restrict foreign competitors.

Whether or not an activity is defined as trade can also determine whether policy issues that affect such activities come under the bureaucratic responsibility of trade officials. Trade officials in most governments have the responsibility to enforce domestic trade laws, to formulate trade policy objectives, and to negotiate international trade agreements. If an activity is labeled trade, it is generally assumed that trade officials will have the primary responsibility to coordinate government policy with respect to such activities and to negotiate international agreements on such policies.

THE SUBSTANTIVE POLICY DEBATE OVER THE DEFINITION OF TRADE IN SERVICES

The intimate relationship between trade in services and other economic activities raises questions about the extent to which the definition of trade in services should cover such activities. When should an international movement of people, information, money, and goods associated with trade in services be treated as trade in services and when should it be treated as immigration, a noncommercial flow of information, an international capital flow, or trade in goods respectively? Perhaps even more to the point, when should policy issues that arise in each of these areas be treated as policy issues concerning trade in services, and when should they be treated as immigration issues or issues of international information, international finance, or international trade in goods?

Similarly, when should international communications and transportation be defined as trade in services and when should they be defined as domestic activities jointly undertaken with foreign entities that provide the same services domestically in the other country involved? When should policy issues affecting international communications and transportation be treated as trade policy issues, and when should they be treated as domestic or international regulatory issues?

Finally, to what extent should an international cross-border transaction in services be defined as trade if it requires a substantial presence in the other country, including investments in local facilities? These questions are addressed in greater detail below.

Immigration

Under the definition of trade in services used by statisticians, someone who travels to Greece from Germany for a vacation is importing services into Germany as long as that person remains a resident of Germany. A person who travels from New York to Ankara to advise a foreign client on the construction of a bridge is exporting services from the United States as long as he or she remains a resident of the United States. There is no fixed definition of a resident, however, since each country has its own laws and regulations on residence. The statistical definition of trade in services involving movement of people is thus closely tied to national laws and regulations defining a resident.

Under U.S. immigration laws and regulations, a foreign exporter who wants to meet clients in the United States can obtain a B-1 visa under the treaty-trader principle. U.S. immigration officials until recently did not recognize the applicability of the treaty-trader principle to trade in services and therefore did not grant B-1 visas to foreigners exporting services to the United States. At the urging of U.S. trade officials, U.S. immigration officials have been willing to consider applications for B-1 visas by foreigners exporting services to the United States, but they have yet to develop a workable definition of trade in services for this purpose. Generally they have granted such requests only where more than half the total value of services sold in the United States is produced abroad.

There are few policy issues as sensitive as immigration policy. What that means is that most countries assign a high priority to the objective of controlling entry by foreigners and lower priorities to trade and other policy objectives. At the same time, international trade in services could not flourish if people could not move from one country to another for temporary periods. The definition of trade in services with respect to the movement of people is therefore one of the most difficult issues that negotiators will have to face in developing future agreements on trade in services.

Trade in Information and Culture

Under the definition used by statisticians, an international flow of information results in trade in services when a resident of another country pays for the information. A letter to Aunt Nellie is not trade in services, nor is a public report on recent events. However, a news report by a press agency or a consultant's report on bookeeping practices in Upper Agraria is counted as trade in services; so is information supplied by corporate headquarters to a subsidiary or branch abroad when that subsidiary or branch has to pay a fee to corporate headquarters.

Some representatives of the press and some representatives of multinational corporations have expressed great concern about the classification of foreign press reports or internal corporate transfers of information as trade in services. They are concerned that a trade perspective could persuade some governments to impose tariffs or other restrictions on such flows in the mistaken belief that it would help protect a domestic industry. This is a rather surprising argument to trade officials since the major objective of trade negotiations is to reduce barriers rather than to impose them, but the concerns that have been voiced are understandable in light of the public debate in France, Brazil, and some other countries on taxing international information flows. Put another way, some people would argue that principles like freedom of the press and the free flow of information are more powerful arguments for maintaining a free flow of information than the free trade paradigm.

Government regulations aimed at a number of policy objectives can affect trade in services in the form of international information flows, including the protection of privacy, the maintenance of records so the government can discharge its fiduciary responsibilities, the protection of intellectual property, and the preservation of reliable public communications. In each of these areas, a balance must be achieved between the trade policy objective of facilitating the flow of information as a channel for trade in services and the domestic regulatory objective.

The conflict over the appropriate scope and definition of information-related trade is particularly difficult in the area of culture. Many governments believe that they have an important responsibility to preserve the national cultural identity as expressed through the media and the arts. Many of these governments also see the media and the arts as channels for public education. These governments tend to take the view that cultural activities should not be treated as commercial activities but as public utilities provided by the state or closely supervised by the state. Those who support this point of view are also inclined to argue that international television and radio broadcasts or international sales of newspapers, books, films, or videotapes cannot be treated as just another form of trade. Most commercial producers of newspapers, books, and so on show little reluctance to seek the help of trade negotiators when foreign barriers limit their sales abroad.

Trade in Finance

Money can move from one country to another for a variety of reasons—in payment for goods and services, for the acquisition of financial or real assets, as a gift to a relative, or to transfer an inheritance. An international movement of money per se is not trade in services, but it can lead to trade in services if a foreign bank or investment house financial management performs services.[7]

Under the definition used by statisticians, the financial management services provided by a London bank to a resident of Hong Kong would be counted as an export of services by the

United Kingdom and an import of services by Hong Kong, though no country has good data on exports of financial management services. Contrary to common belief, however, interest, dividends, profits, or capital gains earned by the money invested in Britain have nothing to do with trade in services. They are treated as a return on capital, a separate category in the balance of payments accounts.

There has been considerable reluctance on the part of banks and finance ministries to recognize that financial management services provided to residents of other countries constitute trade. Banking and other financial activities are viewed as exclusive activities that should be carried out on the basis of their own genteel rules of the game, and not mixed together with the kind of bargaining that takes place in trade negotiations. Finance ministries naturally also have an interest in keeping trade officials off their bureaucratic turf. Some of the more dynamic banks have gradually come to the view, however, that a trade perspective could be beneficial to the removal of restrictions on their activities abroad.

Trade in Goods

When is an international movement of goods trade in services and when is it trade in goods; or when is a policy that affects the international movement of goods a trade in services issue and when is it a trade in goods issue? Does it make a difference? Yes, it will make a difference because there are no current international rules for trade in services, and future rules for trade in services are likely to be somewhat different from the existing rules on trade in goods.

Depending on whether they wanted their activities covered by rules for trade in goods or by future rules for trade in services, representatives of various enterprises have argued over the definition of trade in services that takes the form of an international movement of goods. The most common issues of debate have been the following: 1) Should a machine that has been repaired abroad be treated as an import of a machine or as an import of repair services? 2) Should a computer tape that contains software and accounting information be treated as an import of an unenhanced computer tape, as an import of a computer tape whose value has been enhanced by the addition of the software and accounting information, or as an import of computer software and accounting services?

Is It Trade in Services or Is It a Shared Public Utility?

International trade in support services such as transportation and communications facilitates the international movement of goods, people, money, and information. Under the definition used by statisticians, the sale of shipping, aviation, or communications services is treated as an export of services if such services are sold to the resident of another country. The crucial distinction is whether the buyer and the seller of the transportation or communications service are residents of different countries, not whether the transportation or communication is provided between one country and another. Even transportation and communications provided between two points inside the same country would be treated as exports if they were sold to a resident of another country (provided you can collect such data, which, of course, is very difficult).

A conceptual difficulty arises in connection with the transportation of internationally traded goods. Who is the buyer of the transportation service, the exporter or the importer? Even though the exporter buys the transportation service, isn't the importer ultimately the real buyer of the service? This can be very confusing, and statisticians therefore usually treat all transportation associated with exports of goods one way and all transportation associated with imports of goods another way, no matter who actually buys the transportation service. Under the cash, insurance, and freight (CIF) method of valuing trade, the cost of transportation is treated as if it were purchased by the exporter and, under the free on board (FOB) method of valuing trade, the cost of transportation is treated as if it were purchased by the importer.

The representatives of some transportation firms have argued that all international transportation should be treated as trade in services, even if it is sold to domestic residents. Their argument is that you cannot evaluate the size of the market that is contested between domestic and foreign transportation firms if you treat the sale of international transportation services to domestic residents differently from the sale of international transportation services to residents of other countries, or more to the point, if you do not collect and publish data on international transportation services provided to domestic residents on the same basis as international transportation services provided to foreign residents. This is probably not a very persuasive argument for changing the basic definition of trade, but it is certainly a persuasive argument for the collection and publication of more comprehensive data for analytical purposes.

The representatives of some communications companies have made the opposite argument that international communications should not be treated as international trade since each international telephone call is serviced both by the telephone company in the country where the call was initiated and by the telephone company in the destination country. They argue that basic international communications services should therefore be treated as two separate domestic transactions, one in the country where the call was initiated and another in the country to which the call was made.

Another argument that could be made is that almost all international telephone calls are purchased from a domestic telephone company and, therefore, should always be treated as domestic transactions. The real reason why some well-entrenched communications companies advance these arguments is that they do not want to subject themselves to negotiations that could reduce barriers to international competition in this area. For the same reason, new entrants into the international communications area make exactly the opposite arguments.

Is It Trade in Services or Is It Investment?

Services that are sold in a foreign country usually require additional inputs in that country, and in some cases the value of inputs supplied in the importing country is greater than the value of inputs supplied in the exporting country. For statistical purposes, the utilization of inputs in both the exporting country and the importing country does not pose any difficulties in defining trade in services. The service inputs provided in the exporting country are defined as trade in services, and the inputs provided in the importing country are defined as the domestic production of services. If the facility producing the local inputs in the importing country is owned by the foreign producer, the production of those inputs can also be defined as the product of foreign investment activity.

A problem of definition arises with respect to policies that could affect the ability of a foreign producer to deliver services in the foreign market. Should policies that affect the ability of a foreign producer to supply services to a foreign market be treated as trade issues when the issue concerns the right of the foreign producer to invest in a facility that will supply the necessary local inputs?

Many exporters of services argue that such policies should be treated as a trade issue because they affect their ability to sell services abroad. Others argue that the sale of services that require substantial inputs in the importing country should be treated as a foreign investment issue rather than as a trade issue. The reason for this debate is that it has traditionally been assumed that trade negotiations should address trade issues and not foreign investment issues.[8] Whether a policy is defined as a trade policy issue will therefore determine whether that policy will be subject to rules and agreements negotiated in the trade area or not.

Without the ability to acquire local inputs, the scope for trade in both goods and services would be quite limited. In recognition of the need for local inputs, the existing rules for trade in goods provide that foreign exporters should have the right to be treated the same way as local producers with respect to the acquisition of local inputs; this is the so-called national treatment principle of the General Agreement on Tariffs and Trade (GATT). The national treatment principle in the GATT, however, does not give foreign exporters the right to own facilities (such as a car dealership) that produce the local inputs. Any rules that are developed for trade in services will have to address this issue and come up with an approach that reflects the special character of services. We will explore this issue in later chapters.

CONCLUSIONS

How a transaction is defined thus can have major policy implications, particularly in an area like trade in services, where the issues are complex and governmental objectives are not clearly delineated. The debate over the content and shape of future international agreements on trade in services to a considerable extent revolves around the scope of trade negotiations in services, and by implication around the definition of the term *trade in services* as used in a policy context.

The resolution of this debate may well lead to a new definition of trade in services for policy purposes that will cover some but not all of the activities associated with the international movement of people, information, money, and goods, and the use of facilities in the importing country. At the same time, international communications and transportation issues are likely to be treated as both trade issues and sectoral regulatory issues. Where the boundaries will be drawn no one will know until the end of the negotiations.

NOTES

1. Each country has its own definition of residence embedded in its visa, immigration, and tax laws. For statistical purposes, a resident is normally someone who lives in a country for more than three months, though some might not consider someone a resident unless that person lives in the country for at least one year.

CONCEPTS, ISSUES, AND DEFINITIONS

2. Repairs made abroad are counted as imports of services in U.S. trade statistics, but the United States imposes a duty on foreign repairs when the equipment is reimported into the United States, much as it would on other imports of goods.
3. A majority of an international panel of GATT experts established to look at this issue to resolve some disputes over the application of customs duties has determined that the computer tape as a good should be valued on the basis of its commodity value, that is, in terms of the price charged for an unused tape. By implication, the GATT panel decided that a computer tape full of data should partly be treated as a commodity and partly as a service.
4. For purposes of calculating statistics you assume that everyone working at a factory or office in another country is a resident of that country.
5. Sampson and Snape (1985, p. 172) refer to this as the "residential" concept of national income.
6. The last such survey, entitled *U.S. Direct Investment Abroad: 1982 Benchmark Survey Data*, was issued by the U.S. Department of Commerce in December 1985.
7. Economists disagree whether interest income and other returns to capital should be treated as exports of services. Both for analytical and for policy reasons interest and dividend payments, as payments for the use of capital, should be segregated from payments for services rendered through human effort. Analytically, it makes sense to distinguish income from current economic activity from income generated as a result of the ownership of assets. By distinguishing income received from producing services and income received as a result of the ownership of assets, it also becomes easier to explain to a country's workers why income received from producing services should not be treated differently from income received from producing goods. Including investment income as trade in services confuses the issue. Many economists, however, have taken the opposite view that the use of capital is a service provided by owners of capital, and that income generated from the use of capital should therefore be treated as payment for imported services. See for example Sampson and Snape (1985, p. 176).
8. In the current Uruguay Round of multilateral trade negotiations, trade-related investment measures have been added to the agenda as a legitimate negotiating issue. This represents a major break from the past presumption against the negotiation of investment

issues in the General Agreement on Tariffs and Trade. At the same time, the mandate limits the negotiations to the trade effects of investment measures, rather than the extent to which such measures limit investment opportunities per se.

6
DOES INTERNATIONAL TRADE THEORY APPLY TO TRADE IN SERVICES?

Modern economic theory owes its beginning to Adam Smith and his *Wealth of Nations*, which appeared in 1776, the same year that the United States declared its independence. Both events were heavily influenced by the industrial revolution, which was rapidly changing the economic and political landscape at the end of the eighteenth century, and by the age of enlightenment, which was characterized by a more open and critical approach to the investigation of the world around us.

In his book, Adam Smith articulated the basic mechanism of the market, whereby the pursuit of individual profit leads to the most efficient use of the country's resources in producing what consumers want to buy. It made a virtue out of greed and thus offended the moralists. In fact, Marxist theoreticians and Christian theologians are still struggling with the question how the profit motive and morality can be reconciled.

For Adam Smith, it was a question not of morality, but of how things worked if people were left to pursue their own natural economic instincts. He also showed how the organization of economic activity and government policies could be analyzed to draw conclusions about their impact on the availability of goods and services. Adam Smith thus laid the foundation for modern economic theory and market-oriented policies not only within nations, but also among nations.

The arguments for free trade among countries were more fully elaborated by David Ricardo in the *Principles of Political Economy*, published in 1817. Contrary to popular impressions, it was David Ricardo and not Adam Smith who developed the theory of comparative advantage. One of the most frequently quoted and yet least understood theories of economics, it demonstrates how trade between two countries can be advantageous whenever they have a different mix of resources and skills, even if one country is more efficient in producing all tradeable goods and services. Differences in the mix of resources and skills lead to different price relationships among the goods and services produced in each country, and these differences in price relationships are the basis of all trade between two countries.

The least understood aspect of the theory of comparative advantage is that it does not require exporters to be more efficient or to have lower labor costs than foreign producers; instead, exporters have to be relatively more efficient in utilizing the country's resources than other industries in their own country. Comparative advantage means that every country can gain from trade if it concentrates its energies in the industries that make best use of its resources and skills.

The principle of comparative advantage can be seen at work not only among countries, but also within every national economy, or even within an individual office or household. Thus it is rational for an engineer to hire a draftsman who is less skilled in drawing blueprints, because it allows the engineer to more fully utilize his or her source of greatest comparative advantage, the training and experience in engineering. The engineer's income is maximized by allocating the available time to engineering work. At the same time, someone who is not as talented in drawing blueprints as the engineer, but even less talented in doing engineering work, is well advised to allocate the available time to drafting blueprints rather than engineering.

Over the last two hundred years many economists have expanded the basic theoretical framework developed by Adam Smith and David Ricardo, thus adding to our understanding of the various conditions under which trade leads to gains for the participants. Conversely these economists have also laid out the conditions under which a country is better off by restricting trade. Economists have also tested the extent to which the theory of comparative advantage can be used to explain existing patterns of trade; they have done this by examining whether the composition of a country's resources can explain the composition of its exports and imports.

DOES INTERNATIONAL TRADE THEORY APPLY TO SERVICES?

Adam Smith and David Ricardo largely focused on trade in goods, since they assumed that most services were not tradeable. Most of the theories on international trade developed by later economists were also described entirely in terms of examples involving trade in goods, and the work carried out to test the applicability of those theories under various circumstances has been largely focused on trade in goods. Only in recent years have economists begun to examine how the extensive economic literature on international trade could be applied to trade in services.

Interestingly enough, while Adam Smith laid out his arguments for free trade in terms of trade in goods, he applied the same general principles elsewhere in the book to argue against the Navigation Act, which placed restrictions on the right of foreign ships to bring foreign goods into British ports (though foreign ships were allowed to take British goods out of British ports). Smith argued, "The act of navigation is not favourable to foreign commerce, or to the growth of that opulence which can arise from it. The interest of a nation in its commercial relations to foreign nations is, like that of a merchant with regard to the different people with whom he deals, to buy as cheap and to sell as dear as possible." (1817, p. 431)

Adam Smith thus saw that restrictions on the right of foreign ships to carry British imports were equivalent to an import tax on goods and could be rejected on the same grounds. This is not quite the same thing as saying that services should be imported and exported on the same basis as goods, but it showed that the same economic reasoning could be applied to trade in services.

A half century after Adam Smith, Frederic Bastiat, a French economist and member of the French parliament, applied the same tools of economic reasoning to the construction of the railroad between Paris and Madrid. When the Paris-to-Madrid railroad was being debated in the French Assembly, one member of the Assembly by the name of M. Simiot argued that it should have a gap at Bordeaux, because such a break in the line would enhance the wealth of all the porters, commissionaires, hotel keepers, and bargemen of Bordeaux and thereby would enrich France. To demonstrate the absurdity of the argument, Bastiat wrote, "If Bordeaux has a right to profit by a gap... then Angouleme, Poitiers, Tours, Orleans should also demand gaps as being for the general interest.... In this way we will succeed in having a railroad composed of successive gaps, and which may be denominated a Negative Railway." (Quoted in Heilbroner, 1961, pp. 151–152)

Adam Smith's analysis of shipping services and Frederic Bastiat's analysis of railroad services did not make as much of an impact on economic thinking as their observations about trade in goods, and international trade economists over the last two hundred years have concerned themselves largely with trade in goods.

With the growing interest in trade in services in recent years, however, a number of economists have addressed themselves to the question whether the existing body of international trade theory could be applied to services. Generally, economists have concluded that the application of the existing theoretical framework can lead to useful insights about trade in services. (See, for example, Herman and Holst, 1981; Hindley and Smith, 1984; Oulton, 1984; Sampson and Snape, 1985; Deardorff, 1985; and Richardson, 1987.)

Most of the problems economists have encountered in applying existing trade theories to trade in services can be traced to the fact that trade in services is largely invisible, that it is tied to the international flow of people, information, money, and goods, and that it is closely tied to foreign investment in the importing country. Because trade in services is largely invisible, economists have difficulty in precisely identifying what is being traded. Because trade in services is so closely tied to international movements of people, information, money, and goods, economists sometimes confuse the two. Because trade is linked to investment, some economists have questioned the value of looking at the trade dimension.

The unique characteristics of trade in services do not invalidate the application of existing international trade theory. At the same time, the existing theory will have to be expanded to deal with the unique aspects of trade in services. The close link between trade in services and the international flow of people, information, money, and goods, for example, has major implications for the way economists need to organize their thinking as they probe more deeply into the theoretical, empirical, and policy issues related to trade in services. International trade in services thus has to be analyzed not only in terms of the service products that are traded, but also in terms of the means for transferring such services from one country to another. In order to analyze trade in repair services between two countries, for example, one would need to examine differences in the cost of repairing a machine in the two countries, and the relative costs and economic gains associated with five alternative means for transferring repair services—shipping the machine to be repaired from one country to another, sending a repairman to the country where the machine is located, sending information that will help a local repairman accomplish the task at less cost, bringing the foreign repairman to the factory for training, or establishing a local repair facility in the importing country (the last two options would clearly take more time). In other words, in order to understand trade in repair services, or even just to define trade in repair services, one has to develop a fairly clear concept of the family of services that can fulfill a particular economic objective, and how the alternative means for transferring the service affect the relative costs and benefits of trade in such services.

The difficulty of observing trade in services has important implications for the research strategy economists need to adopt in seeking empirical data to back up their theories. As discussed in Chapter 2, government statistics are not very well organized to shed much light on trade in services, and while current efforts to collect more data will be extremely useful, there is an inherent limit to the government's ability to collect meaningful, detailed data. The implication for economists is that they should not expect to base their research of trade in services on aggregate data. In order to find out what services are being traded, economists will need to pursue case studies based on the experience of individual firms and to use such detailed information to interpret the aggregate data that become available.

NORMATIVE AND DESCRIPTIVE THEORIES OF INTERNATIONAL TRADE

The theory of comparative advantage is both a normative theory and a descriptive theory. As a normative theory, it describes a set of circumstances under which trade is economically advantageous to the countries participating in such trade. As a descriptive theory, the theory of comparative advantage seeks to explain observed trade flows among countries in terms of observed differences in the distribution of resources and factors of production among such countries.

Normative Theories of International Trade

The normative theory of comparative advantage holds that two countries can gain from international trade if 1) supply and demand in the two countries are determined on the basis of market competition, and 2) prices charged by producers adequately measure the cost to society, and the prices paid by consumers adequately measure the value of services to society. To the extent these conditions are met, the theory of comparative advantage demonstrates that trade raises each country's standard of living by allowing each country to devote its resources to what it produces most efficiently. In terms of the terminology used by economists, trade leads to an improved global allocation of resources. To the extent that any of these conditions do not hold, trade may not be in the economic interest of the countries involved under some limited conditions. A large number of books and articles have been written to elaborate on these conditions.

The theory of comparative advantage deals with only one set of economic gains generated by international trade, namely, the increase in output available for consumption that is achieved by producing a more efficient mix of goods with existing national resources. International trade can also generate dynamic gains by putting competitive pressures on domestic producers to adopt more efficient methods of production. Trade thus increases national income by changing both what is produced and how it is produced. On the other hand, sometimes strong competition from foreign producers can deprive domestic producers of the time needed to hone their skills and to develop the economies of scale that could make them fully competitive with foreign producers.

Much of the economic literature in trade has been devoted to identifying the various economic conditions under which trade would not be in the economic interest of one country or another. Where such conditions can be identified in the real world, a rationale can be shown to exist either for restricting trade or for implementing government measures that would bring about the right conditions for beneficial trade.

A corollary set of international trade theories describes the circumstances under which one government or another can improve its gains from trade by taxing imports or subsidizing exports. A government can improve its own gains from trade by imposing duties on imports (or by offering subsidies for exports) whenever domestic demand and foreign supply of foreign goods are responsive to price changes, a relatively common situation. In terms of the terminology used by economists, a country can shift the terms of trade in its favor by imposing duties on its imports whenever the foreign price elasticity of supply and the domestic price elasticity of demand for foreign goods are elastic. It can also be demonstrated, however, that if other governments adopt the same strategy, both countries can end up losing. If each country seeks to adopt an optimal tax on imports and an optimal subsidy on exports, every country can end up worse off than if they all agreed to avoid import duties and export subsidies.[1]

Such circumstances can arise, for example, in industries that are characterized by large economies of scale—that is, where the development of new products requires large expenditures on research and development, where efficient production can only be achieved on the basis of large investments in capital equipment, or where the product can be sold only through an expensive distribution and maintenance network. Many of these industries are often also characterized by steep learning curves; the cost of production and quality of the product are highly sensitive to the training and experience gained from the initial stages of production. In such industries international competitive advantage is not determined by a God-given endowment of resources but rather by being the first firm to develop the necessary economies of scale, either by chance or as a result of government support.[2]

The calculation of economic gains and losses from international trade is based on a concept of national wealth. While the country as a whole can be shown to gain from trade, some industries or groups of workers are likely to experience a loss of income as a result of trade. One of the issues that has concerned economists is the extent to which those who gain from international trade should compensate those who lose. Economic assistance to those adversely affected by the removal of trade barriers can reduce their resistance to such policies. On the other hand, it is argued that economic groups adversely affected by technological changes or by acts of God are not compensated for such losses, and that there is no greater reason to give preferential treatment to economic groups adversely affected by trade.

Descriptive Theories of International Trade

Descriptive theories of international trade seek to explain the pattern of imports and exports found in the real world on the basis of each country's economic endowment of resources and other economic variables. The theory of comparative advantage seeks to explain the pattern of trade on the basis of each country's relative endowment of the major factors of production such as capital and labor.

The descriptive theory of comparative advantage was developed by two Swedish economists, Eli Heckscher (1919) and Bertil Ohlin (1933).[3] The Heckscher/Ohlin theory basically says that a country will have a comparative advantage in goods that require a relatively large input of factors of production that are relatively plentiful and therefore relatively cheap in that country, and that it will have a comparative disadvantage in goods that require a relatively large input of factors of production that are relatively scarce and therefore relatively expensive in that country. A capital-rich country with high wage rates should therefore be expected to export goods that require a large amount of capital and import goods that require a relatively large input of cheap labor.

One of the first economists to examine the empirical validity of the theory was Wassily Leontief (1953), who computed capital and labor ratios for U.S. export industries and import-competing industries. Leontief came up with the surprising findings that U.S. industries that competed with imports had a higher ratio of capital to labor than U.S. export industries. This was a surprising result, because everyone had assumed, on the basis of the Heckscher/Ohlin theory, that the United States would show competitive strength in industries that required a large input of capital, which was plentiful and relatively cheap in this country, and that the United States would tend to import goods with a relatively larger input of labor relative to capital, since labor was considered to be relatively scarce and therefore expensive in this country.

Needless to say, Leontief's findings created considerable controversy in the profession about who was right: Heckscher/Ohlin or Leontief. The final judgment is that both are right. The Heckscher/Ohlin theorem seems to be valid over a broad range of circumstances, but this was not evident in Leontief's findings because he had not considered other factor inputs such as human capital and natural resources, both of which are plentiful in the United States. Other economists such as Baldwin (1971), Hufbauer (1970), and Lary (1968) expanded the analysis done by Leontief to include these other factors, and their work has shown that Heckscher and Ohlin were right after all.

In recent years empirical investigations have focused on the observation that countries often export and import the same type of goods. The Heckscher/Ohlin theory of comparative advantage, which assumes that trade is based on an exchange of goods which contain diffcrent resource inputs, cannot explain such intrasectoral trade. This has led to new theories that seek to explain trade flows in terms of product differentiation, leadership in new technology, institutional factors, and government industrial targeting policies.

Theories based on product differentiation start from the observation that in many product areas goods produced in different countries or by different firms are quite different in quality, performance characteristics, and visual appeal. Two-way trade takes place in these products among countries with similar resource endowments because consumers have different needs and different tastes. Theories based on technology leadership and industrial targeting are based on the observation that competitive advantage in some industries has gone to firms that were first able to produce a product on an efficient scale, either by chance or by government design.

The questions that have been raised about the empirical validity of the Heckscher/Ohlin theory do not undermine conclusions about gains from trade derived from the normative theory of comparative advantage.

DOES THE THEORY OF COMPARATIVE ADVANTAGE APPLY TO TRADE IN SERVICES?

The theory of comparative advantage tells us that trade between two countries creates mutual economic gains provided such trade is based on a competitive market and provided it does not generate other costs to society as a whole that producers do not have to pay. As a theoretical statement about relationships between economic actors and market outcomes, the theory should meet the test of logical consistency for all possible products that can be produced and exported by residents of one country and imported and consumed by residents of another country. In other words, the theory of comparative advantage as a theoretical statement about economic relationships should be equally valid whether the products encompassed by the theory are tradeable physical goods such as shoes and oranges, or tradeable services such as insurance and engineering.[4]

The theory of comparative advantage is nothing more than the extension of classical economic theory to international trade. It builds on the economic principles and theories that describe the behavior of buyers and sellers in domestic markets, and describes the adjustments that occur in isolated national markets when producers and consumers from one country are allowed to participate in another country's market.

Services, like goods, are produced by combining inputs of goods and services to create something of value that can be sold and purchased in the market. One should therefore be able to expect that the production, sale, purchase, and consumption of services follow the same pattern of economic behavior as the production, sale, purchase, and consumption of goods.[5] The remainder of this chapter is devoted to the testing of this proposition through rigorous analysis.

The questions that need to be addressed are the following: Do services have any characteristics that are inconsistent with the normal operation of markets as assumed by the theory of comparative advantage? Does the link between trade in services and international movements of people, information, money, and goods somehow undermine the theory? Does the need for investment in local production and distribution facilities in the importing country invalidate the theory?

In order to answer these questions, this section examines in greater detail whether the economic principles incorporated in the theory of comparative advantage govern economic behavior in services, whether the theory can encompass the related movement of people, information, money, and goods, and whether the need for foreign investment to export some services invalidates the application of the theory to trade in services.

Any conclusion reached about the applicability of the normative theory of comparative advantage to trade in services in general does not directly answer the more important question whether trade in specific services will lead to gains from trade. In order to demonstrate that trade in specific services will lead to economic gains, it has to be shown that trade in such services meets the conditions set out in the theory of comparative advantage with respect to competitive markets and nonmarket costs and benefits. The normative theory of comparative advantage ultimately is only a tool for analyzing the economic benefits of trade.

The following two sections are devoted to testing whether market conditions in services satisfy the preconditions set out in the normative theory of comparative advantage for the achievement of mutual economic gains. The theory holds that trade will lead to mutual economic gains if trade is the result of market competition and if trade does not generate other costs to society not paid by producers, or does not adversely affect the availability of benefits to society not normally paid for by individual consumers. The key issues therefore are whether markets in services are competitive,[6] whether the prices charged by producers adequately reflect the costs of production to society, and whether the prices consumers are willing to pay adequately reflect the benefits to society as a whole. These are particularly important issues in the area of services, and deserve careful consideration.

The final section will go over recent attempts to carry out empirical tests of the descriptive theory of comparative advantage on the basis of currently available aggregate data. The question is not whether trade leads to economic gains, but whether actual trade flows are explained by differences in the basic resource endowment of the countries involved in such trade. While the data available to researchers are extremely poor, as already noted, it is interesting that this work nevertheless seems to support the validity of the descriptive theory of comparative advantage in explaining observable trade in services.

Some Theoretical Issues

A theory about trade in services is likely to be meaningless unless it can encompass and account for the required movements of people, money, information, and goods involved. A closely related issue concerns the link between foreign investment and trade in services. Many services, particularly services sold to households and small business enterprises, can be exported only in conjunction with the local production of services by foreign-owned enterprises. Any conclusions about trade in these services has to be based on an explicit recognition of the link to investment, and a question can be raised whether the theory of comparative advantage can deal with this link.

Brian Hindley (1984) addressed the question whether the movement of people or capital associated with trade in services might invalidate one of the basic assumptions of the theory of comparative advantage, namely, that trade is based on existing differences in the distribution of resources in two countries trading with each other. He rejected this argument on two grounds. First, he pointed out that as long as the distribution of resources remains different in the two countries, a rationale for trade remains. The rationale for trade depends not on the initial distribution of resources, but on the extent to which a difference remains at any one time. Second, he pointed out that unimpeded international factor movements would lead to the same adjustment in global output and prices as unimpeded international trade, and therefore the economic theory of comparative advantage could encompass both trade in services and international factor movements.[7]

Another approach one could take to the issues addressed by Hindley is to establish a distinction between permanent transfers of factors of production from one country to another, and the temporary movement of people or money from one country to another for the purpose of exporting services. International movements of service workers can therefore be treated as trade in services if the stay abroad is temporary and can be treated as international factor movements if the stay abroad is for an extended period of time or is permanent.

Similarly, a distinction can be made between the management of money and the transfer of capital. The temporary movement of money to another country for the purpose of importing foreign financial management services can be distinguished analytically from the more permanent transfer of money connected with a capital investment decision. There is no reason to believe that money placed in a Eurodollar account with a London bank will necessarily be invested in Great Britain, or that money deposited in a large New York City bank will be invested in the United States. Any global financial institution that readily accepts deposits from foreigners also lends money to foreigners, and will seek out the most attractive investment opportunity in a global market context.

Another theoretical issue concerns the close relationship between trade in services and foreign investment in many services. Most services sold directly to consumers require significant investments in local production and distribution facilities, because the production of such services depends on close interactions between suppliers and consumers. It would be difficult for a foreign bank to provide consumer banking services without a local branch, and it would be even more difficult for McDonald's to sell hamburgers without a local facility where they can be cooked and served to customers. While foreign companies that sell consumer services can supply many of the managerial service inputs and much of the technology from the home country, they have to be able to use local facilities to produce and distribute the final product. Besides banking and fast food services, a list of services that require extensive local facilities would need to include hotel services, medical services, and local professional services sold to households and small business enterprises.

As traditionally formulated, the theory of comparative advantage does not directly address investment in foreign facilities. However, as noted earlier, trade and international movements in factors of production such as labor and capital ultimately have similar economic effects on the goods and services that are produced and consumed, the cost of production and the prices paid by consumers, and the income earned by workers. Nothing in the theory of comparative advantage precludes gains from trade that depend on local investments in facilities. International trade and investment flows equally lead to a more efficient utilization of productive resources, as goods, services, and factors of production move from countries where they are relatively cheap to countries where they are relatively expensive.[8]

In summary, the requirement for an international flow of people, money, information, and goods makes trade in services different from trade in goods, but it does not change the underlying economic rationale for such trade as demonstrated by the theory of comparative advantage. The foreign investment required to support trade in some services introduces an added dimension that is not directly addressed in the theory of comparative advantage, but it can be shown that such investments have complementary economic effects.

Although there is no logical flaw in the application of the normative theory of comparative advantage to trade in services, these arguments about theoretical consistency do not prove that an international flow of people, money, and information or foreign investment is good or bad in a broader sense. One country might deplore the more direct foreign involvement in its society, while another country might consider itself enriched by the greater variety of ideas, business experience, and cultural horizons.

In order to complete our evaluation of the economic effects of trade in services, we have to examine how the level of competition and nonmarket costs and benefits of trade in services affect the calculation of gains and losses from trade. The theory of comparative advantage assumes that trade is based on market prices determined by competition, and that trade does not lead to significant nonmarket costs and benefits. Trade can still lead to gains from trade even if there is less than perfect competition and even if there are nonmarket costs and benefits, provided there is some level of competition and provided nonmarket costs do not exceed the net gains from trade, including nonmarket benefits. In order to help define advantageous trade and disadvantageous trade under less than ideal conditions, we will need to examine more closely how limited competition and nonmarket costs and gains affect the achievement of gains from trade.

The Relevance of Competition to Gains from Trade in Services

The theory of comparative advantage, and in fact most of our economic theories, are based on the operation of markets, in which producers compete with each other to sell products at the highest prices consumers will pay and consumers compete with each other to buy products at the cheapest prices at which producers will sell. In an ideal market, no producer and no consumer is so powerful as to be able to determine market prices and the total quantity of goods and services that are bought and sold in the market.

A review of the degree of competition in services leads to the conclusion that in some sectors competition is limited as a result of high overhead costs, while in other sectors competition is limited as a result of government policy. The degree of competition in individual sectors varies from country to country, reflecting both differences in the development of the industry and government policies in individual countries. Whether competition is limited by government policy or by economic realities can make a considerable difference for the potential gains from trade. After all, the opening of trade could in some cases bring about the ideal competitive market conditions assumed by the theory of comparative advantage. Trade will increase competition unless the industry has the economic characteristics of a natural monopoly.

In the absence of perfect competition, individual producers have the ability to set prices above the cost of production and to reap excess profits. The more limited the competition, the greater the flexibility of producers to charge higher prices. Now let us assume that an industry with little domestic competition is opened up to trade. What would happen? Competition among foreign producers would force the price down to the lowest foreign cost of production. Under this scenario, the opening up of trade would bring about the ideal market conditions envisioned by the theory of comparative advantage. The first conclusion one can draw, therefore, is that the absence of adequate domestic competition does not provide grounds for restricting trade if the opening up of trade would bring about competitive market conditions.

The second scenario to be considered is one where the opening up of trade does not lead to vigorous competition among foreign suppliers. In this case the foreign firm would be able to set prices above its cost of production but presumably below the current price set by domestic producers. If it did not set prices below those set by domestic producers, the foreign firm would not have much of a chance to gain a significant market share. The lack of competition thus will enable a foreign producer to extract undue profits, but the importing country is still better off than it would be in the absence of trade. The issue in this case, therefore, revolves around the distribution of gains from trade, not whether trade results in gains. Moreover, the remedy for an unequal distribution of the gains from trade is to pursue policies that would increase the number of potential foreign suppliers.[9]

A more serious situation could arise if a dominant foreign supplier could eliminate weak competitors in the importing country, and with the competition removed raise prices higher than they would be in the absence of trade. In this situation, a country could actually lose from trade. The right remedy would be to pursue policies that would increase competition among potential foreign suppliers. An alternative course would be to provide enough support to the domestic industry to keep it in business as a viable competitor.

The most contentious trade policy issues arise not over insufficient competition among potential foreign suppliers of services but over differences in the level of competition permitted in different countries. Government-imposed limits on competition, whether they affect the ability of new firms to enter the market or the ability of existing firms to expand, ipso facto reduce trade opportunities. Put another way, government-imposed limits on foreign competition are equivalent to a tariff or quota on trade, and such regulations are in practice the most commonly used tool for protecting services industries.

The liberalization of trade between a country that allows open competition and another country that limits competition will enable the country with more limited competition to capture a greater share of the gains than it would be able to obtain with a more competitive regime. In fact, the economic outcome of liberalization of trade between two countries that allow different degrees of competition among suppliers is equivalent to a one-sided removal of tariffs on trade in goods. While it can be demonstrated that under a range of assumptions, a unilateral removal of tariffs can be in a country's economic interest, it could obtain even larger gains if other countries were to remove their tariffs as well. A country will therefore be better off by negotiating a mutual reduction of barriers, than by engaging in unilateral disarmament. Unilateral reductions of barriers, not surprisingly, are also difficult to sustain politically.

The discussion up to now has focused on the absence of sufficient competition among suppliers. An issue could also arise with respect to inadequate competition among buyers. Lack of competition among buyers allows individual buyers to reduce their prices below free market levels by withholding purchases. This situation can arise whenever a government marketing monopoly that has the exclusive right to market certain services in the home market can choose among competing foreign suppliers. Competition among foreign suppliers will enable the government marketing monopoly to extract extraordinary profits from such transactions by shifting the terms of trade in its favor. In effect, the government marketing monopoly as a monopsonist can levy an optimal tariff on foreign producers through its power to determine the purchasing price.

Now let us turn to a broad overview of the state of competition in services, and the implication for the potential gains from trade. Where the provision of services depends on the development and maintenance of an expensive network, economic pressures have limited the number of producers to a single, monopoly producer, or to a very small number of producers. The most obvious examples are found in the areas of transportation and communications. In many countries, transportation services and communications services are provided by government monopolies. In other countries they are provided by private monopolies. Since no single country, however, can assert a monopoly over transportation and communications services provided between two countries, most governments have worked out a duopoly arrangement, under which one producer from each country competes with the producer from the other country under a set of ground rules negotiated by the two governments.

In recent years, advances in technology and the growth of the market have opened up the possibility for a greater degree of competition in both transportation and communications, and a number of governments have taken steps to establish competition in some segments of the market. The emergence of greater competition, however, has not meant that the market structure in these sectors now approximates an ideal market. The level of competition varies significantly from country to country; some countries have not reduced the scope of the domestic monopoly, and in countries that have encouraged the development of some competition, the number of suppliers remains fairly small.

By virtue of its monopoly power, a foreign monopolist can charge higher prices in its own market than it could charge in a competitive market, and these monopoly profits could be used to subsidize exports to other countries. The important question therefore is whether a country that has competition in its own market can gain by allowing a foreign monopolist to participate in its market—that is, whether it can derive economic benefits by accepting imports from another country that does not permit competition. As noted above, a country that limits competition can shift the terms of trade in its favor. Firms that are protected from competition in their home market can also use the resulting monopoly profits to subsidize the sale of services abroad, displacing sales by nonsubsidized foreign suppliers operating in a competitive environment.

Economies of scale could limit the number of firms that would survive under open international competition in segments of the telecommunications and transportation markets characterized by high overhead costs. Such segments of the industry could thus evolve toward a monopolistic market structure or an oligopolistic market structure with imperfect competition. Such a market structure would enable the surviving firm or firms to reap extraordinary profits. This possibility has provided the rationale for extensive regulation of both the telecommunications and the transportation sectors in most countries. In recent years there has been growing recognition that not all segments of these industries have economies of scale so large that they will necessarily evolve toward a monopolistic or oligopolistic market structure. There is wide disagreement among economists as well as policy officials, however, on the potential scope for competition in various segments of the market, and the evolution of thinking will very much depend on the outcome of deregulation in the United States and elsewhere.

We have to conclude that neither the transportation nor the communications sector fits the ideal conditions assumed in the theory of comparative advantage, and that we cannot reach any conclusions with respect to potential gains from trade without a more detailed investigation of possible ground rules under which trade in these sectors could approximate the competitive market conditions necessary for mutual economic gains.

In some countries, a number of services besides transportation and communications are provided through government-owned or government-regulated monopolies. Financial services such as banking and insurance, for example, fall into this category, particularly in developing countries. The argument is made that the small size of the domestic market and the scarcity of domestic financial management expertise make it uneconomical to permit open competition among an unlimited number of small firms.

The argument that the limited size of a domestic market requires government intervention to limit the number of competitors rests on a fairly weak theoretical foundation. If the market cannot sustain more than a certain number of competitors, enough firms will drop out through the normal operation of market forces. The problem in most countries that limit competition in banking and insurance is not too much competition, but rather too little real competition as a result of overregulation.

It has become clear in recent years that an excessive centralization of financial institutions entrenches the economic status quo and limits the availability of financial resources for local entrepreneurs. Even the communist countries are moving away from a monopoly structure in the financial industry. Clearly, many governments in the past have underestimated the economic scope for meaningful competition and the potential gains from competition. More competition can benefit such countries, whether such competition takes the form of more domestic competition or more international competition.

In other service sectors, many governments have chosen to limit competition by regulating the number of participants, or by allowing industry associations to limit the number of practitioners through a licensing process. This is particularly the case with respect to professional services, where even developed countries like the United States allow the professional associations to exercise considerable influence or control over admissions to professional schools and the licensing of professional practitioners. In the same vein, professional regulations frequently prohibit advertising and discourage price competition.

The argument is usually made that the quality and reliability of services provided in these sectors is more important to consumers than the prices at which such services are provided. Were unlimited competition allowed, it is argued, suppliers would be forced to provide cheap services of poor quality and reliability, and consumers would not have the necessary information to make rational choices between price and quality. Moreover, it is argued, consumers themselves are in a poor position to evaluate quality, and it is therefore necessary to impose standards enforced by professional peers who are in the best position to judge quality.

On the whole, these arguments for limiting competition tend to be exaggerated, and indeed they are employed by everyone who wants to justify limits on competition. Governments have a role to play in establishing standards, but there is little justification for explicitly limiting competition among potentially qualified professionals for the purpose of protecting quality.

Any government-imposed limits on competition or government-sanctioned understandings among suppliers to limit competition ipso facto create barriers to trade in services. Such limits on domestic competition, however, do not constitute a sufficent economic rationale for restricting trade. In fact, negotiations aimed at the liberalization of trade in services may usefully force many governments to reevaluate regulations that limit domestic competition. Trade negotiations could thus become an important tool for domestic reform.

The Issue of Nonmarket Social Costs and Benefits

The nonmarket costs of trade are not paid by producers and consumers of services but are imposed on society as a whole. Trade in services, like trade in goods and like most economic activity, can result in adjustment costs for less efficient producers, and some of these costs are passed to the country as a whole through social assistance programs such as unemployment compensation, tax write-offs, and adjustment assistance programs. In fact, many of these programs are part of a broad social compact that redistributes some of the gains from trade to those who are adversely affected by them. A case can be made for limiting the growth of trade in services where a rapid increase in such trade imposes large adjustment costs on less competitive firms and workers. This is the case where the entry of a large number of temporary workers could create major unemployment in an area.

International trade in services can also result in nonmarket social costs if it displaces domestic services industries that yield nonmarket social benefits. Some service industries, for example, could provide unique training opportunities for professional skills in demand in other sectors of the economy. A research laboratory could thus become the training ground for research scientists in related industries, or a software company could provide unique training opportunities for computer programmers in demand throughout the economy. Since firms that subsequently employ such individuals would not have to pay for the initial training, the market will tend to undervalue the economic contribution made by an industry that provided unique training opportunities. It would have to be demonstrated, however, that the training opportunities provided by a targeted services sector were in fact unique and would not be available otherwise. In such circumstances, a rational economic case could be made for limiting imports of the services involved or subsidizing the domestic production of such services.

Trade in services based on an international movement of people can also generate other nonmarket social costs by placing an added burden on infrastructure facilities and social services. Where the stay abroad is very brief, the burden placed on such facilities is probably slight. Even short stays abroad, however, can overload public facilities if the number of people involved is very large, as perhaps best exemplified by the Olympics or the Haj to Mecca. In light of the burden placed on limited public facilities, a government under rare circumstances may well have rational economic grounds for limiting the number of people it is willing to admit in connection with trade in services.

Trade in services, like trade in goods, can also impose more qualitative nonmarket costs on society. Trade leads to greater dependence on foreigners, and this can reduce the government's ability to exercise control over the available supply of services. In the case of war or in the case of an economic emergency, this greater dependence on foreigners could lead to a shortage of critical services. Every country must evaluate these risks on its own. It has to be said, however, that this risk is frequently exaggerated in public political debate. All human economic progress has been based on growing specialization and mutual dependence, both within countries and among countries.

Temporary movements of labor also lead to disputes over taxation and access to subsidized services provided by governments. A temporary service provider most likely will pay income taxes in the home country, and not in the country importing his or her services. At the same time, such a person could make use of social services subsidized by the host government.

It is sometimes argued that services such as transportation, communications, and financial services are more crucial to the functioning of society than goods, and that this makes it more essential to maintain national control over these industries. Moreover, it is argued that the reliability and quality of services are more important to national economic welfare than the cost of producing services, and that the inability of the government to control the quality and reliability of services produced abroad more than offsets what could be gained from the lower cost of services produced abroad.

These arguments underestimate the ability of consumers to judge quality. In any case, consumers who can afford to buy services abroad are likely to be sophisticated enough to know what they are buying. On the other hand, services purchased from foreign suppliers in the home market of the consumer are subject to the full regulatory control of the home government. Claims to the contrary, claims that governments cannot exercise effective regulatory control over foreign suppliers established in the local market, are greatly exaggerated.

Trade in services, like trade in goods, inevitably exposes a country to foreign customs and ideas. Countries that want to resist foreign cultural influences are likely to find trade in services more intrusive than trade in goods. After all, trade in services frequently takes the form of people moving across national borders, and these people inevitably bring along their foreign habits, outlook, and cultural values. In other cases trade in services takes the form of an international flow of information, and inevitably facts and figures are mixed together with qualitative information that reflects different cultural values and a different point of view.

The desire to preserve national culture and identity is understandable; yet, despite the growing influence of global mass media, many countries have seen a revival and renewed interest in ethnic culture. The vast expansion of communication channels in recent years has lead to an expansion of both global informational and cultural material and local and ethnic informational and cultural material.

Instead of being viewed as a social cost, the cross-cultural exposure provided by trade in services could be considered a major social benefit. By offering a greater variety of cultural experience, it could enrich a country's social and cultural life. By increasing knowledge of foreign customs and culture, it can reduce international frictions due to an inability to understand each other and to communicate with each other. An expansion of trade in services thus can be a powerful instrument for ensuring peace in the world.

DYNAMIC GAINS AND LOSSES FROM TRADE IN SERVICES

The discussion of comparative advantage in the last section showed us that trade in most services can lead to the better use of the existing resources of countries engaged in trade. In addition to these allocative or static gains from trade, we have to address possible dynamic effects of trade. Trade in services can affect the development of domestic resources over time, both positively and negatively.

On the positive side, competition from foreign suppliers can stimulate domestic suppliers to undertake a more vigorous effort and to acquire new techniques by emulating foreign competitors. On the other hand, if foreign competitors are too strong, domestic firms may not survive to acquire the skills and economies of scale that would make them effective competitors in the long run. In other words, trade could prevent domestic suppliers of services from developing a potential comparative advantage.

Dynamic Gains from Trade in Services

The production of services, more than manufacturing, is a people business. The quality of the product and the efficiency with which it is produced are highly dependent on personal skills and capabilities, and the motivation of the individual worker to provide a high quality product. The organizational support and the advanced technological tools provided by the enterprise are obviously also important, but most of the technology and the capability to produce a highly competitive service usually reside in the individual service worker.

Trade in services, whether based on an inflow of foreign experts, foreign information, or foreign investment, will expose domestic suppliers of services very directly to the skills and techniques employed by their foreign competitors. Multinational firms that want to sell or buy services abroad usually maintain regular contacts with their foreign customers and suppliers, and frequently they end up hiring and training local personnel in the skills and techniques employed by the firm. Once trained, these local employees can be hired by domestic competitors, or the more dynamic of these employees can start their own businesses. Trade in services, because it is so dependent on personal skills, can lead to a rapid transfer of the skills and techniques needed to produce a world competitive product.

Foreign competition can also have a powerful effect on the personal motivation to excel and to work hard. As we saw earlier, there is a built-in tendency in many services to allow the industry to limit the level of competition. Against this background, increased competition from foreign suppliers can provide an important stimulus to overcome the lethargy and indifference to customers that usually accompanies a lack of sufficient competition.

Dynamic Losses from Trade in Services—The Issue of Infant Industries

The rapid expansion of imports can also create dynamic losses from trade by preventing domestic enterprises from developing the necessary skills, experience, and economies of scale. In other words, local firms may never get the chance to build on a natural comparative advantage they might have as a result of cheap labor or a favorable location because the development of such advantages might take time, and strong competition from foreign firms could force them out of business before they have a chance to build their strengths.

Competitiveness in services tends to depend on

- The personal skills and capabilities of individual employees and the wages paid to such employees
- The ability of the firm to organize a cooperative effort among people with the right complementary skills
- The availability of equipment such as computers and communications facilities

- The institutional support provided by the system of laws, regulations, practices, and traditions found in each country
- Proximity to the market, which enables a firm to develop an intimate familiarity with customer needs
- The potential economies of scale provided by the size of the market

Of these factors, the cost of labor and capital, and physical proximity, are bound by a country's current endowment of resources. The other factors—personal skills, organization, and institutional environment—can be acquired. A country that has cheap labor and can afford the necessary capital therefore may be able to develop a globally competitive industry. Putting together the needed personal skills, organization, and institutional environment, however, takes time, and local firms may not have the opportunity to develop these acquired skills if powerful foreign competitors can keep them from growing or can drive them out of business.

Too much trade too soon could thus prevent a country from developing competitive strengths in a services industry in which it has potential strengths as a result of its plentiful supply of cheap skilled labor. This is the so-called infant-industry argument. Although it has considerable validity, it is rarely applied intelligently in practice. A country that adopts a trade policy based on the infant-industry principle has to avoid a series of traps.

The first trap is total protection. Even though less foreign competition may sometimes give a domestic industry a better chance to become more competitive, this does not mean that the elimination of foreign competition altogether will create the most favorable environment for the development of a competitive industry. If foreign competition is removed altogether, the domestic industry is likely to decide that the current way of doing things is just fine and that difficult decisions can be postponed indefinitely.

The second trap is permanent protection. As an industry acquires the skills, organization, and institutional environment that will make it more competitive, it needs to be exposed to increasing levels of foreign competition in order to push managers to their best performance. Without the pressure of increased foreign competition, the domestic industry could declare itself satisfied with partial progress having been made. In fact, the development of a more sizable domestic industry could increase political pressures for maintaining the status quo with respect to the protection from foreign competition. The adoption of infant-industry protection as a short-term measure thus frequently tends to become permanent protection that defeats the original objective of the protection.

The third trap is comprehensive protection. It is easy to conclude that the infant-industry principle can justify the protection of all noncompetitive industries. This is wrong for two reasons. First, not all noncompetitive industries have the same potential for becoming world competitive, given an individual country's economic strengths and weaknesses. Second, every country has only a limited number of people with the skills needed to foster and facilitate the development of an industry, and the more industries are covered by infant-industry protection, the more the people with the critical skills are spread over too many industries. The scarcity of national resources thus imposes limits on the range of industries in which a country can develop a globally competitive position over a given period of time.

The fourth trap is insufficient market size. The domestic market may not be large enough to provide the economies of scale needed to support the large-scale investment in research and development required to become competitive in a desired industry. If the domestic market is not large enough, no amount of protection for the domestic industry will make that industry competitive in either the short run or the long run. It can cost more than a billion dollars, for example, to develop the software necessary to operate a large public telecommunications switch efficiently. Obviously only a handful of countries with very large domestic markets could support the development of the necessary software, and it is doubtful that more than one or two countries could achieve success on their own.

A country that falls into any one of the four traps associated with infant-industry protection ends up sacrificing both static and dynamic gains from trade without getting the dynamic gains it hopes to get from infant-industry protection.

ECONOMIC DEVELOPMENT

It is often assumed by developing countries that they will not benefit from a liberalization of trade in services. This is a wrong assumption. While a case can be made for selective protection of some service industries for limited periods of time on the basis of the infant-industry principle, developing countries as a rule can derive major economic benefits from expanding both their imports and their exports of services. While many of the arguments are the ones we explored in the earlier sections of this chapter, it is worth reviewing the arguments as they apply to developing countries.

International competitiveness in services is determined by the cost of labor, the knowledge and skills of local service workers and managers, the availability of data processing and communications equipment, the effective organization of service inputs required to deliver the services desired by customers, the institutional environment for the production of services, and proximity to the market. Developing countries can derive an important source of competitive advantage from their low cost of labor because labor constitutes the largest element of cost in most service industries.

The critical handicap many developing countries face is the lack of the right skills, organization, and institutional environment, but these can be developed. Ultimately, the only real competitive disadvantage developing countries face is a relative scarcity of capital. One should therefore expect developing countries to do well in all service industries that require a relatively large input of labor and a relatively small input of capital. Developing countries should be able to develop a competitive advantage in an area such as data input and computer programming, which are labor-intensive activities, but not necessarily in computer processing or information services, which are machine- and capital-intensive activities.

The crucial question developing countries must address is how they can best acquire the skills, organization, and institutional environment needed for the production of world-class services. The optimal strategy is likely to be one that offers foreign producers of services access to an increasing share of the domestic market and encourages them to establish local facilities for the production and distribution of services. By offering foreign producers access to a growing share of the market, a government can help assure a gradual increase in foreign competitive pressure on domestic producers and give foreign producers an adequate incentive to invest in the production and delivery of services to the local market. By encouraging foreign producers to invest in local facilities, a government can speed the transfer of professional and managerial skills, since the foreign producers will have to train local employees and by their presence will give domestic firms a role model to emulate. Foreign firms also tend to play a useful role in putting pressure on officials to modernize local laws and regulations, and in persuading the local industry to adopt more competitive business practices.

One key problem of many developing countries is that their market is too small to support many firms that are large enough to obtain globally competitive economies of scale. This is perceived to be a bigger problem in services than in goods because it is difficult to export many services without sizable investments in service facilities in the importing countries. Protection is clearly not a solution to this problem, however, since protection cannot enlarge a market that is too small to begin with. Indeed, protection is likely to reduce chances of ultimate success by pointing the attention of management toward the domestic market instead of the international market.

One way that service suppliers in small countries can compete successfully with large foreign firms in the international market is to ally themselves with large multinational firms and to use the international infrastructure of such firms for exporting their services. Such allied multinational firms can, in effect, provide the economies of scale otherwise unavailable to small firms.

A highly protectionist policy in services is likely to be very costly for developing countries, not only by delaying the development of competitive domestic services industries with export potential, but by raising the costs of domestic manufacturing. Services constitute a large and growing input into the production of manufactured goods, particularly the production of high-quality manufactured goods that have to compete in world markets. Increasingly, developing countries that seek to expand their exports of manufactured products have to acquire competitive inputs of services in such areas as engineering and design, software programming, communications and transportation, marketing and advertising, financing and insurance, documentation and training, and maintenance. In a highly competitive market, the price and quality of these service inputs can be crucial to competitiveness.

Low productivity in services can also hamper economic development by absorbing too many manpower resources that would otherwise be available to expand manufacturing. While many of the poorest developing countries have not run into labor constraints, those that achieve a high rate of growth do run into labor supply bottlenecks. Beyond constraints on the development of manufacturing, it is a mistake to assume that a country's standard of living is not affected by the efficiency of the services sector. Services constitute a large portion of every person's budget, and the more inefficient the services, the more time is wasted in taking care of daily service needs.

Many developing countries have protected the domestic services industry not only from foreign competition but also from excessive domestic competition. In some countries this policy has been motivated by a belief that an inefficient services industry can help assure full employment, and in other countries it has been motivated by a belief that competition would result in firms that are too small to achieve efficient economies of scale. As already noted, this is a particular concern in smaller developing countries. Whatever the rationale, these policies often end up inhibiting the development process rather than accelerating economic development.

EMPIRICAL INVESTIGATIONS

In recent years a number of economists have begun to test whether the descriptive theory of comparative advantage could be used to explain the observed pattern of world trade in services. Two studies, in particular, have come up with some interesting results. The first study was carried out by André Sapir and Ernst Lutz (1980) for the World Bank. The second study was done by Nicholas Oulton (1984) for the Trade Policy Research Center in London.

Both studies used balance of payments data published by the International Monetary Fund for trade in four categories of services: 1) freight and insurance services, 2) other transportation services (passenger fares and port services), 3) travel services (expenditures by travelers while abroad), and 4) other private nonfactor services (in other words all other services, not including interest payments and labor remittances). The period covered by the two studies is slightly different, 1967–1975 by Sapir and Lutz and 1959–1960 to 1979–1980 by Oulton. The major difference between the two studies, however, was country coverage. The investigation by Sapir and Lutz covered trade in services by both developed and developing countries, while Oulton's study focused exclusively on trade by developed countries.

The study by Oulton showed some fairly consistent patterns of competitive strength by the countries studied in specific services, but not a very clear relationship to the underlying economic resource endowment of the countries involved. The study by Sapir and Lutz showed a clearer relationship between trade patterns and resource endowments. The difference in the results of the two studies is explained by the fact that differences in resource endowment between developed and developing countries are much more distinct than they are among developed countries.

Sapir summarized the results of his work with Lutz in an article he published later in the *Columbia Journal of World Business* (Sapir, 1982, p. 79). His conclusion is that the competitive position of a country in transportation (aviation) is determined by a relative abundance of physical capital, while its competitive position in insurance and other services is determined by the availability of human capital and research and development expenditures. He also found that the size of the country's market (scale economies) was an important factor in determining competitive strength in services more generally.

Both Sapir-Lutz and Oulton were painfully aware of the overwhelming shortcomings of the data, which are highly aggregated, are aggregated differently in each country, and are of dubious quality overall. It is all the more interesting that Sapir and Lutz were able to show that the application of the descriptive theory of comparative advantage to trade in services yields results consistent with empirical observations, however poor the data.

It is highly doubtful that an analysis of more detailed data on trade in services, were such data available, would support the validity of the Heckscher/Ohlin theory with respect to trade in many services, particularly among developed countries. Competitiveness in services is based more on human skills, the institutional environment, and past success in building an international network for delivering services than on resource endowments. These questions about the empirical validity of the Heckscher/Ohlin theorem with respect to trade in services, however, do not undermine conclusions about gains from trade in services based on the normative theory of comparative advantage.

CONCLUSIONS

The basic concepts of international trade theory can be articulated without any reference to what is produced and consumed and what is imported and exported. International trade theory is a logical construct that provides conclusions about market outcomes, no matter what is bought and sold in the marketplace. In other words the normative conclusions that can be drawn from international trade theory are as valid for shoes and oranges as for insurance and engineering.

The real question is whether the underlying conditions specified in trade theory for the achievement of economic gains from trade are met in the real world. This question has been investigated at great length for goods. The process of carrying out an equally detailed investigation for individual service sectors has only begun, and the sectoral studies that have been carried out under the sponsorship of the American Enterprise Institute represent a major contribution to this effort. The analysis provided in the present overview can cover the subject only with the broad brush strokes of an impressionist painter.

A considerable amount of basic theoretical and empirical work also remains to be tackled. While the similarities between trade in goods and trade in services are fairly apparent and the application of traditional trade theory to trade in services has been well explored, the unique characteristics of trade in services remain to be more fully explored. Areas where more work is required include the economics of trade in information services and intellectual property, the growth of specialized communication networks and trade in professional services, and the linkages between traditionally segregated policies in areas such as communications, transportation, immigration, and foreign investment. In short, the investigation of trade in services is a growth field that should provide material for many doctoral dissertations.

NOTES

1. The theoretical literature on this question, considered under the rubrik of the theory of retaliation, goes back to Scitovsky and Johnson and has recently been treated in McMillan (1986). For an assessment of its policy implications, see Bhagwati (1988).
2. A number of economists have contributed to the literature in this area in recent years. One of the best sources for a nontechnical discussion of the recent theoretical work in this area is a

collection of articles published in Krugman (1986). This volume contains a useful introductory survey article by Krugman and papers by a number of economists and political scientists who have done pioneering work in this area, including James Brander, Avinash Dixit, John Zysman, Gene Grossman, and others. Also see Grossman's contribution in Bhagwati (1988).

3. The earlier, classical theory was due to David Ricardo, but was superseded by the Heckscher-Ohlin theory in the postwar period.

4. A number of excellent articles have appeared recently on the application of international trade theory to trade in services. John Richardson (1987) in his article "A Subsectoral Approach to Services Trade Theory" has provided an extremely well-written overview of the current state of thinking on the subject, with extensive references to the available literature. Other important additions to the literature have been provided in recent years by Bhagwati (1984a), Deardorff (1985), Hindley and Smith (1984), and Sampson and Snape (1985). While Deardorff believes that he has found an inconsistency in the Heckscher/Ohlin interpretation of comparative advantage as it applies to trade in services, he and the others agree that the normative theory of comparative advantage can be applied to trade in services, and that trade in services should lead to the expected gains from trade.

5. Alan Deardorff (1985) has pointed out that management services are frequently exported from a country where such services are expensive (where managers command high salaries) to a country where they are cheap (where managers command low salaries). He argued this is a paradox, since the theory of comparative advantage and classical theory are based on the assumption that services are exported from a country where they are cheap to a country where they are expensive. Ron Jones (1985) has pointed out, however, that the apparent inconsistency with the theory of comparative advantage disappears if the price of management is adjusted for differences in the level of quality due to technology. Deardorff, in an exchange recorded in Stern (1985a), replied that quality is a difficult thing to measure, and that economists should not use arguments that cannot be tested empirically to uphold the validity of a theory. The measurement problems cited by Deardorff are not a valid reason for rejecting an adjustment for levels of quality. The fact that economic researchers may find it difficult to measure something is not an argument for rejecting the validity of a particular theory. In addition to the argument made by Jones about

differences in quality, it is worthwhile to note that exports of services are usually an integral part of a broader package of services. Services exported from the United States, for example, contain not only managerial services, but also inputs of computer technology, professional services unavailable in many importing countries, and ready access to sophisticated support services provided by a highly developed infrastructure. Managerial services in this context constitute only one input into the production of an exportable package of services. It is therefore necessary to be very precise in defining the export product in terms of the full package of services that is exported as a unit. Admittedly, it is more difficult to define precisely a homogeneous category of exportable services than exportable goods because it is easier to identify a car than a package of services. The applicability of the theory of comparative advantage to trade in services cannot be evaluated in terms of the individual service inputs that make up the package.

6. To be more precise, the real question is whether markets behave as if they were competitive. In some cases, the potential entry of new suppliers could force existing suppliers to behave as if there were a competitive market, even if the actual number of suppliers was limited.

7. While global output will be the same whether equilibrium in international markets is achieved through trade or factor movements, the distribution of total income and output between the two countries will not be the same. The total output and income of the country losing labor will fall, and the total income and output of the country gaining workers will rise. Countries that measure their wealth and power in terms of total income and output, rather than per capita income and output, will not be indifferent between the two outcomes. This does not detract from the general observation, however, that international factor movements, like international trade, will lead to mutual economic gains in terms of the standard of living in the two countries.

8. Both Deardorff (1985) and Hindley and Smith (1984) develop this argument more fully. Actually, most arguments against foreign investment rest not on economic grounds but on political grounds, namely, that such investment gives "foreigners" control over the use of national assets, thus limiting national control and influence over the deployment of such assets.

9. A small country may not be able to support enough foreign suppliers to create a fully competitive market. As long as the potential entry of new suppliers is not restricted, however, even a limited number of suppliers could behave as if there were full competition. A firm that seeks to derive monopolistic rents will undoubtedly attract competitors even if the market is small.

7
BARRIERS TO INTERNATIONAL TRADE IN SERVICES

Adam Smith formulated his theory of international trade as a means for advocating the removal of tariffs on corn, and most of the subsequent work on international trade theory focused on arguments for and against the imposition of tariffs and quotas on imported goods. The barriers that are likely to be the focal point of theoretical work on trade in services are not so straightforward and simple. Because you cannot see services crossing the border, governments tend to impose barriers on trade in services at points where such trade leads to verifiable transactions. There are four types of transactions or activities associated with trade in services that lend themselves to government controls:

1. Sales of imported services within the domestic borders of the importing country, provided the government regulates the sale of all such services, those produced by both domestic and foreign enterprises
2. Consumption of imported services, provided the government regulates the consumption of all such services, those produced by both domestic and foreign enterprises (an example is compulsory auto or fire insurance)
3. Purchases of foreign exchange in order to pay for imported services, provided the government controls all foreign currency transactions
4. Movements of goods, people, and informational materials that carry services across the border, provided the government controls all such movements indiscriminately

Controls on imports of services rarely serve the exclusive purpose of restricting trade and are usually feasible only to the extent that the government regulates or controls all transactions in a particular category, whether they relate to trade in services or not. Indeed, the basic rationale of the underlying control mechanisms usually has nothing to do with trying to control trade in services per se.

Controls on the sale and consumption of imported services are usually attached to domestic regulatory programs that are aimed at domestic objectives. Controls on the purchase of foreign exchange used to pay for imported services are usually a part of a broader currency control program designed to solve a balance of payments problem. Controls on people moving across the border are usually designed to control the flow of new immigrants who want to settle permanently. This means that trade policy objectives and other regulatory objectives are usually completely intertwined, and this inevitably leads to considerable confusion over the objectives of government policy measures that create barriers to trade in services.

This chapter is devoted to a brief review of the key barriers to trade in services in the major services sectors, as seen by business.[1] Its aim is to provide an indication of the type of policy measures that trade negotiators are asked to address, the extent to which the measures that bother the business management the most in various sectors are similar, and finally whether the issues seem important enough for a major negotiating effort.

The information on barriers summarized in this chapter is drawn from three principal sources:

> 1. A survey of barriers to trade in services carried out by the services committee of the U.S. Chamber of Commerce, in cooperation with the Office of the U.S. Trade Representative (1979). This has come to be known as the USTR Inventory of Barriers to Trade in Services. The data collected from that survey, organized by industry and type of barrier, provided the first comprehensive overview of the barriers faced by businesses engaged in international trade in services.

2. Two comprehensive surveys by Price Waterhouse of the problems encountered by U.S. services industries in selling abroad. Price Waterhouse, an international accounting and management consulting firm, carried out these surveys in order to make a private contribution to the effort undertaken by the government to reduce barriers to trade in services. The first of these surveys was published in December 1983, and the second in February 1985.

3. A report prepared by Peat, Marwick, Mitchell for the Commission of the European Community in 1986. The report was based on an exhaustive analysis of all the available information on barriers to trade in services. It is by far the best analysis of barriers to trade in services that is available.

WHAT IS A BARRIER TO TRADE IN SERVICES?

A barrier to trade in services is a government measure that creates an obstacle to the sale of services produced abroad. Normally there is also an implication that the government measure involved creates a burden on foreign producers that is not borne by domestic producers. Use of the word *barrier* in a trade policy context can also add an analytical judgment that the burden on foreign producers is unnecessry for the achievement of nonprotectionist, domestic regulatory objectives. Finally, when used in the context of public rhetoric, the word *barrier* conjures up value judgments; the government measure is implicitly condemned as unjustifiable, undesirable, or even illegitimate.

A trade barrier could be an added cost that is imposed on services produced abroad, either through a discriminatory tax on imported services or through regulations that require foreign producers to spend money on people or things that they do not need. A head tax on tourists who wish to travel abroad is an added cost on imports of tourism services. A requirement that foreign insurance companies staff sales offices with experts in every area of insurance, even though they are not allowed to sell many kinds of insurance, represents a discriminatory burden on imported insurance services.

A trade barrier could also take the form of a quantitative limit on the services that can be produced by a foreign company, and in some cases foreign companies might be prohibited from producing certain services altogether. Foreign banks operating in Canada, for example, have a ceiling on their permitted level of deposits and loans. Foreign companies until recently have been prohibited from selling life insurance policies, fire insurance on public buildings, or compulsory auto insurance in Korea.

Sometimes governments have to draft different regulations for foreign and domestic producers in order to achieve a domestic regulatory objective. For example, a government may wish to protect buyers of insurance against poor management through periodic audits of the investment portfolios of companies selling insurance. Since governments find it difficult to audit the books of companies located abroad, they may require foreign companies to maintain deposits and investments in local financial institutions, where they are within the reach of local regulatory authorities.

The question in such cases is whether the requirement imposed on foreign producers is reasonable from the point of view of the domestic regulatory objective and minimizes any added burden on foreign producers. In order to determine whether a trade barrier exists, it may therefore be necessary to determine not only whether a government treats foreign producers differently from domestic producers, but whether any differences in treatment that might exist are justified as a means for achieving equivalent domestic regulatory objectives.

In other situations, the imposition of the same regulation on both foreign and domestic producers can be highly discriminatory. Two very different examples can help illustrate the point. Foreign exchange regulations that prevent both domestic and foreign architects from converting local currency receipts into foreign exchange are likely to be highly discriminatory against foreign architects, and could exclude foreign architects entirely. A regulation that freezes the total number of domestic or foreign companies allowed to sell securities could be highly discriminatory, particularly if foreign companies were largely excluded in the past.

Government measures that limit the ability of foreign companies to carry out certain activities in the local market can also create trade barriers. Foreign producers of services, depending on the requirements of the specific industry, may need local sales representatives or agents, freight handlers, insurance adjusters, repairmen, or professionals familiar with the local environment. They may also need access to local communications systems, air and hotel reservation systems, and local transportation systems.

Foreign suppliers of services also have to be able to carry out activities required by government regulations. For example, foreign insurance companies may need to invest a portion of their premiums locally, or they may need to establish themselves locally to satisfy regulatory requirements. Government measures that restrict any of these local activities by foreign producers of services can limit trade opportunities, and it is useful to analyze them as potential trade barriers. In order to determine whether they are in fact trade barriers, one has to examine whether the restricted activity is essential for meaningful trade in a particular services industry.

Barriers to trade in services need to be distinguished from barriers to the establishment and operation of foreign-owned firms producing services. Regulations limiting the local production and sale of services by companies owned by foreigners are usually considered not trade barriers, but investment barriers. Nevertheless, restrictions on foreign investment in services can have a restrictive effect on cross-border trade in services, since trade and investment are often closely linked. Barriers to foreign investment in services thus frequently also constitute barriers to trade in services.

Government measures that inhibit the movement of money, information, people, or goods create barriers to trade in services by limiting the means for transferring services internationally. Controls on the transfer of money thus can create impediments to international trade in banking, insurance, and brokerage services, which depends on the international flow of money. Barriers to the international flow of information create barriers to international trade in data processing and information services that depend on an international flow of information. Travel restrictions create barriers to trade in tourism, education, and professional services that depend on the international movement of people. Restrictions on the movement of goods create barriers to trade in services that add value to material things—repair of equipment or printing of books.

Money, of course, is not only a means for transferring financial services, but also a means of payment. Restrictions on the transfer of money thus create a barrier to all trade in services by limiting the extent to which sales proceeds can be transferred home. After all, how much opportunity is there for real trade if one cannot get paid for it?

Similarly, information flows are not only a means for transferring information services but also a means for providing information about trade opportunities in services. Impediments to the transfer of information can reduce the information available to banks about foreign exchange or securities markets, information available to travel agents and airlines about foreign bookings, and information available to credit card companies about stolen cards. Barriers to international information flows also can make it more difficult for construction companies to coordinate the timely procurement and transportation of cement, bulldozers, building permits, architectural drawings, construction workers, and supervising engineers.

Barriers to movement of people create a barrier to trade in any service that requires frequent face-to-face contacts between an exporter and a foreign client, or between a manager in the home office and a local sales manager in the importing country. Business contracts still depend on personal trust and confidence, which can only be achieved through face-to-face contacts.

Barriers to the movement of goods create barriers to trade in any service that requires the international transfer of a physical information medium. Accountants often need to carry audit tapes, engineers often need to carry technical drawings, computer services companies often need to carry software tapes, and musicians have to carry their instruments. International trade in services also frequently depends on access to compatible equipment in the importing country—a customized crane to unload a special kind of ship, or telecom equipment designed to handle information transmitted in a unique code or requiring transformation into a unique medium in the importing country.

WHERE TO EXPECT BARRIERS TO TRADE IN SERVICES

Since the movement of services across a border is largely invisible, it is generally useless to put up barriers to trade in services at the border. Barriers to international trade in services have to be erected at a point in the transaction where the government can exercise some control over the transaction. A government can limit, or at least it can try to limit, (a) the purchase of foreign exchange needed to pay for imported services; (b) the movement of all people, information, goods, and money across the border; (c) the sale of services inside the country by a foreign business; (d) the employment of foreign service workers in the importing country; or (e) the consumption of services required to meet regulatory requirements.

A government, as a general rule, cannot control international trade in services purchased abroad unless it is prepared to maintain a comprehensive foreign exchange control system, it establishes comprehensive controls on the consumption of services, or it establishes a comprehensive system for controlling the movement of all information, people, money, and goods. The government would also have to develop and maintain a comprehensive system for collecting and compiling information about (a) foreign exchange transactions; (b) the information, people, money, and goods crossing the border; and (c) the consumption of services (e.g., the information drivers have to supply to the government about their liability insurance). Barriers to services purchased abroad, therefore, should be a problem only in countries that maintain such comprehensive control systems. This tends to be the case with respect to a large number of the developing countries and the communist countries, but not with respect to most of the developed countries with market economies. Only a few developed countries in some specific cases try to control the purchases of services abroad by their citizens. Japan, Portugal, and Switzerland, for example, prohibit their citizens from buying insurance abroad.

Even comprehensive foreign exchange control systems and even comprehensive border controls on international flows of information, people, money, and goods are likely to be insufficient and ineffective as long as they are not totalitarian. One should, therefore, expect that most barriers to trade take the form of regulatory measures limiting the right of foreign companies to sell services in the local market or handicapping their sales effort. Since most governments tend to regulate the sale of services domestically, in any case, domestic regulation provides a convenient mechanism for controlling trade in services. Controls on sales in the importing country can cover most potential trade in services since the close interaction required between the buyer and the seller of services makes it difficult to buy such services at a distance.

Government controls on purchases of services at home are likely to be less effective with respect to the purchase of high-value services, since both the cost and the time required to travel to the exporting countries could be relatively small compared with the economic advantage of buying abroad. This is frequently the case with respect to the purchase of high-value business services by multinational corporations. Since large businesses have that option, one should expect governments to recognize the futility of protection in such areas, and one should expect to see a gradual breakdown of domestic controls on business services supplied to large multinationals. This has clearly been happening in the banking area.

Even though less than fully comprehensive controls on the movement of people, information, money, and goods are not able to prevent trade in services, they can create inconvenience and can add to the cost of trade in services. One should therefore expect that any government measures that hamper or add to the cost of moving information, people, money, or goods would be high on any list of barriers put together by the business community.

WHAT SURVEYS SHOW ABOUT BARRIERS

The results of the three surveys on barriers to trade in services are fairly consistent with what one might expect on the basis of the analysis above (see Office of the U.S. Trade Representative, 1979; Price Waterhouse, 1983, 1985; and Peat, Marwick, Mitchell, 1986). On the basis of the responses provided by exporters of services, we can say that most barriers to trade in services are created by regulations that control who is allowed to sell what to whom under what terms and conditions. Restrictions on who can sell what are most frequently cited in the surveys as a significant barrier to trade in services.

Discriminatory terms and conditions imposed on foreign suppliers of services are the third most frequently cited barrier to trade in services. Predictably, controls on the international movement of money, information, and people are also frequently cited. Foreign exchange controls are the second most frequently cited barrier to trade in services, and problems associated with transborder data flows are the fourth most frequently cited barrier.

The most prohibitive barriers are created by regulations that completely prohibit or strictly limit the number of authorized foreign suppliers. These truly prohibitive regulations are found in most countries (even in the United States). In many countries domestic regulators of some service sectors determine who can sell what to whom on a fairly detailed basis. The working assumption in these countries is that enterprises are only allowed to sell service products for which they have obtained a license, and the product can be defined in fairly narrow terms.

Both the USTR and the Price Waterhouse surveys show that most barriers to trade in services take the form of regulations that limit the right of foreign firms to establish themselves in the local market, and limit what foreign-owned firms are allowed to sell.

All industries listed restrictions on establishment and restrictions on products and markets as the most important barriers to trade. In four industries—banking, insurance, advertising, and construction—the concentration of barriers in this first category is particularly high.

In addition to restrictions on what they are allowed to sell, foreign companies frequently face discriminatory taxes, discriminatory fees for services they must buy from the government, and discriminatory access to government facilities. The range of discriminatory practices reported by businesses is quite remarkable. It includes discriminatory delays in required government inspections, approvals, licenses, and clearances. Some businesses have reported discriminatory access to data collected by the government, discriminatory placement of sales offices, and discriminatory treatment in the provision of public utility services.

All in all, both the USTR and the Price Waterhouse surveys show that these kinds of barriers are widespread. The USTR inventory shows that barriers within this category are of particular concern to the computer processing industry, the motion picture industry, the air transport industry, the shipping industry, and the insurance industry. Overall, discriminatory treatment by the government is the third most frequently cited barrier to trade in services.

In some cases, businesses have identified as barriers government policy measures that are not discriminatory per se but have the effect of placing a far greater burden on foreign suppliers than on domestic suppliers. It is not always obvious, however, whether the choice of measures was designed to restrict or place an added burden on foreign suppliers, or, more important, the extent to which the officials responsible for designing the regulations could adopt a less trade-distorting approach without altering regulatory policy goals.

Foreign exchange restrictions and limitations on the transfer of funds from the importing country to the home country are the second most frequently cited category of barriers to trade in services. As expected, most foreign exchange restrictions reported by respondents to the USTR survey are found in developing countries. In some cases, the foreign exchange controls place a ceiling on the amount of local currency proceeds that can be converted into convertible currencies and in other cases the controls impose specific limits on the repatriation of profits, royalties, management fees, or capital. Needless to say, all of these controls are subject to a considerable degree of discretion by local officials. In the USTR survey, the tourism industry, the construction industry, the motion picture industry, the computer services industry, and the car rental industry reported strong concern about foreign exchange restrictions. Interestingly enough, while the banking industry indicated in both the USTR survey and the Price Waterhouse surveys that foreign exchange restrictions were a problem, the degree of concern expressed was not as high as that expressed by other industries.

Another major problem reported by exporters in many service industries is unfair competition from government-owned enterprises. The practices covered under unfair competition include the following list of preferences extended to government corporations: subsidies provided by taxpayers, avoidance of taxes, preferential enforcement of regulations, and greater latitude in permitted practices. As in the case of foreign exchange restrictions, most of the examples of these kinds of practices involve developing countries.

In the first Price Waterhouse survey, a quarter of all respondents indicated a concern about these practices, compared to 71 percent who expressed a concern about the right of establishment (including limitations on what the firms could sell), 49 percent who expressed a concern about foreign exchange restrictions, and about 35 percent who complained about discriminatory treatment. The USTR survey provided a less clear focus on this issue, but descriptions of problems provided by individual respondents nevertheless indicated that this was an area of major concern.

The fourth most important area of concern is related to the transfer of information, or what are often called transborder data flows. Since transfer of information has become an increasingly viable and convenient way of transferring services from one place to another, policies affecting the cost and conditions for transferring information have become a critical issue for trade in services. Increasingly regulations that increase communication costs or limit flexible use of communication facilities are seen as barriers to trade in services. Thirty-eight percent of all companies responding to the first Price Waterhouse survey and 23 percent of all companies responding to the second survey reported difficulties concerning the international transfer of information. The initial USTR survey did not focus on this issue because international data flows had not yet emerged as a key concern, but all later information collected by USTR clearly established the widespread concern about impediments to the efficient and economical transmission of information.

Some of the problems with respect to transborder data flows arise from regulations dealing with privacy and the concern of fiduciary authorities for a full audit trail. Most of the difficulties, however, relate to restrictions on the exploitation of new telecommunications technology at a market-oriented price. Many telecom authorities have been slow to respond to advances in technology, and they have been loath to allow private companies to introduce the new technology because that would lead to an erosion of the traditional post, telephone, and telegraph (PTT) monopoly.

The last major category of barriers concerns regulations dealing with work permits and immigration rules. Interestingly enough, the issue is not primarily a visa issue, though many companies report visa problems, but a work permit issue. Companies report almost as many problems in employing local nationals as in employing foreign nationals. A favorite technique to control the size of a foreign enterprise seems to be to control the number of people it can hire. With respect to foreign nationals, the problem does not seem to be so much a problem of the number of foreign service workers that can be transferred (except in construction), as the ability of a foreign enterprise to bring a critical expert into the country on a timely basis.

REFLECTIONS ON THE NATURE OF BARRIERS

The fact that most barriers to trade in services are not very visible to the general public (in the terminology used by trade negotiators, not very transparent) makes them more difficult to deal with. It also makes them more protective, because businesses are reluctant to undertake major commitments when they do not have very good information about the restrictions they are likely to face. The lack of transparency thus makes barriers to trade in services more costly to society in terms of lost economic opportunities.

Some barriers to trade in services are quite explicit, in the sense that the discrimination against foreign suppliers is written into a country's laws or published regulations. The reason that they remain not very visible is that they are frequently buried in hundreds of pages of domestic regulations. They are also not very visible to the general public because the average person who travels abroad is not faced with a discriminatory tax while crossing the border. (The tax levied on citizens traveling abroad by many countries is an exception.)

In many cases the discriminatory treatment is not written into the published laws and regulations but is a matter of official practice. In some cases the discriminatory practice is the result of an explicit government policy, but more often than not "it is the way things have always been done." The process of writing and implementing detailed regulations offers endless opportunities for discrimination against services offered by foreigners.

Even less visible are barriers created not by open discrimination against foreign enterprises, but by a general bureaucratic tendency not to approve new activities. Even the least protectionist-minded bureaucrat has an incentive to prove his or her worth by exercising control, and to exercise control is a matter of denying or delaying regulatory approval of new businesses, new service products, or changes in prices.

While bureaucratic tendencies are likely to limit the competitive opportunities of new domestic as well as foreign suppliers of services, they tend to have a more restrictive impact on foreign firms because the competitive advantage of foreign suppliers is in their ability to introduce new products and new ideas and to sell at lower prices. Moreover, regulators tend to develop symbiotic relationships with the industry they are regulating, which induces them to use their authority to shield the domestic industry from foreign competition. All of these tendencies are reinforced where the authority to regulate is delegated to the industry itself, as is the case for the professions such as lawyers, doctors, accountants, and brokers. Two examples, one from Japan and the other from the United States, help illustrate the points made here.

In Japan the Ministry of Finance regulates every detail of the insurance business—who can sell insurance, the kind of insurance that can be offered, the specific risks that can be covered by insurance contracts, to whom the policies can be sold, and the prices that can be charged. Everything requires a license that must be approved by an official, who must be persuaded that a proposal makes sense, and persuading the official may take weeks, months, or years. If an enterprising insurance executive has a brilliant idea that there is a promising market for insuring suppliers of telephone poles against damage suits arising from defective poles, it is necessary to obtain a license from the Ministry of Finance. In order to obtain a license, the insurance executive must first initiate informal consultations with ministry officials, who must agree that it would be productive to proceed with a formal application for a license. A new insurance company may have even greater difficulties, because the ministry could have decided that the country has enough insurance companies and no licenses should be granted to any new companies. Needless to say, foreign companies have found it very difficult to gain a foothold and, once there, to develop a significant market share. Foreign companies account for only a small fraction of 1 percent of the insurance market.

In the United States, the authority to regulate the licensing of lawyers and the practice of law has been delegated by the individual states to the various state bar associations. Many of these bar associations have adopted the rule that members admitted to the bar (that is, those licensed to practice in the state) are not allowed to form partnerships with lawyers in other states or other countries. This prohibition against interstate or international partnerships is clearly an arrangement that limits outside competition. Moreover, only a small handful of state bar associations have decided to grant foreign lawyers the right to provide legal advice on the laws of their countries or on international law. A proposal to license foreign legal consultants in the state of Illinois was turned down by the state bar because it might create new competition.

Uncertainty about restrictive regulations governments might impose in the future can be as much a barrier to trade as restrictive measures currently in effect. In fact, many businessmen have expressed greater concern about barriers that might be imposed in the future than about existing barriers.

Advances in communications and computer technology have enhanced the possibilities for trade in services for any firm that is prepared to invest large amounts of money in the latest communications and computer equipment. Numerous firms have invested billions of dollars in such facilities. It should not be surprising that these firms have expressed great concern about the possibility that future government regulations might limit their ability to use these facilities for sending information across national borders. While existing regulations concerning the use of private communications facilities inevitably restrict some potentially profitable trade in services, they can be factored into current investment decisions. Unexpected future restrictions could jeopardize the economic value of multibillion-dollar investments.

Public monopolies create unique barriers to trade in services. The establishment of a monopoly prohibits trade in the set of activities covered by the monopoly. At the same time it can lead to a number of barriers and distortions to trade in services not covered by the monopoly. Barriers to trade in services outside the monopoly can be created where the monopoly is the exclusive supplier of essential support services and it uses its monopoly position to disadvantage foreign producers of services. This problem arises in particular in situations where the monopolist competes with foreign producers outside its area of monopoly. The following two examples illustrate the point.

National airlines are frequently exclusive suppliers of ground handling services to foreign airlines flying into their country, while they compete with the same foreign airlines for international traffic. The natural temptation is to supply foreign competitors with inferior ground services, and many airlines cannot resist that temptation. American airlines flying air freight into Japan have thus argued that Japan Air Lines clears its own refrigerated freight in hours, while the refrigerated cargo of its competitors sits in the baggage handling area for days. Alitalia has been accused of landing foreign charter flights at an airport some distance from Rome, while Alitalia's own charter flights used the international airport closer to Rome.

National communications monopolies are the exclusive suppliers of basic communications circuits in most countries. Many are also allowed to compete with other domestic and foreign companies in the rapidly growing area of value-added communications and information services. Since competing suppliers of such services must acquire the basic communications lines from the same national communications monopoly, a natural conflict of interest exists. The monopoly has every incentive to put its competitors at a disadvantage by dragging its feet in making available new lines, or by charging exorbitant fees. The Bundespost, the German communications monopoly, has thus been accused of changing the pricing structure on international leased lines so that less data traffic is diverted from their own network

CONCLUSIONS

The close relationship between barriers to trade in services and governments regulations aimed at a broad range of policy objectives complicates efforts to reduce such barriers. What may be a barrier to a business could well be an essential regulation designed to achieve mandated domestic regulatory goals. In order to decide whether these barriers can be modified or eliminated in the course of trade negotiations, each of these measures will have to be weighed in terms of the extent to which its removal will adversely affect the achievement of mandated regulatory objectives in other policy areas and the extent to which the regulatory objectives could be pursued by other measures that create less of a barrier to trade. How trade policy can be used to accomplish this objective is the subject of the next chapter.

NOTE

1. For additional information about barriers to trade in services in individual sectors see the other volumes in the Ballinger American Enterprise Institute Trade in Services Series, which cover aviation, banking, construction, films and television, professional services, shipping, and telecommunications. Further information can be found in Carter and Dickinson (1979) on insurance, Böhme (1978) on shipping, and Walter (1985) on banking. Also see the survey on banking of the U.S. Department of the Treasury (1979).

8
APPLYING THE TRADE POLICY FRAMEWORK TO SERVICES

Several years ago, a senior official from the Japanese Ministry of Post and Telegraph called on me in my Washington office. The Office of the United States Trade Representative was not on the list of offices a senior official responsible for international communications would normally visit in Washington. A problem had arisen, however, as a result of a complaint filed by the Control Data Corporation that regulations issued by the ministry were creating a barrier to U.S. exports of information services, and U.S. trade officials had passed on the complaint to Japanese trade officials.

One of the things the official wanted to accomplish in Washington was to explain to U.S. trade officials why the regulations in question were fully legitimate and essential for implementing Japanese communications policy. The issue concerned the use of leased communication lines for accessing data bases stored in U.S. computers. The Japanese regulations did not permit the use of such lines if they were connected to more than one computer in the United States. The Japanese authorities were concerned that such interconnections would enable data base users in Japan to use the data lines for making telephone calls to the United States, thus bypassing the public telephone monopoly.

After thanking the Japanese official for his explanation, I explained in turn why the current regulations made it impossible for Japanese clients to take advantage of the full range of data provided by U.S. vendors of information services. The commercial viability of selling American information services to Japan depended on the use of leased lines (which are cheaper for heavy users) and the ability to access over a hundred data bases stored in dozens of computers all over the United States. This regulation, in effect, made the service unavailable to potential Japanese clients.

Both sides of the issue having been clarified, the question that needed to be considered was whether regulations could be developed that would deal with Japanese concerns about bypass while permitting full access to data bases in the United States. The Japanese visitor said he would think about it. A few months later Control Data and other American companies received the green light to proceed on the basis of agreed precautions for avoiding abuse.

At the time this conversation took place, the United States and Japan had a large number of other trade issues before them. While no direct link was ever made to a number of other issues that concerned Japan, the link had been made implicitly by putting the issue on the agenda for bilateral consultations by trade officials. Having obtained U.S. recognition of the legitimacy of their objectives, and recognizing in turn that U.S. trade officials would continue to pursue the commercial issue, the Ministry of Post and Telegraph decided to solve the problem its way by quietly changing its interpretation of the regulations.

This encounter is cited to illustrate the application of a trade policy framework to international services issues. It provides some insights into

- The reason for adding a trade policy dimension to the consideration of international services issues (to expand trade opportunities by identifying and reducing trade barriers)

- The difficulty of dealing with barriers to trade in services (most barriers to trade in services are embedded in domestic regulations)

- The analytical steps required to define issues in trade policy terms (identify trade opportunities and social costs associated with the relaxation of government regulations that restrict trade, and develop policy options that will lead to expansion of trade at acceptable social costs)

- The process followed by trade officials in tackling issues identified as trade problems (clarifying the issues through dialogue with concerned business executives and regulatory officials, and establishing a reciprocal basis for modifying policy measures that interfere with mutually advantageous trade)

Trade policy is the result of a mixture of economic theory, political pragmatism, and commercial savvy. Trade policy goals have been forged over the years through the interaction of international trade theory with the politics of trade. Most trade policy officials assume that their goal is to obtain for their countries the economic gains from trade and that their task is to persuade both their own governments and foreign governments to adopt policies that will advance that goal. On one hand that means reducing trade barriers at home and abroad, and on the other hand it means establishing domestic laws and regulations as well as international rules to guide commercial enterprises and government policymakers.

The purpose of these laws, regulations, and rules is to assure that commercial enterprises follow market rules, that policymakers do not adopt beggar-thy-neighbor policies that advance one country's interests at the expense of another, and that broader social goals are preserved. Political pragmatism and commercial savvy dictate a certain mercantilist bent to trade policy, which emphasizes the value of exports more than imports, but every trade official knows that ultimately the country benefits both by exporting what it can produce most efficiently and by importing what others can produce at less cost.

THE GOALS AND TOOLS OF TRADE POLICY

The goal of trade policy is to achieve economic gains from trade. To achieve this goal, trade policy thus seeks to establish the right economic conditions for the achievement of economic gains. Trade will lead to economic gains for each country if exporters and importers follow market signals, if intervention by other governments does not excessively distort market results, and if market decisions are adjusted for any nonmarket costs and benefits of trade.

It is the responsibility of trade officials to see to it that the behavior of market participants and governments approximates the conditions necessary for the achievement of mutual economic gains from trade. Trade policymakers pursue this goal by developing and negotiating international trade rules to guide both the behavior of enterprises engaged in international trade and the behavior of governments when they adopt policies that affect trade. Generally, these trade rules are based on principles drawn from international trade theory and are designed to establish the conditions for mutual economic gains from trade.

Trade officials have to be sensitive to the impact of trade policy measures on both the economic interests of different industries and the achievement of policy goals in other areas of domestic and foreign policy. In order to pursue an expansionary trade policy, it is usually necessary to convince a large number of business leaders, workers, and policy officials that proposed measures are fair and advantageous to the economic interests of the country as a whole. The process that is used to manage trade policy is usually as important as the outcome of trade policy.

Trade officials engage in extensive consultations at home with managers of domestic enterprises and officials responsible for other areas of policy, and they meet regularly with officials from other governments to consult on specific trade problems and to negotiate longer term agreements that establish the ground rules for the conduct of trade. The most important trade agreement is the General Agreement on Tariffs and Trade (the GATT), which provides both a set of trade rules that are now accepted by ninety-six countries and an institutional setting for negotiating multilateral agreements on the reduction of trade barriers. Many countries have also negotiated more stringent trade rules bilaterally with individual countries, or plurilaterally with a small number of other countries.

In managing their trade policies, countries have to balance the political concepts of national sovereignty and independence, and the economic reality of interdependence. As we saw, the trade rules reflect this balance by limiting government intervention in trade but not in the domestic market. The rules provide some indications of how this balance is to be maintained but leave a very considerable amount of ambiguity and room for interpretation.

When exactly does a domestic measure create unacceptable harm to the trade interests of another country? When should a country be able to expect its trading partners to accept an action it must take to protect an important domestic social objective? The rules provide some guidance for sorting out differences. The system could never work, however, if countries were not also willing to accept the spirit of the delicate balance built into the rules, both in managing their own policies and in evaluating the policies of their trading partners.

Economic Theory and Trade Policy Goals

The overall goal of trade policy is to maximize the economic gains that can be obtained from an expansion of international trade, while keeping the adjustment costs within politically acceptable limits. Since trade will lead to economic gains only if certain conditions are fulfilled, trade policy has to establish the necessary conditions for mutually advantageous trade. Moreover, since trade will result in a redistribution of income among industries, policy also has to keep the pace and the cost of adjustment for affected industries within socially acceptable limits.

We saw in Chapter 7 that the expansion of trade can adversely affect the economic interests of workers or shareholders in the least competitive industries. Even if the economic gains of the country as a whole far exceed the losses of a few, policy cannot ignore the rights and interests of those who lose. Legitimate government depends not only on the support of the majority but also on the passive acceptance of government policies by those who disagree with them. Trade policy must therefore take account of the interests of those who are adversely affected by an expansion of trade.

We also saw in Chapter 7 that some industries that are not internationally competitive today could become highly competitive if given enough time to develop the necessary skills and to exploit the economies of scale that come from growth. This is the case for so-called infant industries in developing economies. This is sometimes also the case with mature industries in developed economies that have not kept pace with advances in technology and management techniques. Trade policy has to take account of the possible need of such industries for time to develop the means for becoming competitive.

Economic Theory and Trade Principles

The international trade rules contained in the GATT are based on a number of basic concepts that are derived from economic theory. The key principles are as follows.[1]

The Market Principle. Central to broad public acceptance of the redistribution of income that results from trade, the market principle is a cornerstone of the trading system. Market competition is also fundamental to the ability to demonstrate mutual gains from trade on the basis of the theory of comparative advantage. Through a process of negotiations, each government that subscribes to the GATT rules has agreed to limit tariffs on imports to a maximum rate specified for each product and not to erect other barriers to imports. Governments have also agreed not to subsidize their exporters of industrial products, and to limit export subsidies for farm products.

In an ideal world, it would have been desirable not only to limit government intervention in trade but also to establish rules concerning market competition inside national markets. National governments, however, have not been willing to commit themselves explicitly to manage their domestic economies on the basis of market principles. The international trade rules thus do not require competition in domestic markets. Governments are not prohibited from intervening in their economies provided they do not discriminate against foreign producers, and governments are allowed to establish domestic monopolies provided such monopolies follow market rules in their dealings with foreign enterprises.

The Reciprocity Principle. There must be a balance between the benefits that can be obtained from tariff cuts and other reductions in nontariff barriers by other countries, and the obligation to contribute to the general welfare by reducing one's own barriers. This principle is consistent with the theoretical conclusion from international trade theory that an individual country can often gain from the imposition of an optimal tariff, but that it will surely incur economic losses if other countries follow suit.

The reciprocity principle is the source of all discipline in the GATT system. The GATT system works because each country knows that if it seeks to obtain unfair advantages through unilateral actions at the expense of other countries, such countries will surely retaliate. On the other hand, the reciprocity principle also facilitates liberalization, because it enables each government to provide a convincing rationale for reductions in barriers that adversely affect specific economic interest groups. The government can thus say: We cannot expect other countries to take painful steps that will help us, unless we are prepared to take some painful steps ourselves.

The Nondiscrimination or Most-Favored-Nation (MFN) Principle. Governments must treat all foreign exporters alike, regardless of their country of origin. This principle is designed to encourage global market adjustment and avoid the politicization of trade issues. It has the supplementary benefit of simplifying customs procedures. In order to minimize conflicts with the reciprocity principle, negotiations in the GATT are carried out on a multilateral basis, giving each country the opportunity to evaluate the benefits of such negotiations both on a global basis, and on a bilateral basis with individual countries. In recent years, however, the tension between the MFN principle and the reciprocity principle has led to the growing application of the

MFN principle on a conditional rather than an unconditional basis. On the basis of conditional MFN, a country is able to obtain the benefits of a new agreement only if it is willing to sign the agreement.

The Legitimacy of Domestic Regulation Principle. The pursuit of economic gains based on a market calculus should not preclude the attainment of social objectives in areas such as morals, public health and safety, environmental standards, and social equity. The trade rules give governments the right to intervene in trade if trade adversely affects the achievement of enumerated social objectives.

The National Treatment Principle. Governments must implement domestic laws and regulations in an evenhanded manner with respect to domestic and foreign producers. In other words domestic regulations cannot be enforced selectively in a way that favors domestic producers over foreign producers. By limiting the ability of governments to intervene on behalf of their own producers, the national treatment principle reinforces both the market principle and the reciprocity principle. It also protects the legitimacy of domestic regulation by saying that domestic regulations should not be used as hidden barriers to trade.

The Orderly Adjustment Principle. Trade can create difficult social adjustment problems, and countries should therefore have the right to stretch out reductions in trade barriers or to limit the growth rate of imports, if a high rate of growth in imports would create serious adjustment problems for an affected domestic industry. This principle is incorporated in the safeguard provisions, which allow countries to limit the growth of imports under specified circumstances. Application of the orderly adjustment principle has also led to the practice of phasing in any negotiated reductions in trade barriers over a number of years.

The international trade rules contained in the GATT, and the more general trade principles on which they are based, maintain a delicate balance between the right of each country to intervene in its own economy in the way it sees fit and the obligation of each country to allow market forces to determine its trade with other countries. Policy measures that are explicitly directed at exports or imports are quite clearly subject to the limitations on government intervention set by the rules. The difficulty arises with respect to domestic economic policy measures that affect trade. It is difficult for a government to intervene in its domestic market for any tradeable product and not affect trade. The rule of thumb, therefore, is that a country should avoid domestic policy measures that have a disproportionate effect on trade and that significantly injure the trade interests of other countries.

The Political Economy of Trade and Procedural Principles

The smooth operation of the system also depends on certain procedural principles, which help to avoid misunderstandings between countries and provide a way to work out mutually acceptable accommodations when domestic measures create trade problems. These procedural trade principles are incorporated in most trade agreements. The key ones are as follows.

The Transparency Principle. Governments should notify foreign exporters and their governments of the details of policy measures that affect international trade and the intended objectives of such measures. Adherence to this principle can prevent misunderstandings about facts, which occur fairly commonly because of differences in language, culture, and ways of doing business. The more credibility a government can achieve in the clarity and integrity of its policies, the fewer suspicions it will face from its trading partners.

The Consultation Principle. A government that is concerned about the trade effects of a policy measure taken by another government should be able to discuss the issue with the government concerned. In the first instance, such consultations serve to clarify the facts regarding the policy measure in question and its effect on trade. Once there is reasonable agreement on the facts or, at least, once differences in the interpretation of the available facts have been identified, the consultations can provide a mechanism for working out a mutually acceptable accommodation.

The Dispute Settlement Principle. Countries that cannot resolve bilateral trade disputes through bilateral consultations should submit such disputes to an agreed dispute settlement procedure, in which trade experts are given an opportunity to evaluate the facts and arguments presented by the two sides.

The International Trade Policy Tools and Institutions

Trade policy officials advance their countries' commercial policy objectives through bilateral negotiations with individual governments and multilateral negotiations in organizations such as the GATT. The GATT provides a global framework for negotiating the reduction of trade barriers and the development of international trade rules. The GATT serves as the international trade organization, and would be called that if Congress in one of its contrary moods had not turned down the charter for the International Trade Organization (ITO) during the early postwar years. In addition to the trade rules contained in the GATT, the ITO would have established international disciplines in many areas not traditionally covered by the GATT, such as competition policy, investment policy, and services.

Bilateral discussions and negotiations between trade officials of two countries can provide a relatively flexible basis for resolving bilateral trade issues that touch on sensitive areas of domestic policy. While no government may be willing to concede another government's right to interfere with its domestic regulatory policies, it may nevertheless be willing to make some pragmatic adjustments in its regulations to accommodate the commercial needs of one of its trading partners.

APPLYING THE TRADE POLICY FRAMEWORK TO SERVICES

The first step in any bilateral effort to solve trade problems is to initiate consultations with foreign government officials, to apprise them of the problem, and to review the facts in the case. In some cases the problem turns out to have been the result of a misunderstanding, or at least it may help everybody save face by pretending there was a misunderstanding. In other cases, the problem turns out to have been the result of an overly restrictive interpretation of regulations by a regulatory official, and the official is overruled by higher officials. One of the advantages of raising issues in a bilateral trade context is that trade officials in other countries are likely to approach sectoral issues from a broad commercial perspective. Moreover, trade officials in other countries have their own bilateral shopping list of issues they want resolved, and this gives them an incentive to help resolve problems brought to them.

Since the staff available to discuss issues with foreign governments is limited, trade officials have to be selective when adding issues to the bilateral agenda. Problems brought to the attention of trade officials are reviewed with respect to the available facts, the effort that has been made by the company itself to solve the problem through contacts with foreign government officials, and the policy issues at stake in the case. If the problems seem real and pressing, the company has done everything it could to argue its case with the relevant regulatory authorities, and the policy issues at stake seem manageable, the issue is included in the shopping list of bilateral trade issues to be taken up with trade officials of the government concerned.

If bilateral consultations fail to resolve a trade problem, the bilateral process takes on the character of a negotiation. In this stage of the process a direct link is established between resolution of the problem and possible actions the U.S. government might take. Progress on issues that have been raised by the other government are tied directly to a resolution of the problem. Information is leaked about possible retaliatory actions. Hints of retaliation can be a very effective tool for bringing an issue to a head, particularly if the proposed retaliatory action can be designed to have a maximum political impact on industries or regions of the country that might be putting political pressure on the government not to permit greater competition from foreign firms. In some cases, where it is possible to identify specific politicians or interest groups that are resisting resolution of a case, it is possible to tailor the retaliation list in such a way that it will have a maximum impact on a politician's constituency, or an interest group's other interests.

Bilateral negotiations on an issue-by-issue basis are very labor intensive, however, and the limited number of trade officials available for such negotiations sets a practical limit on the number of issues that can be resolved through a bilateral process. Governments therefore often find it useful to negotiate more comprehensive agreements with another government on a broad range of trade issues. Such agreements can establish some general ground rules for the development and administration of government measures that could affect trade. They also give businesses some certainty about the process a government will follow in issuing regulations that are likely to affect trade, and the principles they will apply in seeking to minimize any adverse trade effects. Since such broad agreements cannot deal with all detailed circumstances that could arise, however, they tend to complement and supplement the more ad hoc type of negotiations, rather than to substitute for such negotiations.

The key weakness of all bilateral negotiations is that they can only apply to trade between the two countries involved. Multilateral trade negotiations provide an efficient framework for the development of broadly applicable international trade rules and for significant, across-the-board reductions in trade barriers. In a multilateral negotiation, each country, in effect, is negotiating with the rest of the world simultaneously, and can concentrate all of its commercial leverage on whatever it wants to achieve. The shortcoming of multilateral negotiations is that it is far more difficult to find solutions that fit the great diversity of commercial interests represented and can therefore take a long time. The rules that emerge from the process tend to leave excessive room for national interpretations.

Multilateral trade negotiations take place under the GATT, which was negotiated after World War II. The GATT today also serves as the most widely accepted international trade organization, its rules accepted by ninety-six countries. Significant negotiations in the GATT take place in the context of so-called rounds of multilateral trade negotiations, which take place about once every ten years and last three to five years. The most recent round of negotiations was launched in Punta del Este, Uruguay, in September 1986, and is therefore called the Uruguay Round. The previous round of negotiations was the Tokyo Round, which was held from 1973 to 1979.

It is sometimes argued that bilateral and multilateral negotiations are incompatible because the former inevitably lead to preferential arrangements between any two countries, while the objective of the latter is to provide common ground rules for all the countries willing to accept the international trade rules of the GATT. Multilateral negotiations by themselves, however, can never achieve as much specificity as bilateral negotiations, which thus are always a necessary complement to multilateral negotiations. The real question is whether the results of such bilateral negotiations should result in preferential arrangements, or whether everyone might not be better off if all countries agreed to generalize commitments derived from bilateral negotiations. This is the most-favored-nation principle.

Application of the most-favored-nation principle clearly leads to a superior outcome, provided all countries are prepared to accept equivalent commitments. Where that is not the case, public opinion may not support generalizing bilaterally negotiated commitments that create new, substantive obligations. In such cases, it may be desirable to permit preferential bilateral or plurilateral agreements, and to limit the application of the most-favored-nation principle to issues on which multilateral agreement is possible. Given the complexity of the issues in services, and the great diversity of national regulatory philosophies, a hybrid approach to rulemaking in trade in services may be inevitable.

The Corporate Culture of the Trade Policy Fraternity

Trade policy officials tend to acquire certain attitudes in the course of their work that influence the way they approach issues and how they interact with businessmen and other officials. While it is somewhat foolhardy to generalize about something as ephemeral as attitude and approach across differences in personality, culture, and political organization, the task of trade officials is not very different from one country to the next, and that seems to foster a common culture. The trade policy mindset is as much a part of the trade policy framework as the GATT principles and as the negotiating tools used by trade officials.

One of the hard facts of life in trade policy is that a successful implementation of policies requires the approval and consent of a large number of people—business leaders, politicians, officials from other government departments, and officials from other governments. Another fact of life is that success in expanding trade requires a pragmatic attitude toward issues. It is always easy to impose restrictions on imports, but to persuade other countries to remove barriers requires an ability to reconcile domestic policy requirements with hard trade opportunities. Trade officials also inevitably find themselves arbitrating conflicts among different interest groups.

EXTENDING THE FRAMEWORK TO TRADE IN SERVICES

The goals, principles, procedures, and tools that make up the trade policy framework can be applied to trade in services as well as they can be applied to trade in goods. This means not that trade policy discussions should displace existing international agreements and institutions in individual service sectors, but that trade agreements and institutions can usefully complement existing international sectoral arrangements. International trade theories can be used to show that international trade in services can lead to the same kinds of economic gains for countries as international trade in goods. It follows that countries could gain from efforts to expand trade opportunities through a reduction of barriers to trade in services.

We saw in Chapter 7 that under certain circumstances completely free trade in services, like completely free trade in goods, could create more costs than gains. For example, a sudden and rapid increase in imports of construction services could create major adjustment problems for workers in that industry. In an underdeveloped economy, unconstrained imports can prevent infant industries from developing economies of scale or acquiring the knowledge and experience that would make them internationally competitive. Subsidized or dumped exports of services by a foreign monopoly could drive viable domestic enterprises out of business unfairly and could leave the country open to exploitation.

It is the responsibility of trade officials to identify the circumstances under which trade does not lead to mutual economic gains or creates unacceptable social costs, and to develop a set of policies that will either establish more favorable circumstances for trade or limit trade if other policy measures cannot correct the problem.

Domestic Regulation

The production of services tends in most countries to be more thoroughly regulated than the production of goods. Some have argued that this demonstrates the overriding importance of nonmarket social objectives in services, and that trade in services therefore should not be analyzed in purely commercial terms. The economic efficiency with which services are produced, however, and extensive regulation has so reduced competitive pressures in many industries that economic efficiency is not very high. If anything, the efficiency loss due to heavy regulation of services is an argument for the competitive pressures that trade can generate.

The production and sale of manufactured goods are also regulated for the protection of consumer standards, public health and safety, the environment, morals, and national security. Trade rules allow governments to intervene in trade to achieve these goals, while at the same time committing governments to minimize the trade-distorting effects of such intervention. The Standards Code negotiated in the last round of multilateral trade negotiations provides a model for dealing with regulatory issues.

The difference between trade in goods and trade in services is that most trade barriers in services are embedded in domestic regulations, while relatively few barriers to trade in goods are embedded in regulations. The negotiation of the standards was largely a form of preventive medicine, designed to prevent new barriers. The major barriers to trade in goods have been in the form of tariffs and quotas imposed at the border, and many of the trade rules that deal with issues such as standards were designed to prevent governments from circumventing their commitments to reduce the protection at the border.

For reasons discussed in the first few chapters, governments have found it difficult to control the flow of services across borders, and instead have focused their controls on the domestic sale of services. Since services are extensively regulated, most governments use the domestic regulatory machinery to control the sale of services to foreign suppliers. Any effort to liberalize trade in services has to concern itself principally with regulations, and that is likely to require a somewhat different approach to trade negotiations in services.

Inevitably, the line between legitimate domestic regulation and trade barriers will be more difficult to draw for services than it has been for goods. It will be far less clear when governments violate trade commitments in services. Considerable weight will fall on bilateral consultations and multilateral procedures for dealing with disputes over potential violations of commitments. The temptation in negotiating trade agreements in services will be to negotiate documents covering every regulation in existence, but that not only will prove impossible to negotiate but also could prove to be self-defeating by embedding too many restrictive domestic regulations in trade agreements. The rules that would come out of such a negotiation would inevitably reflect the most restrictive domestic regulatory regime, rather than the most liberal.

While trade negotiations in services cannot be aimed at the detailed harmonization of national regulatory systems, any trade negotiations must address the trade implications of different regulatory regimes. One of the major challenges will be to devise a set of rules to govern trade between countries with highly restrictive domestic regulatory regimes on one hand and countries that have substantially deregulated their own industry on the other hand. Without the recent trend in many countries toward deregulation, the opportunities for liberalization on a multilateral basis would be far more limited.

Any new regime for trade in services will probably have to provide for different levels of market access, depending on the extent to which the domestic regulatory system allows open competition. Thus while the negotiations should not focus on the domestic regulatory regime per se, the domestic regulatory regime has to be a factor in any negotiation.

Public Service Monopolies and Trade in Services

Some services such as transportation and communications are typically provided by monopolies. The most common rationale for a monopoly is that large economies of scale create natural monopolies. Transportation and communications usually require large investments in network equipment, and the establishment of the network tends to account for a large portion of the costs of providing such services. These high overhead costs create large economies of scale.

Another argument advanced is that these services are essential for public welfare and that their suppliers should be responsible for providing uniform service for all segments of the public at all times, regardless of cost differentials. A monopoly is needed, it is argued, because only a monopoly is in a position to cross-subsidize uneconomical segments of the market.

Internationally, these services are typically provided on the basis of bilateral agreements between the two monopolies. Representatives of these industries and regulatory officials argue that the absence of real competition in these industries means that trade is not possible and that trade policy therefore should not play any role. It is argued that the international delivery of these services should be viewed exclusively in terms of a shared regulation of a public utility.

A few years ago these arguments might well have been accepted without much debate. The underlying economic structure of these industries has been significantly altered in recent years, however, as a result of advances in technology and expansion of the market. Competition among a larger number of suppliers has now become possible in many segments of these industries. In light of these fundamental economic shifts, a number of governments have decided to deregulate large portions of these industries, or at least to permit and foster more competition. While competition remains fairly limited in many countries, international competition can no longer be ruled out.

It is becoming increasingly clear that the old rules of the game in both international transportation and communications have become less and less relevant to the more competitive segments of these industries. The divergence among countries with respect to the degree of regulation makes the current rules even less generally acceptable. There is a need to rethink international rulemaking in these industries, with complementarity between rules developed in a regulatory context and rules developed in a trade context. In developing the new rules, it will probably be useful to segment each of the industries into sectors with different degrees of competition, based on common economic criteria.

While differences are likely to remain in the degree of competition allowed or encouraged in different countries, the underlying economic fundamentals should ultimately persuade a majority of countries to adopt somewhat similar approaches to various segments of the market. Thus, for example, we should expect most countries in due time to allow broad competition for value-added and business communications services, to organize a limited form of competition for long-distance public telephone services, and to preserve a form of monopoly for the delivery of local public telephone services. It would make sense to give trade rules greater emphasis and regulatory rules less emphasis in the most competitive segments of the market, and to give trade rules less emphasis and regulatory rules greater emphasis in the least competitive segments of the market.

International Flows of People, Information, Money, and Goods

An important characteristic of trade in services that makes it different from goods is that it is dependent on the international movement of people, money, information, and goods. Services cannot be traded unless they become incorporated in people, money, information, or goods. Trades in goods would be severely hampered without people, money, information, and services moving back and forth across national borders—but it would still be possible to have at least some trade in goods. This makes trade in services different.

The fundamental question is whether issues such as the granting of visas to service workers, foreign exchange controls, and data flow issues should be covered by trade negotiations. The movement of people, money, and information from one country to another are issues that go far beyond trade in services. Yet, as we have seen throughout this book, international trade in services is inextricably linked to movements of people, information, money, and goods.

Policies dealing with the movement of people, money, and information raise sensitive issues of national policy in many countries. While most democratic countries permit a relatively open flow of people, money, and information into and out of the country, national governments have been most reluctant to constrain their freedom to control such flows. It is equally clear, however, that an agreement on trade in services could be frustrated by restrictions on the movement of people, information, money, or goods. Any services agreement therefore will have to address these issues. The question is how.

Immigration. The admission of foreigners into a country is one of the most sensitive issues with respect to trade in services. Few other issues generate as much emotional political debate as the admission of foreign workers, and it is doubtful that countries are prepared to treat this issue on a purely commercial basis. Most countries consider this area of policy a purely internal affair, not subject to negotiation. Despite these sensitivities, most countries permit considerable movement of people in and out of the country for commercial purposes, and many countries have signed bilateral visa agreements.

One approach to this issue could be to build on the treaty-trader principle that has been applied in friendship, commerce, and navigation (FCN) agreements. Under the treaty-trader principle, persons engaged in international trade are granted temporary admission to a country in order to negotiate or facilitate exports or imports. The applicability of this principle to international trade in services, however, remains relatively undefined in most countries. There may be some scope in building on the existing structure of agreements in this area.

U.S. trade officials have intervened from time to time with the immigration authorities in specific cases to obtain the application of the treaty-trader principle to trade in services. The question at issue in most cases has been over the extent to which work performed in the United States as against work performed in the home country should be treated as trade. The emerging practice has been to limit the work performed in the country to less than half of the total value of the services exported.

Some economists have expressed concern that an international trade agreement in services that covers international information or data flows but not the movement of people would result in a distortion of trade patterns. Services that can be delivered in the form of transborder data flows would grow faster than trade in services that depend on the movement of people. That is all very true, but it is not clear that leaving out visa issues would be any worse than leaving out any other set of government policies that affect trade in services. Any partial liberalization leads to a distortion of the patterns of trade, but that does not mean that such a partial liberalization does not lead to economic gains from the trade that is generated.

A more convincing argument has been made by Jagdish Bhagwati (1984a, 1985, 1986) and others that the comparative advantage of some countries lies in the plentiful supply of cheap labor, and that they would lose their major source of potential economic gain if any agreement did not cover the services that could be provided through a temporary international movement of people.

International Monetary Flows. The movement of money is only a little less sensitive than the movement of people. National controls on international financial flows are covered by existing rules of the International Monetary Fund, and the international trade rules of the GATT contain provisions dealing with balance of payments restrictions that affect international trade in goods. Efforts are underway in the Uruguay Round to strengthen the GMT discipline, and this could serve as a basis for equivalent rules for trade in services.

International Data Flows. The issue of international data flows is a relatively new issue, and as such not subject to extensive regulation by an entrenched bureaucracy. The negotiation of international trade rules thus seems a more manageable challenge. Many industry representatives have argued, in fact, that an agreement on international data flows should constitute a core element of any international trade agreement in services. The issue of international information flows is nevertheless a very sensitive issue for some countries, raising questions about national control over the dissemination of cultural material and giving foreigners access to information about national assets. Countries that restrict freedom of the press and the dissemination of information more generally will obviously resist commitments in this area.

Industrial countries took a first step toward the development of an international regime on international information flows with the adoption of the OECD Declaration on International Data Flows in 1985. This declaration commits countries to minimize barriers to the international flow of information. It recognizes the right of countries to establish regulations for the protection of individual privacy and national security, and the maintenance of vital data within national borders, but it also commits countries to minimize the disruption of international flows of data in connection with the enforcement of such regulations.

It has been suggested that another principle that should be established in an international trade in services agreement is the right to plug equipment into the public communications network for the purpose of transmitting services from one country to another.

Foreign Investment

Most services sold to consumers and small businesses are not easily sold across national borders, or even over long distances within a country. The delivery of these services depends on close contacts between producers of services and consumers of services; so they are ideally produced where they are consumed. If foreign suppliers of these services want to sell in a particular market, they have to invest in local production and distribution facilities or have to be able to lease such facilities from local owners.

The work performed in local facilities, however, is usually only part of the production process. Many of the technical, developmental, managerial, and administrative service inputs are typically produced abroad. In light of this close link between trade and investment, one could argue that the right to invest in local facilities for the production and distribution of services should be addressed in any trade negotiations in services. Others have argued conversely that services produced by local facilities do not constitute trade in services, and, therefore, should not be addressed in trade negotiations.

APPLYING THE TRADE POLICY FRAMEWORK TO SERVICES

An even closer link between trade and investment policies is created when a government imposes an investment requirement as a condition for the sale of services. Many countries, for example, require foreign insurance companies and banks to establish local branches or subsidiaries before they are allowed to sell such services locally. In these situations where the government itself makes the link between trade and investment, the right to invest becomes a clear trade issue.

THE RELATIONSHIP BETWEEN TRADE POLICY AND REGULATORY POLICY

Until a few years ago, economists and government officials did not look at the delivery of services as a form of trade. The traditional way of looking at international services was as a stream of services produced by an international delivery system. Thus scholars wrote textbooks and governments formulated policies largely in terms of an international postal delivery system, an international communications system, and an international air transport system.

The international delivery system in turn was seen as nothing more than an international extension of national delivery systems. The systemic view or model of the international delivery of services grew naturally out of a domestic regulatory approach. Services have thus been treated as a special category of economic activity that needed to be supervised more closely by the government than other forms of economic activity. It has just been taken for granted for a long time that the government should be responsible for the way the mail is delivered, how banks and insurance companies manage other people's money, how well doctors, accountants, and architects perform their services, how well the phone system works, and whether trains run on time.

The traditional regulatory approach to international services is well demonstrated by the allocation of responsibilities between domestic regulatory agencies and executive agencies in the United States. Authority to regulate services provided by foreigners is largely in the hands of the domestic regulatory agencies, even though the president is otherwise responsible for foreign relations. The president and executive agencies have had very little authority to decide whether foreigners should be allowed to provide a broad range of services, and the conditions under which they should be allowed to do so.

While regulatory agencies are theoretically not authorized to negotiate with foreign governments, they have been thrust into that role in practice by the need to reconcile differences between domestic and foreign regulations with foreign regulatory authorities. In the communications area, for example, the only power delegated to the president by the Congress is the right to determine the placement of submarine telephone cables from abroad. All other regulatory decisions have been in the hands of the independent regulatory agencies.

Economic analysts and policymakers who thought about international services in the past thus largely thought of services in terms of interconnected national systems for delivering various services internationally: a cooperative arrangement among national postal administrations for delivering the mail internationally, cooperative arrangements among national phone companies that made it possible to make international phone calls, international agreements among airlines that made it possible to transfer tickets and baggage when making connections between national and foreign airlines, international agreements among governments on air traffic rules for planes flying international routes, and cooperative arrangements among banks in different countries that made it possible to transfer money efficiently from one country to another.

An analytical and policy model of international services that puts the emphasis on the system for delivering services internationally has considerable validity. It puts the analytical or policy focus on the capacity of the system to deliver reliable service on a predictable basis. A systemic approach also provides a conceptual basis for deciding what services should be provided by the monopolies that dominate the national delivery of services in many areas such as postal delivery, communications, and transportation. Since monopolies are in a position to exploit the public, most governments have considered it appropriate and desirable to take over the management of the monopolies or to regulate their activities in the public interest. At an international level, this has led to the natural conclusion that the appropriate basis for organizing services provided by monopolies or quasi-monopolies is to divide the market between the national monopolies. Moreover, it has been argued that international services sold by domestic monopolies should not be viewed as internationally traded services, but rather as just another type of service provided domestic customers.

A regulatory approach to the international delivery of services has an inherent weakness in losing sight of the increased efficiency or improvement in quality that could be generated by potential competition. By removing the possible entry of new, competitive suppliers, a government removes a powerful incentive and source of pressure on managers to search out new ways of producing services more efficiently and supplying the services that business users and consumers would like to buy. In a period when the technology for producing and delivering services is changing rapidly, as it has in recent years, the loss of innovation due to the absence of potential competition is particularly costly to an economy.

A regulatory, system-oriented model also does not bring out the possibility that some countries might do a better job, for whatever reason, in performing certain services, or might be able to produce such services at a lower cost. The English might do a better job in economic journalism, the Americans in writing economic textbooks, the Greeks in shipping, the French in designing clothes and hair styles, the Italians in designing fast cars, and the Swiss in providing a safe place to put your money.

A trade policy approach is not likely to prove very effective in addressing systemic issues concerning the operation of delivery networks in services. The trade policy framework is not structured to address such issues; the rules of the trading system are not designed to deal with issues such as the capacity of a network to deliver a reliable stream of services, and trade rules have never proved to be very effective in dealing with monopolies.

A strong case can therefore be made for a complementary relationship in areas such as telecommunications and transportation between international agreements negotiated in a regulatory context and international agreements negotiated in a trade context. Both trade policy and regulatory policy have a contribution to make to the smooth and efficient functioning of the world economy.[2]

International negotiations carried out by trade officials, in a trade policy context, thus should supplement and complement international negotiations carried out by officials responsible for related policy areas. In order to assure a harmonious and complementary relationship, trade agreements that deal with the trade effects of regulatory decisions will have to be negotiated with the participation of regulatory officials or at the very least on the basis of close consultations with such officials. In many cases these negotiations are likely to be carried out by officials from the regulatory departments who have been detailed to the trade negotiations.

Regulatory officials will need to continue the negotiation of international agreements in their sphere of responsibility, and international organizations with sectoral responsibilities, such as the International Civil Aviation Organization (ICAO) and the International Telecommunications Union (ITU), will need to continue to play a major role in their respective spheres. The negotiation of trade agreements will not reduce either the need or the scope of efforts to update and extend regulatory agreements in sectors such as telecommunications and aviation, and in functional areas such as international monetary policy and immigration policy.

Officials from finance ministries will need to continue to address the full range of issues concerning the international movement of money, the regulation of international banking activities, and issues arising from foreign exchange controls imposed by other governments. Consular and immigration officials will need to continue to address the full range of issues related to the movement of people, including visa issues. Officials responsible for the regulation of individual sectors such as communications or aviation will need to continue to pursue negotiations that have a regulatory focus.

The process of meshing trade and regulatory policies and responsibilities will not always be easy, and the struggle over bureaucratic turf is likely to make the negotiations within the individual national governments even tougher than the negotiations among countries. That internal bureaucratic struggle, however, is not a mere inconvenience that should be avoided as a wasteful exercise, since it is part of the whole rationale for pursuing trade negotiations. The objective is to place greater emphasis on the efficiency gains that can come from international competition and specialization in services, and this will require a reordering of priorities in national regulatory policies. The struggle over bureaucratic turf ultimately is over policy priorities, and that is the gut issue in any trade negotiations in services.

The overlap in responsibilities that will result from trade negotiations will be inconvenient not only for some of the officials involved, but also for those in business management who complain that they do not know who is in charge. Managers are often puzzled and frustrated by the division of responsibilities between trade policy officials and officials responsible for other functional and sectoral areas of policy. A sharing of responsibilities is unavoidable, however, because a government has many different objectives that are assigned to different government departments.

Officials in each department and bureau have their assigned area of responsibility and expertise for a given area of policy. Real world problems do not neatly fall into one policy area or another. Each policy measure raises issues in a number of policy areas simultaneously, and just as there are no clear areas of demarcation between one policy objective and another, there can be no clear areas of demarcation between the responsibilities of officials in one department and another.

CONCLUSIONS

Application of the trade policy framework to trade in services provides the means for pursuing the economic gains from expanded trade predicted by the application of classical trade theory to services. While barriers to trade in services are more difficult to identify and to remove because they tend to be embedded in domestic regulations, the concepts and techniques trade policy officials have used to deal with nontariff barriers to trade in goods can be adapted to deal with barriers to trade in services.

NOTES

1. An excellent discussion of the basic concept underlying the GATT is contained in a book written by Clair Wilcox in 1949, entitled *A Charter for World Trade*. Wilcox is one of the officials in the U.S. State Department who played a key role in the formation of the GATT.
2. Feketekuty (1987) contains a detailed discussion of the respective responsibilities of trade officials and regulatory officials in the telecommunications area, as well as the respective responsibilities of the GATT and the ITU.

9

BILATERAL AGREEMENTS WITH ISRAEL AND CANADA: MODELS FOR A FRAMEWORK AGREEMENT

Over the past three years, the United States has negotiated bilateral free trade area agreements with both Israel and Canada, including provisions on trade in services. Services were added to the negotiating agenda with both countries out of a desire to create useful precedents for future multilateral negotiations. In both cases, the negotiations provided trade negotiators with useful experience in negotiating trade agreements in services.

The two agreements differ substantially with respect to both the scope and the legal character of the commitments. The services agreement with Israel covers all areas of cross-border trade in services, with no exclusions. It does not cover foreign investment or the production of services in the local market. It is also not legally binding, and instead commits the two countries to implement its principles on a best efforts basis, and to pursue sector-by-sector negotiations with the aim of filling in enough details so the agreement can be converted into a legally binding document.

The services agreement with Canada covers not only cross-border trade in services but also foreign investment in services. Unlike the Israeli agreement, the agreement with Canada is legally binding. All existing regulations are grandfathered, however, and the application of the principles of the agreement to existing regulations that are inconsistent with the agreement will have to be pursued through future negotiations. Key service sectors are also completely excluded from the agreement, including basic telecommunications, air transport, shipping, and legal services. Banking services are not covered by the general services agreement, though they are covered by a separate agreement.

The bilateral agreements with Israel and Canada thus provide two separate approaches to the negotiation of trade agreements in services. Each can provide some useful insights into the negotiation of a multilateral agreement on trade in services in the Uruguay Round of multilateral trade negotiations. The basic purpose of this chapter is to draw some practical insights from the bilateral negotiations with Israel and Canada for the negotiations in the Uruguay Round.

U.S./ISRAELI AGREEMENT ON TRADE IN SERVICES

On April 22, 1985, the United States and Israel signed a Declaration on Trade in Services. The declaration establishes a set of principles for trade in services between the United States and Israel. The provisions of the declaration are not legally binding, but the two countries have committed themselves to apply the provisions on a "best efforts" basis. More recently, the two countries have conducted sectoral reviews of trade in tourism, telecommunications, and insurance services and have prepared sectoral annotations that describe with greater precision how the general provisions are to be interpreted with respect to each sector.

From the beginning of the negotiations between Israel and the United States, it was clear that the volume of trade in services between the two countries is limited, except in tourism. There have also been few pressing commercial issues that needed to be resolved. This raised the question why the two governments should commit resources to such a negotiation, particularly since the negotiation of an agreement made it necessary to address a number of sensitive regulatory issues that could otherwise have been avoided. One reason the negotiations were pursued despite these negative considerations is that both countries realized trade in services would become a more important factor in their relationship in the future. Another reason is that these negotiations were expected to help both countries define the issues that will have to be addressed in the broader negotiations on trade in services in the Uruguay Round. Officials on both sides have also enjoyed the intellectual challenge involved and have found it a useful vehicle for bringing out the broader economic implications of many sectoral regulatory issues.

The Contents of the Declaration on Trade in Services

The principal provisions of the Declaration on Trade in Services by the United States and Israel deal with market access, national treatment, obligations of governmental authorities below the national level, domestic regulations, public monopolies, due process obligations, the resolution of trade problems, and the negotiation of a legally binding agreement.

Open Market Access. The agreement establishes open market access as a basic principle, within the constraints imposed by the differences in the regulatory regimes in effect in the two countries in specific service sectors.

National Treatment. Trade in services between the two countries is given national treatment. National treatment is defined in terms of the ability of producers from the other country to market or distribute services under the same conditions as like services sold by domestic producers. The commitment is framed in terms of cross-border trade in services, but also covers any commercial presence that may be required in the importing country to facilitate the export of services. A footnote to this provision defines commercial presence for banking as the establishment of representative offices, but not agencies, branches, or subsidiaries of a foreign bank.

Political Subdivisions. National authorities are expected to consult with the authorities of political subdivisions in order to assure that their regulations are consistent with the principles contained in the declaration.

Domestic Regulation. The national treatment principle is explicitly applied to domestic regulations, but at the same time its application is limited to the area of discretion available to domestic regulatory authorities under current laws. Since this is a best efforts agreement, the reservation makes explicit what is otherwise implicit: that the declaration does not alter any domestic laws. This provision also commits trade officials to consult with officials in regulatory agencies in order to assure consistency in their actions with the principles of the declaration.

Public Monopolies. Each country has the right to establish public monopolies to supply certain services, but such monopolies are expected to abide by the principles of the declaration insofar as they make sales or purchases that affect exports or imports of services from the other country.

Due Process. Each country is committed to publish domestic laws and regulations affecting trade in services and to notify its trading partner of any laws and regulations that discriminate against foreign producers. The provision also gives foreign suppliers access to established domestic procedures for reviewing regulatory proposals and to established judicial proceedings for resolving disputes over the application of regulations.

Problem Solving. Each country agrees to consult periodically on specific problems that arise concerning trade in services between the two countries and to review the existing regulatory regime that applies to services in each country insofar as it affects trade. These reviews have led to the negotiation of sectoral annotations.

Negotiation of Binding Commitments. The two countries are committed to review the operation of the agreement after eighteen months, and to explore the possibility of transforming the provisions of the declaration into a legally binding agreement. The review was held in fall of 1986, and the decision was made at that time to pursue the negotiation of a legally binding agreement through the development of sectoral annotations.

Issues Addressed during the Negotiations

One difficult issue was the relationship of the bilateral agreement on trade in services to the bilateral treaty on friendship, commerce, and navigation (FCN). Israel is one of the countries with whom the United States has negotiated such treaties. Drafted in fairly broad terms, the FCN treaty between the United States and Israel appears to give all businesses of each country the right of establishment and national treatment in the other country. Since the provisions of the treaty apply to services as well as to goods, the question arose whether a trade agreement in services was needed at all, or whether it would overlap with the FCN treaty and create conflicting obligations.

Careful review of the FCN treaty led to the conclusion that it was deficient in a number of respects, and that a conflict between a trade agreement and the FCN treaty could be avoided. First, the FCN treaty primarily focuses on investment obligations, rather than trade obligations. Second, major sectors in services had been carved out of the national treatment provision of the FCN treaty. U.S. legislation restricts the activities of foreign investors in many of the principal service sectors, and it appeared easier at the time the FCN agreement was negotiated to carve out the whole sector rather than to tailor the provisions of the treaty to the requirements of the U.S. law. Third, the FCN treaty was drafted in the early 1950s when trade in services was not a major issue and was not well understood. Services are included only incidentally, and not in a manner that is relevant to the problems faced by exporters of services. Fourth, the dispute settlement provisions of the FCN treaty are not very strong, providing only for voluntary consultations and referral of unresolved issues to the International Court of Justice. This undermined the effectiveness of the agreement.

One approach considered was to expand the coverage of the FCN treaty, but that would have led to too many legal questions. The simplest approach, in the end, was to separate trade issues from investment issues. While it had been the original intention of U.S. trade negotiators to draft an agreement that would cover both trade and investment issues, it was now clear that a potential legal conflict could be avoided by giving the U.S./Israeli services agreement a trade focus. Establishment issues are thus covered only insofar as a commercial presence is required in the other country to carry out cross-border trade. Since most current restrictions on the sale of services by foreign enterprises in the United States take the form of restrictions on foreign investment, it also became possible to minimize sectoral exceptions to the agreement by excluding investment commitments. A fuller description of the debate over these issues is found in Carol Balassa's article in the *Journal of World Trade Law*, "Negotiation of Services in the U.S.-Israel Free Trade Area."

A closely related issue was how the agreement should deal with banking services and the establishment of foreign branches. It was decided that the establishment of a foreign branch would be considered an investment issue and that the agreement would only cover the establishment of representative offices by foreign banks. In effect, commercial presence in banking was defined as the establishment of representative offices. The decision not to cover the establishment and operation of branches and subsidiaries in the importing country significantly reduced concerns expressed by bank regulators that the agreement would undermine their fiduciary authority.

Another key issue was the application of the agreement to political subdivisions and, in particular, to the state governments in the United States, which enjoy considerable authority in regulating services. An agreement that would not commit the state governments in the United States would reduce the value of an agreement to Israel and raise questions about appropriate reciprocity. At the same time, it was equally clear that the United States could not negotiate an agreement binding the states without extensive consultations with the state governments and a great deal of work. Such a process could not be completed within the time available; it therefore made more sense to negotiate a best efforts agreement that could be used as a basis for subsequent consultations with the states.

Consultations that have been held with state authorities on the basis of the Declaration on Trade in Services have not brought out any major substantive issues, and the ground has now been laid for getting over the sensitive political issue of state rights. What has to be made clear to the states is that the federal government is not planning to federalize regulatory responsibilities now reserved to the states.

Consultations with national regulatory authorities in the course of the negotiations revealed that the application of the national treatment principle and the market access principle to domestic regulations raises difficult issues in a number of sectors that will require in-depth consultations with regulatory officials to resolve. It also became apparent that it is difficult to persuade regulatory officials to accept the discipline of a trade agreement in services without a sector-by-sector review with full participation of regulators. The decision to pursue the negotiation of sectoral annotations to the general principles thus emerged naturally out of the internal debates in each government over the extent to which the principles would be applied to specific sectors. Regulatory officials were willing to go along with the signing of an interim best efforts agreement without the sectoral details only because it was not legally binding.

One of the first issues that had to be sorted out was who would have the responsibility for negotiating a broad agreement on trade in services. In the United States the responsibility of the U.S. Trade Representative for the negotiation of such an agreement had been established in both law and practice. No department in the Israeli government had a similar set of responsibilities. A team of Israeli officials with the necessary responsibility was constituted from government ministries. Some of the officials have maintained their involvement in the process despite transfers from one ministry to another.

Sectoral Annotations on Tourism, Telecommunications, and Insurance

Sectoral reviews have followed a standard pattern. The first step has been to discuss the scope of activities that should be covered in the discussions of the sector and the relevant policies that affect trade in services in that sector. The second step has been to develop national papers that specify the regulatory regime that applies to the covered activities and how trade in the covered services is treated under the regulations. The third step has been to conduct bilateral exchange on the basis of the papers, with each side raising pointed questions regarding the treatment of foreign suppliers under a broad range of circumstances. The fourth step has been to develop an initial draft of a sectoral annotation, which is then subjected to detailed review to identify key issues. The most difficult part of the process has naturally been the last step, namely, the resolution of politically difficult issues that involve important conflicts between principle and political reality.

Each sectoral annotation follows the structure of the declaration. Since the first provision in the declaration deals with the definition of trade in services, each sectoral annotation also begins with a detailed description of the sector—the activities covered by the sector, the various ways in which trade in services is conducted in that sector, and the major functional activities associated with trade in services in that sector. This is followed by sections dealing with the meaning of market access in the sector, the application of national treatment to trade and to the commercial presence of foreign suppliers inside the importing country, application to political subdivisions, adherence to the provisions of the agreement by domestic regulatory authorities, the responsibilities of public monopolies, and due process.

Since the sectoral annotations are still under negotiation, it is too soon to discuss the substantive details. A few general comments, however, could be added with respect to the scope and definition of the sectors covered. In the Annotation on Tourism, there was considerable discussion of the scope of activities that should be covered, and it was agreed to cover a very wide range of activities. Since tourism is very popular and is supported by strong domestic political groups, tourism proved a useful context for addressing a broad range of issues. In the Annotation on Telecommunications, it proved extremely useful to specify both supplier interests and user interests, and to distinguish between the interests of small and large users and suppliers. The most important definitional issue, however, has not surprisingly been the dividing line between basic telecommunications services and value-added telecommunications services.

U.S./CANADIAN AGREEMENT ON TRADE IN SERVICES

President Reagan and Prime Minister Mulroney signed the U.S./Canadian Free Trade Agreement on January 2, 1988. The agreement must now be ratified by the U.S. Congress and the Canadian Parliament. The provisions on services are an integral part of the Free Trade Agreement and will become legally binding once the two legislatures ratify the agreement.

In contrast with the situation that exists between Israel and the United States, Canada and the United States have a large volume of bilateral trade in services. This is not surprising, given the proximity between the two countries. In some sectors such as insurance, the United States and Canada also have fairly similar regulatory systems, and businesses reported few problems in these sectors. In other sectors, the United States and Canada have very different regulatory systems and these differences inevitably constrained the scope of the agreement in these sectors. The air transportation sector and the basic telecommunications sector, for example, were excluded from the provisions of the agreement because it proved too difficult to establish a reciprocal basis for trade in these sectors.

Unlike the agreement with Israel, the agreement with Canada covers investment in local facilities as well as the movement of business persons between the two countries (this category is meant to cover white-collar professionals as well as independent entrepreneurs, but not blue-collar workers). Moreover, the agreement with Canada includes detailed sectoral agreements with respect to architecture, tourism, computer services, and telecommunications-network-based enhanced services.

Provisions on Services, Investment, and Temporary Entry

Coverage. Covered services include (a) the production, distribution, sale, marketing, and delivery of a covered service and the purchase or use thereof; (b) access to, and use of, domestic distribution systems; (c) the establishment of a commercial presence (other than an investment) for the purpose of distributing, marketing, delivering, or facilitating a covered service; and (d) subject to the provisions of Chapter Sixteen on investment, any investment for the provision of a covered service and any activity associated with the provision of a covered service.[1]

National Treatment. Each country agrees to give firms from its trading partner treatment no less favorable than that accorded in like circumstances to its own firms. States and provinces are expected to give firms from the trading partner the same treatment they would give firms from another state or province within their own country, or the same treatment they give their own firms, whichever is better.

Treatment of producers from the trading partner can be different, however, provided the difference in treatment is no greater than that necessary for prudential, fiduciary, health and safety, or consumer protection reasons, and such treatment is equivalent in effect to the treatment accorded local firms. The burden of proof is on the country taking a regulatory action to show it is consistent with national treatment.

The national treatment provision does not apply to existing laws and regulations that are inconsistent with national treatment, or to future amendments of them, provided they do not increase the level of protection.

Nonestablishment. Each country agrees not to require establishment or commercial presence by a supplier from its trading partner insofar as such a requirement would create a barrier to cross-border trade in services covered by the agreement.

Licensing and Certification. Each country agrees that in principle licensing and certification requirements should be used only to establish competence or the ability to provide covered services, and not have the purpose or effect of restricting market access by professionals from its trading partner.

Future Negotiations. The two countries agree to pursue negotiations to extend coverage to excluded sectors and to existing regulations that are inconsistent with the agreement.

Temporary Entry for Business Persons. Chapter Fifteen of the agreement commits each country to provide for the temporary entry of "business persons" from its trading partner. Business persons are defined as citizens who are engaged in the trade of goods or services or in investment activities. In practice, this definition is meant to include businessmen as well as white-collar professionals engaged in producing services, but not blue-collar workers.[2] Implementation will take the form of a special visa that will be issued by the immigration authorities of the two countries to eligible persons.

Lessons Learned

One of the important lessons learned from the negotiations on trade in services with Canada is that it is difficult to establish a basis for free trade in a sector where there are large differences in domestic regulations, particularly if one country has a regulatory regime that permits open competition among domestic firms and the other country has a regulatory regime that limits domestic competition. In both long-distance telecommunications and air transport services, deregulation in the United States has resulted in open competition among domestic firms in these sectors, while Canada has maintained tight regulatory controls over these sectors. Extending national treatment provisions to these two sectors would have meant, in effect, that Canadian firms would have had unlimited access to the U.S. market, while access of U.S. firms to the Canadian market would have remained under the administrative control of Canadian regulatory authorities.

Not surprisingly, Canadian firms were in favor of applying the national treatment obligation to these sectors, while U.S. firms in these sectors vigorously argued against such treatment. U.S. negotiators expressed a willingness to extend the national treatment commitment to both of these sectors, provided Canada was prepared to permit open domestic competition. Since this would have required major regulatory reforms, Canada could not agree to this U.S. request, and the United States in turn refused to commit itself to national treatment in these sectors.

In the area of banking, the shoe was on the other foot. Canada permits commercial banks to engage in investment banking activities while the Glass Steagall Act prohibits commercial banks in the United States from engaging in such activities. Canada argued that it would be willing to give American banks national treatment in Canada, provided Canadian banks in the United States were allowed to engage in investment banking activities. This would have given Canadian banks in the United States preferential treatment as compared with local banks, unless the United States had been prepared to abandon the Glass Steagall restraints on investment banking activities by commercial banks.

While there is growing sentiment in the United States in favor of a relaxation of the Glass Steagall Act, the Treasury was not in a position to tackle this issue in the context of the U.S./Canadian negotiations. Treasury officials, instead, came up with a compromise. They agreed to allow commercial banks in the United States to handle securities issued by the Canadian government, thus opening the way for Canadian banks to pursue this lucrative business in the United States. In return, the Canadian authorities agreed to relax regulatory restraints on the growth of some American banks in Canada.

The shipping sector was excluded from the agreement because of determined opposition by the U.S. shipping industry. Canadian negotiators asked for exemption from the Jones Act, which limits shipping in American waters to U.S.-owned and-crewed vessels. After resisting Canadian pressures, U.S.

negotiators proposed a compromise, exempting Canada from future extensions of the Jones Act to new areas. Even that proved more than the industry could accept, and it succeeded in mobilizing congressional opposition, forcing the administration to withdraw its compromise proposal.

CONCLUSIONS

The negotiation of the agreements between the United States and Israel, and between the United States and Canada has given trade officials in the three countries a good hands-on experience in negotiating a comprehensive agreement on trade in services and in applying trade concepts to a variety of sectoral issues. It has provided the trade policy community everywhere with functioning models of trade agreements in services.

NOTES

1. The following service activities are covered by the agreement:

    Agriculture and Forestry Services

    Soil preparation services
    Crop planting, cultivating, and protection services
    Crop harvesting services (primarily by machine)
    Farm management services
    Landscape and horticultural services
    Forestry services (such as reforestation, forest firefighting)
    Crop preparation services for market
    Livestock and animal specialty services (except veterinary)

    Mining Services

    Metal mining services
    Coal mining services
    Oil and gas field services
    Nonmetallic minerals (except fuels) services

Construction Services

    Building, developing, and general contracting services
    Special trade contracting services

Distributive Trade Services

    Wholesale trade services
    Vending machine services
    Direct selling services

Insurance and Real Estate Services

    Insurance services
    Segregated and other funds services (managed by insurance companies only)
    Insurance agency and brokering services
    Subdivision and development services
    Patent ownership and leasing services
    Franchising services
    Real estate agency and management services
    Real estate leasing services

Commercial Services

    Commercial cleaning services
    Advertising and promotional services
    Credit bureau services
    Collection agency services
    Stenographic, reproduction, and mailing services
    Telephone answering services
    Commercial graphic art and photography services
    Services to buildings
    Equipment rental and leasing services
    Personnel supply services
    Security and investigation services
    Security systems services
    Hotel reservation services
    Automotive rental and leasing services
    Commercial educational correspondence services
    Professional services, such as
        Engineering, architectural, and surveying services
        Accounting and auditing services
        Agrology services

    Scientific and technical services
    Management consulting services
    Librarian services
    Agriculture consulting services
 Nonprofessional accounting and bookkeeping services
 Training services
 Commercial physical and biological research services
 Commercial economic, marketing, sociological, statistical, and educational research services
 Public relations services
 Commercial testing laboratory services
 Repair and maintenance services
 Other business consulting services
 Management services
    Hotel and motel management services
    Health care facilities management services
    Building management services
    Retail management services
 Freight forwarding and arrangement services
 Packing and crating services

Other Services

 Computer services
 Telecommunications-network-based enhanced services
 Tourism services

2. The range of professions covered by the term *business persons* is enumerated as follows:
   - accountant
   - engineer
   - scientist
     - biologist
     - biochemist
     - physicist
     - geneticist
     - zoologist
     - entomologist
     - geophysicist
     - epidemiologist
     - pharmacologist
     - animal scientist
   - agriculturist (agronomist)
   - dairy scientist
   - poultry scientist
   - soil scientist
   - research assistant (working in a post-secondary educational institution)
   - medical/allied professional
     - physician (teaching and/or research only)

- dentist
- registered nurse
- veterinarian
- medical technologist
- clinical lab technologist
- psychologist
- scientific technician/technologist
- disaster relief insurance claims adjuster
- architect
- lawyer
- teacher
  - college
  - university
  - seminary
- economist
- social worker
- vocational counselor
- mathematician (baccalaureate)
- hotel manager (baccalaureate and 3 years of experience)
- librarian (MLS)
- animal breeder
- plant breeder
- horticulturist
- sylviculturist (forestry specialist)
- range manager (range conservationist)
- forester
- journalist (baccalaureate and 3 years of experience)
- nutritionist
- dietitian
- technical publications writer
- computer systems analyst
- management consultant (baccalaureate, or equivalent professional experience)

10
A GENERAL AGREEMENT ON TRADE IN SERVICES

In the early morning hours of September 20, 1986, trade ministers from around the world successfully concluded a meeting in Punta del Este, Uruguay, by agreeing to launch a new round of multilateral trade negotiations. After days of virtually nonstop negotiations, exhausted delegates agreed to the text of the Ministerial Declaration on the Uruguay Round, which specified the agenda for the negotiations. One of the most controversial and historic decisions of the Punta del Este meeting was to initiate, for the first time, negotiations on trade in services as a major negotiating item.

The seeds for the negotiations on trade in services were planted in legislation passed by the U.S. Congress in 1974 to authorize the participation of the United States in the Tokyo Round of multilateral trade negotiations. The Trade Act of 1974 directed U.S. negotiators to seek the elimination of barriers to trade in services. Getting agreement among a large number of countries to initiate comprehensive negotiations on a new topic, particularly a topic as new and different as trade in services, however, proved difficult. The most the United States was able to achieve in the Tokyo Round was a sprinkling of references to complementary services in a number of the codes dealing with nontariff barriers to trade in goods.

The first major step forward came in 1979, when the United States succeeded in persuading the other industrial countries of the Organization for Economic Cooperation and Development to undertake a study of trade in services, with the objective of identifying areas for future negotiation. The analytical work and the discussions that have taken place in the OECD over the past eight years have created a substantial consensus among developed countries on the desirability of launching negotiations on trade in services in the GATT. In line with that consensus, OECD countries agreed in spring 1987 to release a paper titled "Elements of a Conceptual Framework for Trade in Services," which sets out the key elements to be included in an agreement on trade in services. It has made a substantial contribution to the development of an intellectual foundation for the negotiations.

The first serious discussion of trade in services in the GATT took place in 1982, when the GATT began to lay the groundwork for a new round of multilateral trade negotiations. The United States proposed that the work of the GATT include a study of trade in services. In support of that objective, the U.S. trade representative put forward ideas on a future multilateral agreement on trade in services in an article entitled "A Simple Plan for Negotiating Trade in Services," in *The World Economy*, a publication of the Trade Policy Research Center in London (see Brock, 1982). After a prolonged debate between developed countries, which generally supported a GATT study of services, and developing countries, which generally opposed such a study, trade ministers agreed in November 1982 that countries that were so inclined should undertake national studies of trade in services and exchange information on trade in services on the basis of those studies.

The United States was the first country to circulate its national study, in spring 1984; eventually more than twelve countries completed such studies. The work on trade in services was given more formal recognition at the end of 1984, when the GATT Contracting Parties agreed to set up a working group under Ambassador Jaramillo of Colombia to examine whether or not services should be included in the new round of negotiations. In light of the prolonged and contentious debate, the Ministerial Declaration on the Uruguay Round offers remarkably clear guidance to the negotiators.

The first phase of the negotiations will focus on the negotiation of a set of overall principles and rules that will establish the basic ground rules for trade in services and will provide a framework for the subsequent negotiation of more detailed commitments in individual sectors. These overall prin-

A GENERAL AGREEMENT ON TRADE IN SERVICES

ciples and rules will, in effect, constitute a general agreement on trade in services that will parallel the General Agreement on Tariffs and Trade, which has guided trade in goods for the past forty years.

This chapter will explore in detail the major issues that have to be addressed in the negotiations.[1] We will start by looking at the language of the Uruguay Declaration and by analyzing its content. In examining these issues, we will go back and review some of the debates that preceded the agreement at Punta del Este, because the different points of view represented in those past debates continue to be reflected in the negotiations.

THE URUGUAY DECLARATION

The Uruguay Declaration is divided into two parts. Part I deals with negotiations on trade in goods and Part II deals with negotiations on trade in services. Part I sets up a Group of Negotiations on Goods (GNG) and Part II sets up a Group of Negotiations on Services (GNS). This division recognizes that the negotiations on goods and the negotiations on services are legally different.

Under Part I, the GATT Contracting Parties have agreed to negotiate a liberalization of trade in goods and a reform of trade rules within the framework of the existing GATT Articles of Agreement. Under Part II, the ministers as representatives of interested governments have agreed to negotiate a new agreement or agreements on trade in services. Both parts, however, are contained in a single political document, the Ministerial Declaration on the Uruguay Round, and both the Group of Negotiations on Goods and the Group of Negotiations on Services report to a single Trade Negotiations Committee (TNC), which provides overall political management of the negotiations. The declaration and the TNC thus recognize the two parts of the negotiations as a single political undertaking.

Part II of the Uruguay Declaration, under the heading Negotiations on Trade in Services, reads as follows:

Ministers also decide, as part of the Multilateral Trade Negotiations, to launch negotiations on trade in services.

Negotiations in this area shall aim to establish a multilateral framework of principles and rules for trade in services, including elaboration of possible disciplines for individual sectors, with a view to expansion of such trade under conditions of transparency and progressive liberalization and as a means of promoting economic growth of all trading partners and the development of developing countries. Such framework shall respect the policy objectives of national laws and regulations applying to services and shall take into account the work of relevant international organizations.

GATT procedures and practices shall apply to these negotiations. A Group of Negotiations on Services is established to deal with these matters. Participation in the negotiations under this Part of the Declaration will be open to the same countries as under Part I [dealing with trade in goods]. GATT secretariat support will be provided, with technical support from other organizations as decided by the Group of Negotiations on Services.

The Group of Negotiations on Services shall report to the Trade Negotiations Committee.

The Objectives of Trade Negotiations in Services

The Uruguay Declaration establishes three levels of objectives for the negotiations on trade in services. At the operational level, the declaration says that the "negotiations in this area shall aim to establish a multilateral framework of principles and rules for trade in services, including elaboration of possible disciplines for individual sectors." In other words, the declaration says that the negotiations should seek to develop a system of principles and rules for trade in services generally, to be supplemented by rules for specific sectors.

This conclusion resolved a major debate over the feasibility and desirability of negotiating trade issues in services as diverse as banking, insurance, professional services, data processing, and transportation within a common framework. Some argued that because each services sector raises unique issues, it made no sense to organize negotiations as a single undertaking. Others argued that many of the principles and rules of the GATT could be applied to trade in services and that a general framework of principles and rules would be more likely to succeed in achieving a broad liberalization of trade in services than a sector-by-sector approach.

The language in the Uruguay Declaration supports the traditional trade policy view that general, across-the-board rules are needed to advance the liberalization of trade barriers. At the same time, the Uruguay Declaration also recognizes that sectoral differences are more fundamental in services than in goods and that effective negotiations ultimately have to get down to a sector-by-sector level.

A framework approach puts the emphasis on general economic principles that are difficult to oppose in the abstract, and once agreed can provide a basis for challenging restrictive arrangements that serve narrow sectoral needs and interests. A purely sectoral approach, on the other hand, emphasizes sectoral differences and the unique characteristics in each sector that justify the status quo. A purely sectoral focus would have made it much more difficult to bring out the broader economic reasons why a liberalization of policies would further the general public interest. The decision to negotiate a general framework first thus was closely tied to the broader liberalization objective.

After setting out the operational objectives of the negotiations, the Uruguay Declaration goes on to say that the purpose of the negotiations on trade in services is to achieve an "expansion of such trade under conditions of transparency and progressive liberalization." This language not only makes it clear that the primary focus of the negotiations should be the expansion of trade in services but also plots a path for pursuing that objective: 1) establishing transparency in policy measures that restrict trade in services and 2) progressively liberalizing measures that restrict such trade. This language clearly resolved the dispute over whether it was appropriate to expand trade in services through a process of liberalization.

Alternative objectives that could have been adopted include 1) an equitable or fair distribution of market shares in world trade in services, 2) the harmonization of national regulations affecting trade in services, or 3) the resolution of regulatory conflicts whenever traded services are subject to overlapping jurisdiction (for example, when two countries have responsibility for regulating a common activity like a commercial flight from one country to another).

The last part of the long sentence on objectives establishes the negotiations "as a means of promoting economic growth of all trading partners and the development of developing countries." This language serves to remind negotiators that the ultimate purpose of their efforts should be to promote economic growth and economic development. It is also a statement of conviction that liberalization of trade in services and the development of an agreed framework of rules for trade in services can advance the economic growth of all countries, as well as the development of developing countries.

Relationship to Nontrade Objectives

In the course of the debate over the inclusion of services, the fear was often expressed that a GATT framework agreement on trade in services would undermine the achievement of national regulatory objectives. The Uruguay Declaration addresses these concerns by stating that "such framework shall respect the policy objectives of national laws and regulations applying to services." This language spells out the obvious, that any trade agreements on services will have to leave countries enough flexibility to pursue domestic regulatory objectives.

By focusing on the objectives of national laws and regulations rather than the laws and regulations themselves, the language of the declaration leaves open the possibility that the liberalization of trade might require changes in the way national laws and regulations implement policy objectives. This is a distinction the GATT has made before with respect to the application of technical and regulatory standards to internationally traded goods. The Standards Code, negotiated in the Tokyo Round of multilateral trade negotiations, gives countries the right to pursue national regulatory objectives but requires that they pursue such objectives in a manner that will minimize distortions of trade.

Another concern often voiced in the course of the debate over services was that GATT negotiations could conflict with existing international agreements negotiated in sectoral organizations such as the International Telecommunications Union (ITU). In recognition of this concern, the declaration provides that a framework agreement "shall take into account the work of relevant international organizations."

Clearly, the negotiations will have to address the relationship between any new trade agreements in services and sectoral agreements in transportation, telecommunications, and tourism. Here too, GATT agreements negotiated in previous rounds of negotiations provide useful models. In the area of standards, for example, governments had to define complementary responsibilities for the GATT and the International Standards Organization (ISO). While the challenge to define a division of responsibilities may be somewhat greater in services than it was in goods, the language in the Uruguay Declaration is based on the proposition that such a division of responsibilities can and should be worked out.

Negotiations on Trade in Services and Negotiations on Trade in Goods

Considerable time was devoted to the relationship between negotiations on trade in services and negotiations on trade in goods. Actually, this argument was not only over the relationship between two sets of negotiations but also over the relationship between the eventual agreements that might come out of the negotiations. The United States, which led the campaign for the inclusion of services, wanted a close relationship between the negotiations on services and the negotiations on goods, while Brazil and India, which led the opposition to the inclusion of services, wanted a distant relationship between any negotiations on trade in services and the negotiations on trade in goods.

Basically, the United States wanted to make sure that the negotiations on services and the negotiations on goods were seen as a single political undertaking and that it was clear from the outset that the negotiations could not be concluded successfully without an agreement on services. Those who were opposed to the negotiations wanted to have as loose a relationship as possible so that the continued liberalization of world trade in goods would not be tied to a successful outcome of the negotiations on services.

Looking into the future, the group of countries led by Brazil and India wanted to minimize the likelihood that an eventual agreement on trade in services would be made an integral part of the GATT, thus giving countries the legal right to link performance on trade in goods to performance on trade in services. To put the issue more simply, would countries have a right to put restrictions on trade in goods in retaliation against another country's failure to live up to obligations on trade in services? Since Brazil and India felt that it was not in their interest to tie their hands in services, they did not want to expose themselves to retaliation in goods in response to barriers they might impose or maintain on trade in services.

While the United States has not taken a position on the legal relationship between the GATT Articles of Agreement and a new agreement on trade in services, the United States in recent years has taken the view that trade in goods and trade in services are linked both commercially and politically, and therefore cannot be separated in the management of trade policy. Congress also seems to have taken this approach by adding services to existing legislative provisions dealing with trade in goods, rather than drafting entirely new provisions to deal with trade in services. Section 301 of the Trade Act thus directs the president to retaliate against unfair trade practices by foreign countries in both goods and services, without making any distinctions between the two.

A GENERAL AGREEMENT ON TRADE IN SERVICES

In pushing for a close relationship between the negotiations on trade in services and the negotiations on trade in goods, the United States also wanted to emphasize that many of the principles and concepts contained in the GATT Articles of Agreement could be applied to trade in services. The United States recognized that the GATT articles did not cover trade in services and that the existing rules of the GATT for trade in services could not be extended to trade in services without major adjustments. At the same time, U.S. officials believed that a number of concepts and principles embodied in the GATT could be applied to the development of new rules for trade in services, and more generally that thirty years of GATT experience would prove useful.

By dividing the negotiations into two parts, the Uruguay Declaration recognizes that the negotiations on goods and the negotiations on services are legally different. Both parts, however, are contained in a single political document, the Ministerial Declaration on the Uruguay Round, and both the Group of Negotiations on Goods and the Group of Negotiations on Services report to a single Trade Negotiations Committee, which provides overall political management to the negotiations. The declaration thus recognizes that the negotiations on trade in goods and the negotiations on trade in services are a part of a single political undertaking.

The Relationship of Trade Negotiations in Services to the GATT

The text of the declaration says that "GATT procedures and practices shall apply to these negotiations" and that "GATT secretariat support will be provided." Thus, even though the declaration recognizes that the negotiations on trade in services do not legally come under the GATT Articles of Agreement, it brings the negotiations on services institutionally into the GATT and makes the accumulated knowledge and experience of the GATT directly accessible to the negotiators on trade in services. The relationship between a new General Agreement on Trade in

Services and the General Agreement on Tariffs and Trade will ultimately have to be worked out at the end of the negotiations.

THE GOAL OF MULTILATERAL NEGOTIATIONS

The most fundamental issue with respect to multilateral trade negotiations in services is whether the liberalization of trade is an appropriate objective in services. It is fundamental because the motivation for all multilateral trade negotiations has been to liberalize trade and the whole intellectual framework that supports trade negotiations is based on the proposition that the reduction of trade barriers will generate economic gains as trade expands. There would be very little reason to pursue trade negotiations in services if liberalization were not an appropriate objective. Alternative objectives that can be postulated, such as the harmonization of domestic regulations in services, could be carried out much more efficiently by officials responsible for such regulations, in negotiations carried out in sectoral organizations like the International Telecommunications Union that have developed great expertise in national regulatory systems.

The question whether the liberalization of trade in services is a desirable goal rests on the theoretical question whether trade in services will lead to mutual economic gains for the countries participating in such trade. Application of the theory of comparative advantage to trade in services leads one to conclude that trade in services under a broad range of circumstances will lead to mutual economic gains for participating countries. Those who question the desirability of liberalizing trade in services make four key arguments against liberalizing trade in services.

    1. Trade liberalization will undermine the contribution made by the services sector to the achievement of broad social goals. It is argued that in many service industries the achievement of nonmarket social goals is more important than the achievement of economic efficiency and that the high priority assigned by society to the

achievement of social goals in services is reflected in the extensive regulation of most services.

2. Liberalization of trade will lead to excessive competition. It is argued that quality and reliability are more important considerations than price in the production of services and that competition based on price will lead to a deterioration of both the quality and the reliability of services. Those who make this argument therefore believe that increased competition from foreign suppliers does not result in economic gains. In support of this argument, it is pointed out that competition in many services is limited either by government regulation or by government-sanctioned professional regulations.

3. Trade liberalization is largely irrelevant since most services require a close interaction between service providers and service consumers and therefore cannot be sold without extensive investment in local production facilities and international movement of either service providers or service consumers.

4. In many service industries existing suppliers are able to exclude or limit market opportunities for new suppliers through exclusive arrangements with customers and other restrictive business practices. It is argued, for example, that exclusive arrangements between shipping conferences and shippers makes it difficult for new shipping companies to develop a viable business.

The counterarguments are as follows:

1. The desire to satisfy social objectives does not remove cost as a consideration. Since services account for more than 50 percent of output and employment in most countries, the cost of services has a large impact on a country's standard of living. The need to take account of social goals does not eliminate the need to give considerable attention to the cost of services. In fact,

many a country has discovered in recent years that the poor performance of its economy is due to inefficiencies in the services sector.

2. Empirical evidence would suggest that quality as well as price can deteriorate when there is insufficient competition. The fact that market pressures or government regulations have led to only limited competition in many service industries may be an argument more in support of trade liberalization than against trade liberalization. The increased competition generated by trade could force domestic producers to adopt more efficient production methods.

3. Trade in services complements foreign investment in services where foreign investment is allowed and provides an alternative to foreign investment where it is not permitted. Foreign trade in services complements foreign investment in services since foreign-owned service enterprises often derive their competitive strength from business service inputs imported from abroad. The competitive strength of fast food chains such as Baskin-Robbins or Kentucky Fried Chicken, for example, depends on the design of the facilities, the development of managerial techniques, and centralized procurement of equipment and food, service inputs that are generally imported. Where foreign suppliers of services are not allowed to invest in local facilities, trade can provide a second best alternative. The requirement for an international movement of information, people, money, or goods to transfer services does not eliminate the advantages of removing barriers to trade. As long as the movement of information, people, money, and goods is not completely restricted, the liberalization of barriers to trade in services can improve economic welfare. It is equally true, of course, that the freer the international movement of information, people, money, and goods, the larger will be the expansion of trade in services resulting from the removal of barriers to trade, and

many a country has discovered in recent years that the poor performance of its economy is due to inefficiencies in the services sector.

2. Empirical evidence would suggest that quality as well as price can deteriorate when there is insufficient competition. The fact that market pressures or government regulations have led to only limited competition in many service industries may be an argument more in support of trade liberalization than against trade liberalization. The increased competition generated by trade could force domestic producers to adopt more efficient production methods.

3. Trade in services complements foreign investment in services where foreign investment is allowed and provides an alternative to foreign investment where it is not permitted. Foreign trade in services complements foreign investment in services since foreign-owned service enterprises often derive their competitive strength from business service inputs imported from abroad. The competitive strength of fast food chains such as Baskin-Robbins or Kentucky Fried Chicken, for example, depends on the design of the facilities, the development of managerial techniques, and centralized procurement of equipment and food, service inputs that are generally imported. Where foreign suppliers of services are not allowed to invest in local facilities, trade can provide a second best alternative. The requirement for an international movement of information, people, money, or goods to transfer services does not eliminate the advantages of removing barriers to trade. As long as the movement of information, people, money, and goods is not completely restricted, the liberalization of barriers to trade in services can improve economic welfare. It is equally true, of course, that the freer the international movement of information, people, money, and goods, the larger will be the expansion of trade in services resulting from the removal of barriers to trade, and

achievement of social goals in services is reflected in the extensive regulation of most services.

2. Liberalization of trade will lead to excessive competition. It is argued that quality and reliability are more important considerations than price in the production of services and that competition based on price will lead to a deterioration of both the quality and the reliability of services. Those who make this argument therefore believe that increased competition from foreign suppliers does not result in economic gains. In support of this argument, it is pointed out that competition in many services is limited either by government regulation or by government-sanctioned professional regulations.

3. Trade liberalization is largely irrelevant since most services require a close interaction between service providers and service consumers and therefore cannot be sold without extensive investment in local production facilities and international movement of either service providers or service consumers.

4. In many service industries existing suppliers are able to exclude or limit market opportunities for new suppliers through exclusive arrangements with customers and other restrictive business practices. It is argued, for example, that exclusive arrangements between shipping conferences and shippers makes it difficult for new shipping companies to develop a viable business.

The counterarguments are as follows:

1. The desire to satisfy social objectives does not remove cost as a consideration. Since services account for more than 50 percent of output and employment in most countries, the cost of services has a large impact on a country's standard of living. The need to take account of social goals does not eliminate the need to give considerable attention to the cost of services. In fact,

therefore the greater will be the economic gains from such liberalization.

4. The existence of restictive arrangements among foreign producers of services is an argument for the removal of such restrictive arrangements, not an argument against the liberalization of trade.

After weighing these and other arguments, the world's trade ministers decided at Punta del Este that an effort to expand trade through the progressive liberalization of barriers to trade in services made economic sense. At the same time, they made it clear that the negotiations on trade in services should "respect the policy objectives of national laws and regulations applying to services."

The argument comes down to one of balance between the pursuit of the economic gains that will result from a liberalization of trade in services and the pursuit of national as well as international regulatory goals. Trade negotiations aimed at the liberalization of barriers to trade in services can make a contribution to the achievement of greater economic efficiency in the production of services, even while respecting the achievement of domestic regulatory goals.

A Framework versus a Sectoral Approach to Trade Negotiations in Services

The second issue in the debate over goals was whether the negotiations on trade in services should be carried out within a common framework of principles and rules, or on a sector-by-sector basis. Those who favored the development of a common framework of principles and rules argued that the economic issues involved in removing barriers to trade in services were quite similar, regardless of the unique circumstances found in each services sector, and that it is therefore more efficient to develop generic principles and procedures for dealing with barriers to trade in services. Those who favored a sectoral approach argued that each sector in services is so different that it would be impossible to reach any conclusions about barriers to trade across the board, and that any effort to define common principles and rules would be either counterproductive or doomed to failure.

The trade ministers at Punta del Este bought both sides of the argument. They agreed that the negotiations should lead to the development of a common "multilateral framework of principles and rules for trade in services," and to supplement such rules with the "elaboration of possible disciplines for individual sectors." By concentrating first on the development of a multilateral framework of principles and rules, negotiators will be able to develop common ground rules for the negotiations that will safeguard the liberalization objective of the negotiations. At the same time, the ministers recognized that there are some important differences among sectors that will require the "elaboration of possible disciplines for individual sectors."

The Role of Developing Countries

The ultimate purpose of multilateral trade negotiations is to increase the output of goods and services and thus the economic growth of countries participating in the negotiations. Many developing countries have expressed the view, however, that the liberalization of barriers to trade in services would not advance their economic interests since they do not believe that they could compete with developed countries in the production of services at their current stage of economic development.

Developed countries argued, however, that developing countries were underestimating both their capacity to export services and their gain from the liberalization of barriers to trade in services. Developed countries pointed out that a number of developing countries have become major exporters of services such as construction, data entry, printing, computer programming, and engineering.

In the end, the developing countries agreed to launch multilateral trade negotiations in services, provided the developed countries agreed that the negotiations should promote the development of developing countries. One of the key issues in the negotiations will be how the negotiations should achieve this objective.

THE BASIC FRAMEWORK OF A GENERAL AGREEMENT ON TRADE IN SERVICES

The Uruguay Declaration points to the negotiation of a framework of principles and rules as the first task of the services negotiations. Such a framework of principles and rules will, in effect, constitute a General Agreement on Trade in Services.[2] The basic purpose of such an agreement is to establish what countries hope to achieve through multilateral negotiations on trade in services and how they hope to achieve it. The agreement will thus provide a common framework for trade in services. Three sets of activities will be affected by such an agreement: 1) the commercial operations of enterprises engaged in international trade in services, 2) the development and implementation of government policies that affect trade in services, and 3) the subsequent negotiation of more detailed agreements that will cover trade in specific services or that will cover the use of specific policy instruments.

Since the objective of a framework agreement is to define the means for achieving the economic benefits of mutually advantageous trade, the logical structure of the agreement has to reflect the theoretical conditions for the achievement of mutual gains described in the section on economic theory. It also has to accommodate the reality of the current pattern of measures that affect trade in services, because changing existing measures is likely to involve a protracted process of negotiation. In other words, the agreed framework has to establish a process for getting from here to there, from the policies in effect today to a modified set of policies that will more closely approximate the ideal conditions for mutually advantageous trade. Thus, while the framework needs to point toward an ideal world, it must also encompass the current reality.

Finally, the framework has to take account of the political dynamics that drive the development of sectoral policies in each country. The few who have a very large stake in the outcome of a policy measure devote a great deal more political energy to defending those interests than the very much larger number of people who stand to lose from a policy that benefits one specific sector. The negotiating process therefore has to be structured in such a way that it forces a continuing balancing between broad consumer interests and sectoral interests, as well as between general economic policy goals and sectoral regulatory goals.

Trade negotiations inevitably take on the appearance of gladiatorial contests between industries and between bureaucracies, even though the ultimate purpose of such negotiations is to obtain higher quality services and cheaper services for consumers. These fights over profits and bureaucratic turf nevertheless serve the very useful purpose of forcing negotiators to consider the various goals of a society that have to be factored into the final outcome of negotiations.

In constructing a framework agreement for trade in services, it should prove instructive to examine the underlying framework of the GATT Articles of Agreement.[3] Trade in services is sufficiently different from trade in goods that a general agreement for trade in services will have to be different from the GATT for trade in goods.

An analysis of the basic GATT framework and the reasons for its key principles should, nevertheless, prove instructive. By comparing the policy measures that have traditionally distorted trade in goods with the policy measures that restrict trade in services, one should be able to draw some conclusions about the framework that might be developed for trade in services. There are also two other powerful arguments for starting with an analysis of the GATT articles. First, these negotiations are the result of lobbying by the business community in favor of the negotiation of a GATT-like agreement for trade in services. Second, the GATT has shaped the thinking of all the trade officials who will lead these negotiations.

A GENERAL AGREEMENT ON TRADE IN SERVICES

The Basic GATT Framework for Trade in Goods

Stripped down to its basic elements, the GATT framework for trade in goods can be described as follows:

- *Trade barriers should be imposed at the border, and once a good is inside the border it should receive national treatment, which means that it should be treated like a domestically produced commodity.* By narrowing trade barriers to the border, the GATT framework narrowed the range of policies that need to be addressed in trade negotiations, made it easier for enterprises engaged in trade to identify the barriers they would have to overcome, and discouraged the use of domestic regulatory measures as trade barriers.

- *Barriers at the border should preferably be in the form of tariffs rather than quotas.* Tariffs allow some adjustment in trade flows in response to market forces, while quotas freeze trade patterns. The GATT therefore strictly limits the use of quotas.

- *Tariffs should be negotiable.* The GATT provides procedures for exchanging commitments by member countries with respect to the tariffs that apply to individual categories of goods.

- *The results of tariff negotiations should be bound.* The binding of a tariff commits the government not to impose a higher duty or to take any other policy measures that would result in a higher level of protection. A tariff bound in the course of negotiations can be higher or lower than a tariff currently in effect.

- *Tariff cuts negotiated with another GATT member country are automatically extended to all other GATT member countries on a most-favored-nation (MFN) basis.*

- *If a government takes any action that leads to the "nullification or impairment" of its commitment not to increase the level of protection, it must consult with the affected government, and if necessary agree to submit the issue to a dispute settlement procedure. Ultimately, other governments have the right to reestablish "the balance of concessions" by imposing equivalent duties on the country's exports.*

The GATT articles include other provisions dealing with subsidies, dumping, government procurement, economic development, adjustment problems, balance of payments problems, and national security. Through its various provisions, the GATT seeks to establish a balance between the pursuit of open trade on a market-oriented basis and policies aimed at a broad range of other individual national objectives. Some provisions are designed to minimize government interference with market-oriented trade. Other provisions are designed to give governments adequate leeway to protect broader social objectives such as the protection of health, morals, and national security, the development of infant industries, and the adjustment of mature industries.

The GATT articles also prevent countries from trying to improve their terms of trade through unilateral tariff increases, by making it clear that other countries have the right to impose equivalent tariff increases that would wipe out any gains. The GATT rules thus closely parallel the theoretical requirements for mutual gains from trade described in the section on economic theory.

The GATT articles set up a negotiating process that takes account of the political resistance any government must face when it seeks to change policies that affect the interests of specific groups. GATT negotiations are therefore structured to match "concessions" in the form of tariff cuts or policy adjustments by the home government with "benefits" received as a result of equivalent actions by foreign governments. Similarly "obligations" to observe certain rules are carefully matched with "rights" connected with the obligation of other countries to follow rules.

A final point that needs to be made about the GATT framework is that it provides negotiating procedures where governments had to make major changes in policies at the time the GATT was initially negotiated, and it imposes rules where governments did not have to make major changes in policy. Most trade barriers at the time the GATT was negotiated were in the form of tariffs and quotas imposed at the border. The GATT framework established a procedure for phasing out the quotas and for negotiating the reduction of tariffs. Domestic regulations were generally not used to restrict trade, and most countries therefore did not find it very difficult to agree that domestic regulations should be applied equally to domestic and foreign goods—that is, to provide national treatment for all domestic regulations.

In contrast with the situation that existed with respect to goods at the time the GATT was negotiated, most barriers to trade in services are not imposed at the border and instead are embedded in domestic regulations. In services, the application of national treatment will have to be achieved through a prolonged process of negotiation, rather than through the adoption of a rule as was the case in goods.

Identifying Barriers to Trade in Services

Most barriers to trade in services are embedded in domestic regulations for two reasons. First, the production and consumption of many services is heavily regulated by the government, and such regulations provided a convenient basis for restricting trade. Second, governments have great difficulty in controlling the flow of services across national borders because such flows are invisible. Governments have therefore found it easier to restrict the right of foreign suppliers to sell services in the local market or to restrict the right of domestic consumers to use services produced by foreign suppliers to meet domestic regulatory requirements.

Some have argued that despite this basic difference between goods and services, an agreement in services should follow the basic structure of the GATT framework—that trade barriers should be imposed only at the border, that the protection provided by border measures should be quantifiable like a tariff, and that national treatment should prevail with respect to domestic regulations. Since most barriers to trade in services are embedded in domestic regulations, however, the GATT model cannot be transferred to trade in services without major modifications.

Each element of the GATT framework, nevertheless, contains an underlying principle that could be applied to trade in services in another form and accomplish the same purpose. The goal of the GATT framework—making import barriers more visible, more focused, and more price-sensitive—should also be a goal of the framework of principles and rules for trade in services.

The GATT rule that trade measures should be imposed at the border would not work for services because few barriers are at the border today and a wholesale conversion of regulatory barriers into border measures would absorb too much time and energy that negotiators should put into the liberalization of barriers. Moreover, border measures in services are not easily enforced, and if enforced would prove very unpleasant. In order to identify and control trade in services, the government would have to amass an enormous amount of information about the people, information, money, and goods crossing the border, and that would lead to both an excessive invasion of personal privacy and an excessive disruption of the international movement of people, information, and money.

While it does not make sense to impose barriers to trade in services at the border, it does make sense to identify discriminatory barriers to trade and to separate them functionally from domestic regulations. The clear identification of barriers and their separation from domestic regulations would substantially facilitate the process of negotiating the reduction of such barriers. It is difficult to negotiate a reduction of barriers if you do not know whether you are negotiating over import restrictions or over domestic regulations. Separating import restrictions from domestic regulations would also reduce the protective effect of existing barriers by removing or reducing the uncertainty that businesses now face with respect to the rules of the game. If any regulatory decision can be turned into a protective device arbitrarily, how can a business know what it will cost to meet regulatory requirements in the future?

Separating import restrictions from domestic regulations will also encourage good government by clarifying decision-making responsibilities within a government. It will force governments to identify the officials responsible for trade decisions and the officials responsible for domestic regulatory decisions, and the ground rules for making each set of decisions.

The process of identifying barriers and separating them from domestic regulations will not be an easy or simple process. In many cases, the achievement of domestic regulatory objectives legitimately requires different treatment of foreign and domestic suppliers, and deciding when different treatment constitutes equivalent treatment (national treatment in the GATT terminology) may require qualitative judgments. Two examples can illustrate the problem.

Insurance regulators, for example, can require domestic insurance companies to keep their capital invested in stable financial assets, but they are likely to find it difficult to enforce such a provision with respect to foreign insurers. In order to achieve their regulatory objective, they may therefore require foreign insurance companies to maintain local deposits. The vexing question for trade negotiators is the following: What is a reasonable deposit in order to assure that domestic policyholders will be able to collect a claim? What level of deposit will result in the same degree of consumer protection as the asset requirements imposed on domestic insurance companies? In other words, what is national treatment in this case?

An even more vexing question regarding equivalent treatment arises when the total number of authorized suppliers, both domestic and foreign, is controlled through a licensing procedure. What criteria do you use to decide whether foreign suppliers have been given national treatment when it is up to regulators to decide who is given a license? Typically, regulators consider a large number of factors in awarding a license to one of a number of competing applicants, and it may be quite difficult to decide whether foreign applicants are given the same consideration as domestic applicants.

Establishing transparency with respect to barriers to trade in services will take time, since governments will have to sift through a large number of regulations and they may need to organize detailed discussions of both the objectives and the effects of discriminatory measures. Some may argue that a process of separating regulations that serve as barriers from regulations that serve legitimate domestic regulatory purposes is at best useless and at worst an unnecessary source of debate. Those who make this argument will point out that a process of identifying barriers will inevitably degenerate into a debate over the motivations behind a particular measure and that such a debate is fruitless because it is impossible to determine objectively whether the motivation behind a particular measure is to protect the domestic industry or to further a domestic regulatory objective. Why not just get down to a negotiation of the regulations that have a protective effect, as against a protective intent?

There has to be a process, however, for determining which regulations are negotiable and which regulations are not negotiable. The purpose of trade negotiations is to reduce barriers to trade, and by common consent this is to be achieved without infringing domestic regulatory objectives. In the words of the Uruguay Declaration, the objective of the negotiations is to achieve an expansion of trade "under conditions of transparency and progressive liberalization," while at the same time the framework resulting from the negotiations "shall respect the policy objectives of national laws and regulations applying to services." It follows that the framework agreement should provide the means for identifying restrictive measures that are not essential for the achievement of domestic regulatory objectives.

In deciding whether or not a particular measure should be treated as a barrier subject to negotiation, one has to consider both the protective effect of a discriminatory measure and its regulatory objective. Neither criterion by itself is likely to provide a sufficient basis for identifying the measures that should be covered by such negotiations. Whether or not a measure creates an impediment to trade is best established on the basis of the effect of the measure on trade. Whether or not a measure that creates impediments to trade should be treated as a negotiable barrier or not, however, depends on whether or not it is essential for the achievement of legitimate domestic policy objectives. Identifying barriers therefore necessitates identifying measures with restrictive trade effects and deciding which of these measures are essential for the achievement of domestic policy objectives.

Exporting countries are probably in the best position to determine whether a particular measure has restrictive trade effects, and the importing country is in the best position to identify the extent to which such measures are necessary for the achievement of domestic policy objectives. A natural division of labor thus suggests itself. Exporting countries should be asked to draw up lists of regulatory measures in importing countries that create impediments to trade, and importing countries should be asked to identify the extent to which such measures are essential for the achievement of domestic policy objectives. Naturally, exporting countries would be asked to explain why the measures on their list are restrictive, and importing countries would need to defend their claim that certain provisions are essential for domestic regulatory purposes.

Reconciling differences between exporting countries and importing countries over what is a barrier will be an extremely useful exercise for both. Exporting countries will obtain a better understanding of the regulatory systems of importing countries and importing countries may find that many practices they have always accepted as the normal way of doing things in fact are restrictive measures.

In summary, a services agreement should establish the principle that barriers to trade in services should be clearly identified as barriers to trade and functionally separated from domestic regulations. The framework agreement should also include a procedure for implementing this principle, whereby regulations that create barriers to trade are identified and separated from purely domestic regulations. How this is to be accomplished is addressed in greater detail below.

This reformulation of the GATT rule that barriers should be at the border will accomplish the same purpose as the GATT rule. It will identify the regulations that restrict trade and subject them to negotiation. This will reduce the likelihood that purely domestic regulations will be used as hidden trade barriers, and lead to better government by separating domestic regulatory objectives and domestic regulatory instruments from trade policy objectives and trade policy instruments. Ideally it will also lead to a separation of domestic regulatory procedures from trade policy procedures, and a clear separation of roles between officials responsible for the achievement of domestic regulatory objectives and officials responsible for the achievement of trade policy objectives.

Rules for Negotiating Bindings and Reductions in Barriers to Trade in Services

The second element of the GATT framework is the principle that barriers to trade should generally take the form of tariffs because tariffs leave more room for adjustment to changes in market conditions than quotas. It would be impractical to incorporate this principle in a framework for trade in services for the same reason that it would be impractical to require barriers to trade in services to be at the border. The rationale for the GATT preference for price-sensitive measures over quantitative measures, however, is as valid for trade in services as for trade in goods. Negotiators will therefore need to consider whether the underlying principle that price-sensitive measures are to be preferred over quantitative measures should be applied to trade in services in another form.

A framework agreement could include the principle that barriers to trade in services whenever possible should take the form of price-sensitive measures rather than quantitative measures. What that means is that barriers to trade in services should take the form of an added financial burden imposed on services supplied by foreign suppliers, rather than a quantitative limit on the services that can be sold by foreign suppliers. Any government measure that imposes an added cost on foreign suppliers would satisfy this principle, including taxes, reserve requirements, a requirement to serve disadvantaged regions, or a requirement to train nationals. Where a government believes that it must impose a quantitative limit on foreign suppliers, it could auction licenses to potential foreign suppliers.

Foreign suppliers of services that have gained access under current quotas could be expected to resist adoption of this principle, since they could end up losing a privileged economic position. They not only would face new costs, but also would lose the extraordinary profits they can now earn. In order to make the adoption of this principle acceptable to current foreign suppliers, it would have to be implemented gradually, in the context of the liberalization of current barriers. They would lose their privileged position but would gain the opportunity to expand their business.

Barriers to trade in services, like barriers to trade in goods, should be negotiable. In the context of trade negotiations, to label a government policy measure a trade barrier is tantamount to saying that it falls within the legitimate scope of trade negotiations. This does not mean that a government has any obligation to alter or to remove a trade barrier, but rather that it will be under moral pressure to talk about it in the context of trade negotiations.

Any negotiated reductions in barriers to trade in services should lead to clear and firm commitments by the government making the offer not to increase the level of protection above negotiated levels. In the terminology used by the GATT, reductions in barriers should be bound. Bindings with respect to most regulatory measures that restrict trade in services will not have the same degree of precision as the binding of tariffs, since it will be difficult to calculate the protective effect of such measures with any precision. It will be all the more important for negotiators to define the outcome of negotiations on individual measures with as much precision as possible.[4]

National Treatment—The Core Concept in a Trade Regime for Services

The GATT principle that all barriers should be at the border, for the sake of logical consistency, requires a complementary principle that domestic policy measures should not be used as trade barriers; that is, domestic policy measures should not be used to protect domestic industry. This companion principle is the so-called national treatment principle, which requires governments to treat imported goods that have satisfied border measures as they would treat goods produced within the country.

Since it is not practical to require that barriers to trade in services be erected at the border, the national treatment principle cannot be applied to trade in services in the same way that it has been applied to trade in goods in the GATT. To apply national treatment to trade in services across the board would be tantamount to ruling out the possibility of protecting domestic services industries, and this would not be acceptable to many governments. The underlying concept is, nevertheless, crucial to development of an effective regime for trade in services, and the only question is how the GATT national treatment principle should be modified to fit the requirements of a service regime.

In discussing the GATT principle that barriers to trade in services should be at the border, we came to the conclusion that the equivalent principle for services should be that barriers to trade in services should be transparent, that is, that they should be identified as barriers. It follows that all domestic policy measures not identified as barriers should receive national treatment. In fact, one could define as a barrier to trade in services any regulatory measure that is not applied on a national treatment basis.

In applying national treatment to services it is also necessary to recognize that the same regulation may affect services produced abroad differently from services produced in the importing country, or it may affect services produced by a foreign firm in the importing country differently from services produced by domestic firms. Moreover, regulations may achieve the desired regulatory objective when applied to services produced at home but not when applied to services produced abroad, or they may achieve their regulatory objective when applied to domestic firms but not when applied to foreign firms. National treatment in services therefore has to be defined as equivalent rather than identical treatment.

So much for logic and semantics. The question that needs to be addressed is whether a framework agreement should require governments to provide national treatment (defined as equivalent treatment) for all regulatory measures not identified as barriers. As indicated earlier, such a process could take a considerable amount of time, and it would not be possible to put such a rule into effect until governments have completed a thorough examination of all regulations that affect trade in services.

There is an important reason why governments may not be willing to commit themselves to provide national treatment for all measures that have not been identified as barriers. The reason for this reluctance is that a commitment to provide national treatment may not result in equivalent market access when countries have very different regulatory regimes. A regulatory regime that allows open competition among domestic as well as foreign suppliers provides more trade opportunities than a regulatory regime that limits competition, both by domestic suppliers and by foreign suppliers. Countries that permit unlimited domestic competition may wish to withhold a firm commitment to provide national treatment, thus reserving their future bargaining leverage.

National treatment for specific services could thus become the subject of negotiation. This does not mean that a national treatment binding would need to be an all-or-nothing proposition. A commitment to provide national treatment in a specific area could be viewed as equivalent to a zero tariff binding in the GATT. A country could, instead, commit itself to provide national treatment with respect to all policy instruments except certain enumerated policy instruments.

Of course, in addition to negotiating a national treatment binding for nonprotective policy tools, governments would be asked to put a ceiling on the potential protection provided through policy measures not covered by a national treatment commitment. The negotiations would thus consist of two components—a negotiation over the list of policy tools for which governments would bind national treatment and a negotiation over the extent of protection offered through the application of policy measures excluded from the application of a national treatment commitment.[5]

Reducing the Distorting Impact of Domestic Regulations

It was mentioned earlier that a commitment to provide national treatment in the application of domestic regulations can lead to widely different results with respect to market access. It is not always easy to determine what constitutes national treatment when the regulations leave considerable room for discretion by the regulators. The larger the number of regulations that are applied in any given area, the larger the ambiguity created by the discretion available to the bureaucrats that administer the regulations. In fact, practice shows that a large number of the complaints lodged against foreign regulatory measures are directed not at the measures themselves but at the interpretation of the measures by officials.

Another, even more serious problem arises with respect to licensing regimes that limit the number of firms, domestic and foreign, authorized to supply a given service. A country that has decided to freeze the number of firms can offer national treatment and yet exclude foreign competition altogether. Even if foreigners are not excluded altogether, how is anyone to know whether foreign suppliers are allocated a fair share of a limited number of licenses?

The question is whether the national treatment commitment can be made less ambiguous, less subject to the whims of regulators, and less subject to distortion through licensing decisions. This could be accomplished by reinforcing the national treatment principle. A number of additional principles could be considered to reinforce the national treatment principle. Each would remove some degree of uncertainty with respect to the achievement of the market access that could be expected to result from national treatment.

One such principle might be called the least trade-distorting regulation principle. This principle would require governments to design their regulations as much as possible in terms of desired regulatory performance criteria, rather than in terms of the specific means for achieving a desired level of performance, and to allow firms in different circumstances to develop their own means of achieving the mandated objective. Governments would have to specify what they want to achieve with respect to specific regulations, and they would be obligated to work out alternative means for accomplishing their regulatory objectives when current provisions create unnecessary distortions of trade. Implementation of this principle will be useful not only for minimizing regulatory barriers to trade but also for minimizing the economic cost of achieving domestic regulatory objectives.

The least trade-distorting regulation principle presented here is patterned after the Standards Code of the GATT. That code, negotiated during the Tokyo Round of multilateral trade negotiations, establishes rules for minimizing the trade-distorting effects of health, safety, environmental, and product standards. The Standards Code recognizes the right of individual governments to set their own social objectives with respect to health, safety, and the environment but at the same time commits governments to pursue such goals in a manner that minimizes the restrictive effect on trade. In particular, the code requires governments to develop standards on the basis of performance criteria rather than design criteria.

Under the Standards Code, a government cannot, for instance, base standards on a particular technology that is used domestically, since that might be discriminatory against foreign companies that use a different technology to achieve the same regulatory objective. In effect, the code provides an elaborate interpretation of national treatment with respect to the development and implementation of standards and goes beyond a nominal interpretation of national treatment to require that standards not impose a greater burden on foreign suppliers than on domestic suppliers.

Adoption of the least trade-distorting regulation principle would go a long way toward correcting some of the inherent weaknesses of the national treatment principle. It probably would not deal adequately, however, with the trade-restrictive aspects of regulatory regimes that place a fixed ceiling on the number of enterprises authorized to supply any given services. It is probably impossible to construct a principle that would establish clear, operational commitments for the management of restricted licensing regimes. Nevertheless, it would be useful to include in a framework agreement what might be called the equivalent competitive opportunity principle or the effective market access principle.

If the equivalent competitive opportunity or effective market access principle were adopted, countries that restrict the number of authorized suppliers would have to set up transparent, objective, and competitive procedures for awarding limited licenses. Countries would be expected to demonstrate that the criteria employed to allocate available licenses were based on defensible economic principles. Moreover, in order to make this even more concrete in operational terms, countries that are prepared to bind their regulations in a specific sector would be expected to spell out the steps they intend to take to assure foreign suppliers of effective market access and equivalent competitive opportunities.

In summary, a framework agreement on trade in services should go beyond a simple definition of the national treatment principle to assure that the design and implementation of domestic regulations do not impede access to the market by foreign exporters of services. Among the principles that could be considered as a basis for elaborating the national treatment principle are the least trade-distorting regulation principle and the equivalent competitive opportunity (or effective market access) principle.

Reciprocity and Most-Favored-Nation Treatment

The beauty of the GATT framework is that it provides a basis for a bilateral exchange of tariff reductions on the basis of reciprocity and at the same time it makes the results of such bilateral negotiations available to all other GATT member countries on a most-favored-nation basis. Enforcement of a country's rights under the GATT depends on reciprocity of the eye-for-an-eye concept in the Old Testament, since the most powerful incentive to adhere to the rules of the GATT comes from the expectation that countries affected by a unilateral action are likely to retaliate with measures aimed at the offending country. This raises the question whether this hybrid system combining reciprocity and most-favored-nation treatment should be incorporated in the framework for trade in services.

Both the reciprocity principle and the most-favored-nation principle should be included in a framework for trade in services. First, all the provisions of a General Agreement on Trade in Services should apply equally, on a most-favored-nation basis, to all countries that agree to adhere to the obligations of the agreement. Second, each country should be expected to table a list of services for which it is willing to grant national treatment to all member countries on a most-favored-nation basis, subject to enumerated barriers and reservations.

As is currently the case with respect to negotiations on goods under the GATT, each country will have to evaluate the commercial value of the commitments it is offering, versus the commercial commitments it is being offered by other countries. In other words, countries will be able to apply a general reciprocity test to any commitments that are made. If the value of commitments made by others is inadequate, a country can adjust its offer by not making as many reductions in barriers affecting some services, or by withholding commitments on other services.

The scope for a general exchange of commitments on a general most-favored-nation basis is constrained by the value of the commitments made by the most restrictive countries. While it is difficult to assess in the abstract the potential scope of the commitments countries will be willing to offer in a first general exchange of commitments, the large differences among regulatory systems will inevitably limit the scope of a general exchange of commitments on a most-favored-nation basis. Countries with relatively few regulatory restraints will be reluctant to provide full national treatment commitments in sectors where other important member countries maintain tight regulatory controls.

A framework that gives all participants the same level of benefits regardless of the restrictiveness of the domestic regulatory system will thus not fully exploit opportunities for trade liberalization. The services framework therefore needs to give countries with relatively unconstrained domestic competition an opportunity to negotiate supplementary agreements that would enable firms from other countries with an equivalent market structure to compete freely on an international basis. In effect, such countries would agree to bind themselves to a regulatory regime that permits open competition. Any country that adheres to the general agreement should have a right, however, to join such an agreement provided it is prepared to accept the obligations of such an agreement. This is usually referred to as conditional most-favored-nation treatment.

Countries that are prepared to exchange higher levels of obligation with each other on a conditional most-favored-nation basis should have a right to do so, though there should be a commitment to include as many other countries as possible. Countries with a substantially more open regulatory regime than other countries could withhold a national treatment commitment in that sector, and seek to negotiate an exchange of commitments with other countries with similar regulatory systems. In other words a country with a nonrestrictive regulatory regime could exclude that sector from the list of sectors for which it is prepared to bind national treatment, and enter into a subsequent exchange of commitments on national treatment with countries that had an equally nonrestrictive regulatory regime.

Extensive government ownership and control in service industries like aviation and communications have led over the years to a network of bilateral sectoral agreements in which governments have exchanged limited access commitments on a basis of reciprocity. It is highly unlikely that governments will want to eliminate these agreements in the context of multilateral trade negotiations in services. Any framework for trade in services will therefore also have to accommodate reciprocal arrangements in some sectors.

A multilateral framework has to be based on market-oriented competition among a substantial number of enterprises. Where this condition is not met, it would be counterproductive to adopt a multilateral framework since it probably will ultimately not work, will create intergovernmental frictions, and will lead to frustrated expectations. To the extent that a small group of countries are prepared to allow free competition among their air carriers or communication carriers, however, they should be allowed and encouraged to do so under the conditional most-favored-nation concept.

The most important challenge for the negotiators of a trade agreement in services is to develop a framework that will achieve clarity and reciprocity with respect to the trade effects of domestic regulations, without getting into a detailed negotiation of domestic regulations. The Uruguay Declaration specifically reserves the right of each country to pursue its own regulatory objectives in services: "Such framework shall respect the objectives of national laws and regulations applying to services." The declaration in this respect reflects both good politics and practicality.

Each country's approach to the regulation of services is part of its national culture and not something easily sacrificed for the sake of trade negotiations that are only poorly understood in the first place. If the negotiations were to get too deeply involved in each country's regulatory goals, there would be little prospect for substantive progress any time soon. The negotiations would get hopelessly bogged down in philosophical debates over regulatory minutiae. On the other hand, countries will not be willing to bind their hands with respect to their future actions without a clear idea what they can expect from others, and a sense that the bargain involves an exchange of roughly equivalent commitments. A services framework must therefore allow countries that are prepared to limit their regulatory options to enter into a restricted agreement among themselves, provided they are prepared to keep the door open for others.

How to Fit Monopolies into a Trade Regime for Services

A monopoly precludes trade by definition. How can a framework for trade in services encompass a monopoly that precludes trade by its existence? The decision of a country to establish a government-owned monopoly or a government-sanctioned private monopoly is a sovereign regulatory decision that each country must make for itself. From the point of view of other countries, however, a monopoly is equivalent to a prohibition of trade, and they can be expected to treat it as such in evaluating a country's trade commitments. That is their sovereign right. From the perspective of negotiations, monopolies can be treated the same way as any other restrictive domestic regulatory regime.

Monopolies raise broader issues, however, because monopolies inherently have market power and can use this market power for their own ends. A trade problem can arise when a domestic monopoly is allowed to compete with private firms in producing services that fall outside the scope of their legitimate monopoly. A monopoly could, in such a situation, transfer monopoly profits from its monopoly activities to its competitive activities, or it could threaten to withhold monopoly services from firms that produce competing products.

The key principle that should be adopted with respect to the production of competitive services by domestic monopolies is that monopolies should be required to maintain an arm's-length relationship between their monopoly activities and their competitive activities, and that they should follow normal commercial practices in producing services outside the legitimate scope of their monopoly.

Monopolies are also large buyers of service inputs, and another issue that must be addressed is whether such monopolies should be required to use competitive bidding procedures to acquire service inputs, and whether foreign suppliers should be given national treatment in such purchases. While the GATT articles specifically allow countries to discriminate against foreign suppliers in government purchases, GATT countries negotiated a Government Procurement Code during the last round of multilateral trade negotiations.

The GATT Government Procurement Code prohibits governments from discriminating against foreign suppliers in purchases made by government enterprises covered by Government Procurement Code. Trade negotiators responsible for this code in fact have already been discussing the possibility of extending the code to trade in services. While no conclusions have been reached with respect to the procurement of services, the issue is on the negotiating table.

Exceptions

Every agreement has its list of exceptions and so does the GATT and so must a new general agreement on trade in services. The GATT articles allow countries 1) to impose temporary import restrictions in order to give an industry more time to adjust when it is seriously injured by a rapid increase in imports, 2) to restrict imports across the board in order to deal with a serious balance of payments deficit, 3) to restrict imports that threaten public health, safety, morals, the environment, or the general public welfare, 4) to restrict imports that threaten national security, and 5) to restrict imports where that would facilitate the development of infant industries.

When a country restricts imports under the first of these provisions, it must notify other countries of the measures it has taken and agree to consult with any other country that feels that its exports have been unreasonably disrupted by the measures involved. Moreover, the right to restrict imports for any of the reasons cited above does not remove a country's obligation to maintain the overall balance between the market access it provides to exporters from other countries and the market access its own exporters receive from such countries. If other countries insist, it must either offer tariff reductions in other areas or accept an equivalent increase in tariffs by countries adversely affected by its restrictions.

A framework agreement for trade in services will need to include a similar list of exceptions and an obligation to maintain the value of past commitments when a country imposes temporary restrictions on imports. An ambitious agreement in services that extends into related policy areas such as investment, information flows, or perhaps even immigration will inevitably have to have a long list of exceptions.

Fair Trade Provisions

The GATT articles contain several provisions dealing with specific unfair trade practices like dumping and government subsidies. The provisions prohibit dumping of goods abroad and the subsidization of exports (except on primary products); they also give countries injured by foreign dumping or subsidies the right to impose duties that are equivalent to the dumping or subsidy margin. What is different about the right to act in response to subsidy and dumping practices as against the right to act against other types of unfair trade practices is that the GATT does not require governments to seek approval for antidumping and countervailing duty actions. In contrast, before a government can retaliate against other unfair trade actions that are illegal under the GATT, it must first submit its complaint to a GATT dispute settlement panel, and the panel as well as the GATT council must agree that retaliation is warranted.

Government subsidies and dumping practices create trade problems in a number of service industries, particularly in construction, aviation, and shipping. This is particularly a problem with respect to government-owned domestic monopolies that also supply related services on a competitive basis. A number of characteristics of services, however, make it very

A GENERAL AGREEMENT ON TRADE IN SERVICES

difficult to identify objectively the subsidy or dumping margin for any given service, and it would be extremely difficult, if not impossible, to apply the GATT system of antidumping duties and countervailing duties to trade in services. Moreover, the subsidy problems that arise in individual sectors of services are different in different sectors. A framework agreement for trade in services will therefore need to include a system of disciplines and remedies for export subsidies that fit the needs of the individual sectors.

Among the most fundamental characteristics of services are their invisibility and elusiveness. While it is possible to identify the inputs that are used to produce a stream of services over time, it is extremely difficult to identify and measure on an objective basis the cost of a standard unit of service. A system that is based on the calculation of subsidy and dumping margins associated with trade in individual units of a service would not be practical.

A different kind of problem arises with respect to services such as transportation and communications, where fixed costs account for a large portion of the total cost of producing individual services, and variable costs are relatively low. Individual enterprises, on solid commercial grounds, could choose radically different strategies with respect to the amortization of fixed costs and with respect to the development of a price schedule for different segments of the market, reflecting the demand elasticities in each market segment. In terms of economic theory, it always makes sense to price the sale of marginal units on the basis of marginal costs. It is therefore extremely difficult, with respect to the sale of individual units, to determine objectively whether they are being dumped and, if the government owns the enterprise, whether such sales are being subsidized.

A framework agreement in services should contain the general principle that exports of services should not be subsidized or dumped in a manner that distorts the market and injures the commercial interests of other enterprises. The provisions of the agreement should give countries adversely affected by a pattern of injurious subsidy and dumping practices the right to seek compensation or to take remedial steps against the offending country. Before taking action, however, a country that wanted to pursue such remedies should have to go through the normal dispute settlement procedure provided in the agreement. This is necessary, because cases of dumping and subsidization will be extremely difficult to prove objectively with respect to individual transactions, and a country should have to be able to demonstrate that there has been a consistent pattern of subsidy or dumping abuses. In addition to the general principle and related provisions contained in the framework agreement, more detailed disciplines and remedies will need to be developed in individual sectoral agreements.

The Dispute Settlement System

The GATT provides an elaborate system for settling disputes. A government that believes that its commercial interests have been hurt by an action by one of its trading partners can initiate a dispute settlement procedure. The first step in this procedure is to request and hold consultations with the other government, both to clarify the issues involved and to seek to resolve the issue on a bilateral, informal basis if at all possible. If such bilateral efforts fail, it can request the GATT council to establish a dispute settlement panel of GATT experts from third countries. The panel has to examine the issues in the case and the relevant provisions of the GATT and submit a report of its findings to the GATT council. The council must then decide whether the country that brought the complaint has sufficient justification to retaliate. Needless to say, at each step of this process, the two countries involved in the dispute are expected to make repeated bilateral efforts to resolve the dispute, and in practice most disputes are settled before they get to the final stage.

The GATT system for settling disputes is cumbersome and no one is quite happy with it, and yet it has worked reasonably well most of the time. Its greatest failure has been its inability to deal with disputes involving politically sensitive issues like agriculture. The prolonged nature of the process has led to growing impatience. To some extent the delays built into the process are helpful in letting grass grow on the issue and helping governments to back off gracefully. More and more, however, countries have run out of patience with the process and have initiated retaliatory steps before the final approval of the GATT council. An effort is being made in the Uruguay Round to remedy these problems, and whatever conclusions are reached with respect to improvements in the GATT system will undoubtedly have some relevance for the dispute settlement process that is established for trade in services.

Overall, there is no reason to believe that a dispute settlement process that works for trade in goods will not also work for trade in services. In fact, the enforcement procedures built into the GATT through the dispute settlement provisions are one of the important reasons why the services industries in the United States supported the development of new rules for trade in services in the context of the GATT.

The dispute settlement process will be even more important in services than in goods because the outcome of negotiations on trade in services will inevitably leave more ambiguity than the outcome of negotiations on trade in goods. Since it will generally prove impractical to reduce barriers to trade in services to a single number like a tariff, it will be far more difficult to evaluate the protective effect of any changes in the regulations identified as trade barriers. Moreover, changes in purely domestic regulations will frequently have a significant impact on competitive opportunities available to foreign suppliers, and it may be quite difficult to sort out when such changes in domestic regulations result in an unjustifiable increase in the level of protection. Even with the best intentions of the governments involved, differences will arise over the interpretation of negotiated commitments and the effects of national regulatory measures.

In designing the dispute settlement process for trade in services, it may also be useful to borrow an idea from the GATT Standards Code. The code establishes two separate panels for the resolution of disputes: first, a panel of technical experts who are asked to clarify the technical issues in the case, and second a panel of GATT experts who are asked to clarify the interpretation of the provisions of the code. Given the highly technical nature of many of the regulations in services, it will probably make sense to create the same division of responsibilities in a services agreement. Given the complexity of the issues in services, it would probably be useful to involve both the industry and the regulators in a dispute in the GATT process itself. Direct involvement might facilitate a greater understanding of all the issues related to the dispute and contribute to greater acceptance of the outcome.

The dispute settlement system should also include a conciliation procedure that might be invoked at the request of two parties to a dispute. Such a procedure might be particularly helpful with respect to disputes that do not involve violations of binding commitments. Government measures that adversely affect the substantive commercial interests of another country can lead to disputes even though no legal commitments are violated, and such disputes could potentially lead to retaliatory actions. A conciliation procedure could be useful in defusing such confrontations.

Procedural Rules to Avoid Disputes

The GATT articles also contain a number of rules designed to reduce the possibility of disputes. Many of the disputes that arise result from a poor understanding of domestic laws and regulations by foreign exporters and foreign government officials. The GATT therefore requires governments to notify other members of the GATT of any changes in laws and regulations that will affect foreign exporters or importers. This notification requirement covers not only specific import or export regulations but also domestic regulations in such areas as standards.

Some GATT agreements also guarantee foreign exporters and importers the right to consult with government regulators in order to clear up misunderstandings or to work out adjustments in regulatory provisions, where such regulations create special hardships and an adjustment would not undermine the achievement of regulatory objectives. Foreign enterprises are also given the right to appeal to domestic courts or other adjudicatory bodies when such enterprises feel they have been wronged by regulatory decisions. All of these procedural rules, which generally fall under the general concept of due process, should be included in a general agreement on trade in services. Full use of domestic procedures can help to minimize the extent to which minor problems related to the implementation of regulations become disputes between governments. Once an issue is raised to the governmental level, it inevitably becomes political, and in some cases that actually makes it more difficult to resolve.

International Flows of Information, People, and Money

In addition to the pervasive role of regulation, trade in services differs from trade in goods in terms of its dependence on an international movement of information, people, money, and goods. The most difficult challenge facing negotiators of a framework for trade in services thus concerns the international movement of information, people, and money. It is hard to conceive of a more emotionally charged agenda.

The fact that trade in services is affected by government policies that affect the flow of information, money, and people is not necessarily a sufficient argument for dealing with these issues in the negotiation of a general agreement on trade in services. After all, the GATT articles did not deal with transportation issues, even though trade in goods is totally dependent on transportation. Nor did the GATT articles deal with issues related to communications, commercial visas, foreign exchange restrictions, and foreign investment, even though trade in goods is affected by policies in each of these areas. Nevertheless, trade in services is so dependent on policies in these areas that it will be difficult to ignore them altogether. In fact, these issues already are at the core of much of the debate during negotiating sessions of the services group in Geneva.

The issues in each of these areas of policy are complex and touch on sensitive areas of national policy. The framework agreement is unlikely to establish substantive, legally binding commitments in any of these policy areas. It could, however, establish the principle that governments should provide as much freedom of movement for information, money, and people, and as much freedom for foreign investment as is consistent with the achievement of national policy objectives. The framework agreement could also establish procedures for the subsequent negotiation of binding commitments. Such commitments could be negotiated as an integral part of commitment covering specific services.

A commitment on professional services, for example, could include provisions dealing with immigration issues as well as the establishment of a professional practice; a commitment on financial services could include provisions dealing with monetary transfers and foreign investment; and a commitment on data processing could include provisions dealing with the international transfer of information. Alternatively, interested countries could decide to negotiate broad agreements establishing ground rules for the international flow of information, the international transfer of money, the international movement of service workers, or foreign investment in connection with trade in services.

Information Flows. The purest form of international trade in services is trade based on international data flows. Services produced anywhere in the world can be made accessible almost instantaneously to users in other countries, provided they can be transmitted electronically, both producer and user have access to the necessary communications and computer equipment, and government regulations do not restrict either the use of the equipment or the transfer of the information. Given the central role of information flows to trade in services, high priority should be given to the negotiation of an agreement covering such flows. A generic agreement on international information flows could build on an agreement negotiated among OECD countries in 1985. Called the Declaration on Transborder Data Flows, the agreement commits OECD governments to minimize barriers to the international flow of data and to develop cooperative solutions to any problems created by the introduction of new communications and data processing technologies.

A GATT in this area might also establish the right to use the public communications network to deliver services across national borders and the right to plug network compatible equipment into the communications network for the purpose of sending or receiving information related to trade in services. Other issues related to the international transmission of information could be dealt with in the context of a sectoral agreement on international trade in telecommunications, information, and data processing services.

Monetary Flows. The ability to transfer money is not only central to financial services, but also necessary to effect a transfer of payments received for services rendered. An agreement covering monetary transfers in connection with trade in services could commit countries subscribing to such an agreement to avoid restrictions on foreign exchange transactions associated with international trade in services, except when warranted by serious balance of payments problems. In reviewing restrictions imposed for balance of payments purposes, members of the agreement could seek the advice of the International Monetary Fund, as is currently the case with respect to GATT review of balance of payments restrictions imposed on trade in goods.

Movements of People. Every country in the world seeks to control the flow of people into its territory. At the same time, most countries have established criteria and procedures for the admission of foreigners for various purposes, and many countries have negotiated bilateral visa agreements. It should be possible, in the context of negotiations on trade in services, to build on existing bilateral agreements. As a first step, it would be useful to develop a compendium and an analysis of existing visa regulations and bilateral visa agreements.

Foreign Investment and Foreign Trade: The Right of Establishment and the Right of Nonestablishment

International trade in consumer services typically requires an extensive presence in the local market, and foreign exporters therefore often find it necessary to establish themselves in the foreign market by investing in local facilities, or by appointing local representatives and agents.

The first set of arrangements raises the emotional issue of foreign investment. Like all other issues of an equal degree of sensitivity, the foreign investment issue will need to be broken down into its component parts if it is to prove manageable. First, a framework agreement should define a minimum presence in the importing country that would be granted to all foreign suppliers that have been granted national treatment. Such a minimum presence should include legal establishment (insofar as that is required by local regulations as a precondition for selling specific service products), establishment of local representative offices, the ability to use local business enterprises as agents for distributing and supporting the services product, and any investments that have to be made to satisfy regulatory requirements. This minimum presence should be incorporated in the definition of national treatment included in the framework agreement.

Beyond the minimum presence, the framework agreement should make provisions for the exchange of higher levels of commitment with respect to foreign investment. Since foreign investment is absolutely essential in some sectors such as banking and most consumer services, any commitment on market access in these sectors should cover foreign investment. Moreover, given the importance of foreign investment to trade in virtually all services, every sectoral agreement will need to include provisions on foreign investment. International trade in business services, on the other hand, frequently takes place in the exporting country, and the foreign buyer takes responsibility for transferring such services to the importing country. Looking to the future, one can envision new techniques for selling services abroad electronically. Foreign exporters of services might in the future sell services through the mail, market through advertisements in local papers, and deliver electronically to home computer terminals. An international trade regime in services should address potential barriers to such future methods of marketing, selling, and delivering internationally traded services.

Selling services to foreign buyers directly from abroad raises the issue of nonestablishment. Should exporters have the right to sell services to foreign customers in their own market without establishing themselves in the importing country? This is generally not a major operational issue today. In practice, anyone living in a country without comprehensive foreign exchange controls can buy any services abroad he wishes (even though he may not be able to use such services to fulfill local regulatory requirements). As international sales of services through the local advertising, mail order, and electronic delivery routes expand, however, we can expect governments to exert increasing controls over such transactions. It should be easier to deal with this issue before it becomes a major problem, rather than after it has become a problem. The framework for services should therefore include a provision dealing with nonestablishment.

Activities of Local Governments

Since international trade in services is largely controlled through domestic regulation, trade in services much more than trade in goods is affected by regulations under the authority of local governments. If international agreements on trade in services are to have any meaning, they will have to cover not only the regulatory activities of national governments but also the regulatory activities of state, provincial, and local authorities. This requirement can raise constitutional issues in countries with federal systems, and these constitutional issues will have to be addressed. In the United States the issue is less a constitutional than a very difficult domestic political issue. It should be possible to resolve it through close coordination between the federal government and state authorities during the negotiations.

Standstill Commitment

The road to the negotiation of comprehensive, legally binding commitments on trade in services is likely to be a long one. This raises the question whether it is possible to adopt a standstill commitment at the time the General Agreement on Trade in Services is adopted. Countries adopting such an agreement could, for example, agree not to impose new regulations that would reduce market access for foreign firms. Countries adopting the agreement could also agree to do their best to resolve individual trade problems that arise in services on a case-by-case basis. These two commitments, a standstill commitment and a best efforts commitment to resolve problems, would give the framework agreement immediate practical value. They would put a ceiling on trade restrictions in services and provide a process for resolving problems while countries seek to negotiate more detailed rules for trade in services over the long run.

RELATIONSHIP BETWEEN THE GATT AND THE GATS

The last issue a framework agreement must resolve is the relationship between the GATT and the new General Agreement on Trade in Services (GATS). This is partly a legal issue, partly an institutional issue, partly a practical trade policy issue, and ultimately a political issue. Before analyzing these issues in detail, it may well be worthwhile to review the relationship established in the Uruguay Declaration between the negotiations on trade in goods and the negotiations on trade in services, because the issues are largely the same. Moreover, the political balance achieved in the Uruguay Declaration may well provide a model for the legal, institutional, practical, and political relationship between the GATT and the General Agreement on Trade in Services.[6]

The Uruguay Round of multilateral trade negotiations is legally divided into two separate negotiations: a negotiation on trade in goods within the framework of the GATT, and a negotiation on trade in services among interested countries that attended the meeting in Punta del Este. Each of these negotiations is supervised by a separate body, the Group of Negotiations on Goods (GNG) and the Group of Negotiations on Services (GNS). Both sets of negotiations are supported by the GATT secretariat. Both sets of negotiations also come under the common political mandate established by ministers in the Uruguay Declaration. The two negotiations are thus legally separated, but politically linked.

The principal legal issue with respect to the future relationship between the GATT Articles of Agreement and the new General Agreement on Trade in Services concerns the linkage, if any, between the rights and obligations of the GATT and the legal rights and obligations of a General Agreement on Trade in Services. It is conceivable that the two agreements could be merged into a new, more comprehensive agreement on international trade, along the lines perhaps of the stillborn International Trade Organization, which was negotiated at the end of World War II but never implemented because the U.S. Congress refused to ratify it. The path of least resistance, however, will be to adopt the General Agreement on Trade in Services as a separate legal agreement. This will make it possible to conclude the negotiation of an agreement on services even if not all GATT countries are ready to join at the same time. It would also remove concerns that legal rights and obligations negotiated in one agreement could be adversely affected by legal rights and obligations negotiated in the other agreement.

The institutional issue with respect to the relationship between the GATT and the GATS is whether the GATT secretariat should be asked to administer the new agreement on services, in addition to the GATT articles and the related codes on trade in goods. The answer to this question is probably yes. Having the GATT secretariat administer the agreement not only would be practical from a housekeeping point of view, but also would preserve a pragmatic link between trade in services and trade in goods. With the GATT secretariat organizing meetings of the GATT as well as the GATS, trade officials attending meetings on trade in goods would thus be able to schedule parallel meetings on services at the same time. The accumulated experience of GATT officials in dealing with trade matters in goods would also remain available to officials wrestling with trade issues in services. It would probably make sense, however, to establish a separate division in the GATT on trade in services, and nonmembers may insist on separate financial contributions to support a services division.

The practical issue is whether countries would be able to make a link between the enforcement of rights and obligations with respect to trade in goods and the enforcement of rights and obligations with respect to trade in services. The answer is that such a link could not be made in legal terms, but that countries will probably find a way of establishing a linkage in political terms. There are endless ways in which countries can affect the commercial interests of other countries without violating any GATT obligations, and it would be surprising if countries did not establish a broad political linkage between their commercial interests in goods and their commercial interests in services.

CONCLUSIONS

A General Agreement on Trade in Services will provide a framework of principles and rules for the negotiation of binding commitments by governments with respect to policies affecting trade in services. Such a framework agreement should address transparency of barriers to trade in services, national treatment, foreign investment, temporary admission of foreign service workers, international data flows, international financial transfers, and the acquisition of essential equipment and materials. Other issues that will have to be addressed in a services framework include the design and implementation of domestic regulations, the administration of restricted licensing regimes, the establishment of a local presence in the importing market, and the right of nonestablishment where foreign exporters wish to deliver services electronically or through the mail. A range of options are available to the negotiators in framing these issues, from statements of principle without commitment to the establishment of full legal obligations. To the extent that the framework does not establish legal obligations, it can establish procedures for the subsequent negotiation of binding commitments. These options are described more fully in Chapter 12.

NOTES

1. The negotiations on trade in goods are being carried out by the Contracting Parties of the GATT under the rules and procedures of the GATT. The negotiations on trade in services are being carried out by the negotiators acting as government representatives of interested countries.
2. The first person to label the outcome of negotiations on trade in services a General Agreement on Trade in Services was the Brazilian foreign minister who represented Brazil at an informal meeting of trade ministers in Stockholm in June 1985.
3. The first person to examine the potential structure of an agreement on trade in services by analyzing the structure of the GATT was Mel Clark, a retired Canadian trade negotiator, who was commissioned by his government in 1982 to undertake an examination of the applicability of the GATT to trade in services. See Clark (1983).
4. For a discussion of the negotiation of detailed commitments see Chapter 12, on negotiating strategies.
5. For a detailed discussion of such negotiations see Chapter 12, on negotiating strategies.
6. John Jackson, in a monograph to be published by the American Enterprise Institute in 1988, describes in detail the legal structure of an agreement on services, and the various provisions that would have to be included in such an agreement to make it a functional agreement. See Jackson (forthcoming).

11
ELABORATING THE GENERAL AGREEMENT ON TRADE IN SERVICES FOR THE INDIVIDUAL SECTORS

There are obvious differences among individual sectors in services—differences in market structure and the scope for competition, differences in regulatory objectives and the nature of government regulation, and differences in the historical development of domestic and international institutions. Any meaningful regime has to reflect the institutional and market realities of each sector.

As noted in previous chapters, however, a negotiation carried out purely along sectoral lines would be dominated by the sectoral regulatory agenda and would inevitably focus on major philosophical differences among countries with respect to the proper role of government and the optimal regime for achieving regulatory objectives. The development of a general, trade-oriented framework of principles and rules makes it possible to approach the issue of services on the basis of a common desire to obtain the mutual economic gains from trade. The expansion of trade opportunities thus establishes a focus for the development of a common framework.

What is clearly needed is a dual approach to the negotiation of an international trade regime for services—an approach that combines the trade-liberalizing thrust of a generic set of principles and rules and the down-to-earth aspects of a sectoral focus. The Uruguay Declaration, therefore, called for the negotiation of general rules and principles as well as the elaboration of possible disciplines for individual sectors. In this chapter, we will examine the elaboration of the General Agreement on Trade in Services for the major sectors.

One option for combining the benefits of both a general and a sectoral approach would be to record all sectoral deviations and exceptions in the general framework agreement, alongside the statement of general principles and rules. The risk of such an approach would be to dilute the liberalizing thrust of the general principles and rules by creating a confusing and ambiguous document. The alternative approach, recommended here, is to develop separate annotations of the general agreement for individual sectors.

The development of sectoral annotations could follow and build on the exchange of information on barriers and regulations described in Chapter 10, and a subsequent analysis of the applicability of the principles and rules of the general framework to individual sectors. A somewhat similar process is currently under way in the OECD Trade Committee, which is examining the applicability of the concepts contained in the Conceptual Framework Paper (OECD, 1987) to individual sectors.

Some have argued that the sectoral agreements negotiated under the general framework should contain the substantive, binding commitments for the liberalization of trade barriers to services. This would mean that the negotiation of substantive commitments would primarily have a sectoral focus. This would be undesirable, because it would constrain the scope of liberalization and give excessive emphasis to the regulatory issues. The approach recommended here, therefore, is to treat the sectoral understandings as interpretations of the general rules and principles with respect to individual sectors, and to organize the negotiation of substantive commitments on the basis of a general exchange of requests and offers across all sectors. Such a negotiation would follow, in effect, the pattern of past GATT negotiations in tariffs and quantitative restrictions.

Whatever route is chosen, the negotiation of a set of agreements that remain true to the overall liberalizing thrust of the general agreement, while accommodating sectoral realities, poses a real challenge. By its nature, the process of liberalization has to involve a confrontation between purely sectoral regulatory objectives and the broader economic objectives that are served by trade liberalization. This will inevitably lead to a certain tension between the principles, rules, and procedures of the general agreement on one side, and the rules and procedures developed in a sectoral context. It will also, inevitably, lead to bureaucratic clashes between government departments, each of which acts as the guardian of governmental objectives.

The key to the success of the whole enterprise will be to achieve and maintain a proper balance between the general rules and procedures on one side, and the sectoral disciplines on the other. Too much emphasis on the general framework could leave the whole process too far removed from the real world, with the result that it does not lead to many substantive changes in policy measures at the sectoral level. On the other hand, too much emphasis on the sectoral issues could get the whole process bogged down in regulatory minutiae without a clear focus on trade liberalization. The resulting agreements could end up creating new obstacles to global economic adjustments in individual sectors rather than facilitating market adjustments.

SECTORAL ANNOTATIONS OF A GENERAL AGREEMENT ON TRADE IN SERVICES

The most sensible way of achieving an elaboration of the general discipline for individual sectors is to develop sectoral annotations of the general rules. Sectoral annotations can add greater precision to the general rules and principles as they are applied to individual sectors. They can take account of sectoral differences in market structures, differences in regulation, and differences in institutional arrangements.

Sectoral annotations have been used to develop the U.S.-Israeli agreement on trade in services further and have proved extremely useful in familiarizing regulatory officials with trade concepts and in familiarizing trade officials with the basic sectoral concepts.

It will not be necessary to negotiate sectoral understandings for every conceivable sector in services. For some sectors such as management consulting, the provisions of the general agreement will provide an adequate basis for liberalizing trade. Barriers affecting trade in such sectors would be reviewed and negotiated according to the procedures established in the general agreement.

It needs to be clearly established that the principal purpose of such annotations is to *interpret* the general rules and procedures, not to *displace* them with sectoral rules and procedures. The primacy of the general principles, rules, and procedures will need to be preserved, except in those few cases where the structure of the market or the structure of existing agreements is fundamentally inconsistent with the principles and rules in the general agreement. Where trade is dominated by monopolies, as in basic telecommunications services, for example, it obviously does not make sense to impose trade rules that assume free and open competition on the basis of market criteria. Where market access today is dominated by a comprehensive system of bilateral reciprocity agreements, as in air transport, it would not make sense to adopt a multilateral framework *ab initio*. In such cases, the annotations need to spell out the scope of the exceptions clearly.

The sectoral annotation of the principles and rules of the general agreement would not create substantive, binding obligations with respect to market access and national treatment. These would be negotiated as part of the general exchange of concessions envisioned under the provisions of a General Agreement on Trade in Services. The sectoral annotations would offer guidance on how the principles and rules of the general agreement should be interpreted in the context of a particular sector. The agreed interpretation of the market access commitment or the national treatment commitment with respect to specific service activities or specific policy instruments would not come into force until a government had agreed to bind market access with respect to such services or to bind national treatment commitment with respect to such policy instruments.

The challenge in framing the sectoral annotations will be to avoid getting bogged down in debates over differences in regulatory philosophy or a particular country's choice of trade measures. The annotations should be based on facts and not on normative judgments, facts such as the operations that have to be performed in order to produce particular services. It should then be possible to define national treatment in terms of the ability of a foreign firm to carry out such operational activities on the same basis as domestic firms supplying the same services. Market access would be defined in terms of a new firm's being able to carry out the operational activities associated with the sale of particular services.

Outline of Sectoral Agreements

In order to be manageable the sectoral annotations should be rather general, and should not get into national regulatory differences. They should take a generic approach in highlighting the most important characteristics of a sector that are unique to the sector across a wide range of countries. Each sectoral annotation would have four major sections: 1) a description of the sector, 2) an interpretation of the provisions contained in the general agreement for the sector, 3) supplementary provisions applicable to this sector, 4) general exceptions with respect to the sector.

Descriptive Section. This section would describe the scope of activities covered by the sector, the structure of the market (including differences among key segments of the industry), how domestic and international activity is regulated among member countries (in very general terms), the key policy objectives served by the regulations applicable to this sector, the way services in this sector are traded, the form of barriers to trade in the sector, and existing international agreements applicable to the sector.

Interpretive Section. The interpretive section would describe how all the key provisions of the general agreement are to be interpreted in the context of the industry. In other words, this section would describe how the national treatment principle, the least trade-distorting regulation principle, the equivalent competitive opportunity principle, the public monopoly provisions, the fair trade provisions, and the balance of payments, travel, and international data flow provisions are to be interpreted with respect to trade in services in the sector. If no sectoral interpretation was considered necessary with respect to certain provisions, one could merely indicate that no sectoral interpretation was necessary and that the provisions apply as written.

The sectoral annotations would provide an opportunity to relate the rules and principles of the general agreement in a fairly direct way to the specific functional and operational activities that have to be performed by foreign firms that wish to supply specific services covered by the sector. For example, in order to export shipping services, one has to be able to dock the ship in an accessible harbor, one needs access to secure warehousing facilities, one has to be able to maintain a sales office and carry out a marketing effort, and so on. The elaboration of the general rules with respect to each of these activities could provide a fairly concrete notion of what national treatment means with respect to shipping.

Sectoral Rulemaking Section. The sectoral rulemaking section would supplement the general rules and procedures contained in the general framework with additional rules and procedures that are deemed necessary to further international cooperation and the liberalization of trade in the sector.

Exceptions to the General Rules. This section would address general exceptions that arise from fundamental characteristics of an industry. It would not cover individual national exceptions that arise from the regulatory regime of an individual country. National exceptions would be covered in the context of the subsequent negotiation of binding, substantive commitments discussed in the next chapter. As foreseen under the procedures of the general agreement described in the preceding chapter, substantive national commitments would be negotiated as part of a general exchange of commitments covering all sectors.

It could be argued that the negotiation of a detailed sectional annotation would be a waste of time since it would add another step in the negotiations before substantive commitments are negotiated. Such sectional annotations need not be very long, however. As already noted, many of the principles and rules will not require sectoral elaboration, and it will be sufficient to note that the general provisions apply without the need for further elaboration. Much of the work related to the preparation of these sectoral annotations can be carried out through the preparation of background papers by the secretariat.

The experience with the U.S.-Israeli negotiations and the U.S.-Canadian negotiations has shown that the process of working through a sectoral annotation can be extremely helpful in clarifying sectoral issues that arise under the more general trade agreement. Without a clear understanding of the sectoral interpretation of the general principles contained in the overall framework agreement, it will be difficult to persuade many countries to assume binding obligations with respect to the management of sectoral regulations. While it might be possible to achieve this objective through an informal work program, it will be impossible to achieve meaningful results without a sectoral review of some kind.

Relationship between Trade Policy and Sectoral Regulatory Policy

In order to understand how the various elements could fit together, and how the process would work, we have to probe more deeply into the relationship between the trade negotiations and domestic regulations. We have established that most barriers to trade in services are embedded in domestic regulations. In some cases, the barriers to trade embedded in domestic regulations are not essential for the achievement of the legislated regulatory objective and have been added for purely protectionist reasons. In other cases, the barriers embedded in the regulations are an unavoidable by-product of the domestic regulatory regime.

Both the general rules and procedures and the sectoral annotations basically are aimed at the first set of barriers to trade in services, barriers embedded in domestic regulations that are not essential for the achievement of regulatory objectives. The second type of barriers, which cannot be divorced from the domestic regulatory regime, could be tackled in more ambitious negotiations that would address the regulatory regime itself. These are the higher level sectoral agreements that would be negotiated on a conditional most-favored-nation basis. The negotiation of such agreements is beyond the mandate established in the Uruguay Declaration.

Trade officials do not have a comparative advantage in debating regulatory objectives or philosophies. They can ask whether mandated regulatory objectives are being pursued in the least trade-distorting manner possible. They can also examine the commerical consequences of alternative regulatory systems and devise appropriate strategies and tools for protecting a country's commercial interests in light of the regulatory systems employed by its trading partners.

While the negotiating mandate places an obligation on negotiators to respect each country's regulatory objectives, that does not require them to ignore the commercial consequences of a country's decision to pursue certain regulatory objectives. Moreover, it is perfectly consistent with that mandate to say that countries with similar regulatory regimes should have an opportunity to expand trade opportunities with each other in a manner consistent with their national regulatory objectives.

Trade officials within the context of their own turf do not have either the mandate, political clout, or resources necessary to pose a fundamental challenge to any country's regulatory regime, even where such regimes pose major hurdles for trade. This limitation of the scope of trade negotiations inevitably limits the possibility for major breakthroughs toward liberalization, since domestic regulatory systems pose the greatest barriers to global liberalization. This does not preclude the possibility, however, that regulatory officials interested in pursuing major regulatory reforms within one industry or another might seize on trade negotiations in services as a vehicle for pursuing such reforms among a group of like-minded countries.

To put this issue more bluntly, trade officials have no business negotiating over regulatory objectives. At the same time, the prospects for expanded trade opened up by trade negotiations could persuade the relevant regulatory authorities to negotiate a common approach to various regulatory issues, and this in turn could open up the possibility for the negotiation of an expanded market access agreement.

ILLUSTRATIVE SECTORAL ANNOTATIONS

To offer a more precise description of possible sectoral annotations, the remainder of this chapter will focus on some of the principal sectors in services. Since this is an overview, we will not be able to probe very deeply into each sector; the suggestions provided with respect to the contents of individual sectoral annotations are merely illustrative. The illustrative sectoral annotations provided here are probably on the ambitious side, and should be viewed as ideal models. In order to be manageable, the scope of the actual agreements that are negotiated may well have to be more modest. The parallel volumes of the American Enterprise Institute Trade in Services Series (also published by Ballinger) provide more in-depth analysis of the major sectors, as well as suggestions for possible agreements.

Sectoral Annotation on Tourism Services

On the face of it, tourism seems to be an unlikely candidate for an early sectoral focus in negotiations on trade in services. Trade barriers in this sector are not immediately obvious. At first glance, trade negotiations on tourism might seem frivolous.

Tourism provides an excellent basis for starting work on trade in services for a number of reasons, however. Tourism is an industry where most countries, and in particular developing countries, can gain from expanded trade. Negotiations on tourism services can also provide early tangible benefits for a broad cross section of the public. Who has not been frustrated by the unavailability of accustomed services while traveling abroad?

Negotiations on tourism would give travel agents, an extremely well-organized group of people with a large presence at the grass roots level, a stake in the negotiations. The discussion of policy issues affecting trade in tourism would also touch on regulations covering a large number of other sectors in services and thus provide useful precedents for subsequent negotiations in such sectors.

Trade in tourism covers not only the opportunity of the tourist to travel abroad but also the opportunity of those who sell services that support tourists to market and deliver their services in other countries. An annotation on tourism thus could cover the activities of travel agents and tour operators, the sale and use of traveler's checks and credit cards, charter flights, cruise ships, air and hotel reservation systems, automatic cash machines at airports, flight travel insurance, travel regulations, and the management of global hotel chains.

Each of these services associated with tourism opens a window on a much wider range of regulatory issues. The development of a sectoral annotation on tourism thus could provide a dry run for a large number of other sectors. In other words, tourism provides the possibility for a useful experiment and learning experience in a sector where everyone can gain and where commercial and regulatory conflicts are minimal.

The regulations that create barriers to trade in tourism services usually are not the result of an explicit policy to protect the domestic industry. Rather, they tend to be a by-product of policies aimed at a variety of domestic regulatory objectives or policies designed to reduce foreign exchange outlays. This makes it simultaneously easier and more difficult to deal with these issues—easier because resistance from the domestic industry is likely to be less pronounced than in other industries, but more difficult because officials will need to consider the regulatory implications. On balance, the annotations on tourism are likely to prove easier to negotiate than the other sectoral annotations. (For further material on trade in tourism services see Richter, 1987, and Feketekuty, 1987.)

Descriptive Section. This section would describe the various activities to be covered by the annotation on tourism, including the sale of travel and hotel services, the sale of tour packaging services, the operation of reservation systems, the sale of flight insurance, credit card, traveler's check, and check cashing services, the sale of cruise ship and air charter services, and the provision of hotel services. Presumably it would also cover the right of residents to travel abroad.

The text of the descriptive section would state clearly that the obligations extend both to the opportunities provided to travelers to vacation abroad, and to the opportunities provided to suppliers of tourism services to market and to supply tourism services abroad. The last point cuts two ways: local suppliers of tourism services in foreign resorts have to be able to market their services on a competitive basis in the home market of the vacationer, and suppliers of tourism services from the home country of the vacationer have to be able to deliver tourism services to vacationers at the foreign resort.

The descriptive section would also enumerate governmental policy objectives served by regulations that affect the production, marketing, and delivery of services covered by the sectoral annotation. The annotations would undoubtedly point out that the regulations affecting international travel and trade in tourism services serve broad policy objectives that go beyond public policy concerns in tourism. The annotations might refer to fiduciary, immigration, balance of payments, transportation, and communication policy objectives.

Interpretive Section. This section would relate the principles, rules, and procedures of the general agreement to the needs of international travelers and the needs of businesses that support international travelers. The section would translate the general principles into terms that are meaningful to international travelers as well as travel agents, tour operators, vendors of credit card, traveler's check, and flight insurance services, operators of cruise ships and charter flights, automobile leasing companies, and companies that manage hotels.

This section would apply the general provisions dealing with monopolies to the specific problems faced by foreign exporters of travel services who have to both procure certain services from monopolies and compete with the monopolies in supplying related services. Foreign charter airlines, for example, may well have to depend on the national airline for ground handling and customer services, while competing with them for the charter business. Companies operating air and hotel reservation systems depend on the communications monopoly with respect to access to the public communications system, while at the same time competing with the communications monopoly with respect to the provision of electronic message services.

The interpretive section could also apply the general provisions regarding the international movement of people, money, information, and goods to such travel-related issues as the international transfer of information on travel and hotel arrangements, foreign exchange controls on expenditures by tourists, and visa regulations related to tourism travel. It could also apply any general provisions regarding investment to such operational issues in tourism as building and operating hotels, car leasing companies, or travel agencies. As noted earlier, the annotation would not establish substantive obligations in these areas but would help frame the issues in order better to set the stage for the exchange of substantive, binding commitments in the subsequent phase of the negotiations.

Section on Exceptions. The section dealing with exceptions would make clear what activities in each functional area (for example, financial services, transportation services, communications services) are not covered by the provisions contained in the sectoral annotation.

Sectoral Annotation on Telecommunications and Data Processing

The technological revolution in telecommunications and data processing has been central to the rapid growth of international trade in services in recent years. Regulations that limit the use of the new technologies are considered major barriers to trade in services by the business community. The new technologies have created three sets of issues.

First, the new technology has led to the creation of new services dependent on communications facilities, services related to data processing, electronic data bases, banking, insurance, and transportation. Since the competitive position of firms offering these services often hinges on the terms and conditions of access to communications facilities, disputes over communications charges and restrictions placed on the use of the communications facilities have become trade issues.

Second, the new technology has made it economically feasible and commercially advantageous for many corporations and industry associations to develop their own internal communications networks and to use such networks not only for internal management purposes but also for the distribution of specialized services to customers. This has created disputes over the extent to which private entities should be allowed to build such networks and to interconnect them with the public system to deliver services to clients around the world. It has also created disputes over the communications equipment that firms are allowed to interconnect with the public network.

Third, the new technology has made it economically feasible to supply many telecommunications services on a competitive basis. Inevitably there have been disputes over the degree of competition that should be allowed in various segments of the market and over the ground rules that should govern competition between the communications monopoly and competing firms, where both are allowed to compete in the same segment of the market.

The emergence of competition in international telecommunications services in some countries, while the provision of such services remains a monopoly activity in other countries, has created commercial problems for both sets of countries. International telecommunications obviously requires the cooperation of public communications companies in at least two countries, the country in which a call originates and the country where the call is received. Firms that supply international telecommunications services have to negotiate so-called interconnect agreements with their counterparts in other countries. International telecommunications firms in a country such as the United States that permits competition naturally find themselves in a poor bargaining position vis-à-vis foreign telecommunications monopolies. Countries that have retained an international communications monopoly on the other hand have trouble finding a practical and equitable way of channeling outgoing calls to competing foreign firms in countries that permit competition.

What is unique about this sector is that user issues are as important in this sector as supplier issues. Thus the annotations on telecommunications and data processing services will have to distinguish clearly between the principles and rules that apply to users on one hand and to suppliers on the other hand.

Trade-related *user* concerns generally relate to services purchased from communications monopolies. Fundamentally, this covers basic telecommunications services and some value-added or enhanced services, to the extent the government involved has limited competition in these services.

Trade-related *supplier* concerns generally relate to services provided on a competitive basis. This category covers data processing and information services, and value-added or enhanced telecommunications services subject to international competition.

There has been considerable debate over the tradeability of telecommunications services and therefore over the extent to which basic telecommunications services raise trade issues. The view taken here is that basic telecommunications services raise critical trade issues for users whenever such services are provided by monopolies and for suppliers whenever international telecommunications services are provided on a competitive market basis.

These are controversial, hotly debated domestic regulatory issues in each country. They have also become major trade issues that can no longer be treated as purely internal, domestic issues. Any international trade agreement in services will have to address these issues. A trade agreement, and in particular an annotation of general principles and rules on trade in services more generally, will not be able to resolve all the difficult issues and establish a fully satisfactory framework for everyone; but such agreements can help to clarify the issues involved from a trade point of view and establish a framework for sorting out the trade issues that arise and for structuring meaningful commitments that could be included in the negotiation of substantive, binding commitments.

Any trade agreements negotiated in this sector will have to be coordinated closely with the negotiation of agreements within the framework of the International Telecommunications Union. In fact, substantial negotiations are currently under way in the ITU to update many of the agreed guidelines and recommendations of the ITU.

The GATT and the ITU have complementary roles. The GATT and trade officials are best equipped to deal with international commercial issues that arise in the context of competitive markets and the relationship between competitive and noncompetitive markets. The ITU and communications officials are best equipped to deal with issues that arise from the operation of an international communications network, and the relationship between noncompetitive suppliers.

For a more detailed discussion of the trade issues in this sector, see Aronson and Cowhey (1988) in the same series. Also see Feketekuty and Aronson (1984a), a comprehensive article on the issues.[1]

The primary function of an annotation in this sector will be to establish a framework for the negotiation of substantive commitments over a number of years. It should not be so specific that it will be out of date before the ink is dry. Given the continuing rapid pace of change in both technology and government policies, there is a danger that the wrong kind of agreement could become an impediment to market adjustments. In order to avoid these pitfalls, the annotation should not become too detailed, and in particular, it should not be too specific in spelling out which activities should be open to competition and which activities should remain the prerogative of public monopolies.

The annotations should establish different principles or rules for different competitive situations. For example, there could be a set of principles or rules for trade in services produced and sold in competitive markets, a set of principles or rules for the participation of communications monopolies in competitive markets, and a set of principles or rules that would apply to communications services that are supplied by communications monopolies in some countries and competitive suppliers in other countries. Each country could then decide whether to permit or not to permit competition with respect to specific telecommunications services.

Descriptive Section. The descriptive section of the annotation on telecommunications and data processing services would need to describe the range of activities covered, the needs of users, the role of public communications monopolies, public regulatory objectives, and the impact of changing technology. This section would also have to note the differences in regulatory policies among member countries, the resulting differences in market structure, and the various types of trade issues that arise as a result of the intermingling of competitive and monopoly activities, with many national variations.

The annotation would contain separate sections dealing with users' and suppliers' issues. The separate interests of different classes of users would be identified, including those of small end users (small business entities that must depend entirely on the public network), large end users (large business entities that can lease their own lines or build their own satellite-based network), and users who are themselves suppliers of enhanced or value-added telecommunications services or data processing and information services.

The descriptive section would also need to address the relationship between trade in services and equipment issues. The services that can be provided through the telecommunications network may depend significantly on the equipment that can be attached to the telecommunications network. Needs differ with respect to the security required, the nature of coding or decoding, the speed of transmission, and other matters.

Finally, the descriptive section should describe the existing international agreements on telecommunications negotiated within the framework of the International Telecommunications Union and should establish a relationship between trade-oriented agreements on telecommunications negotiated within the framework of the General Agreement on Trade in Services, and agreements negotiated within the framework of the ITU.

Interpretive Section. This section could relate the key principles and rules in the general agreement to the needs of enterprises that supply enhanced or value-added telecommunications services, data processing services, and information services. It would also relate the general principles and rules to the specific needs of users engaged in international trade of other information-based services.

This section could apply the nonestablishment principle to the ability of data processing and information companies to offer their services across national borders without establishing themselves locally. It could also apply any principles contained in the general agreement on foreign investment and on the right of presence to the establishment of facilities for the provision of enhanced or value-added services.

The interpretive section would also need to relate the general provisions dealing with public monopolies to the problems faced by competitive foreign suppliers of enhanced or value-added services, who must both depend on the telecommunications monopolies as users of basic telecommunications services and compete with them as suppliers of enhanced and value-added telecommunications services.

Sectoral Rulemaking Section. This section would contain added principles and rules to deal with the needs of users. The general rules are geared to deal with market access problems faced by suppliers, rather than problems experienced by users in gaining access to services provided by monopolies. Such user-oriented principles or rules could address, for example, access to leased lines and the terms and conditions for such access.

The sectoral rulemaking section may also have to address issues related to the importation of telecommunications equipment, where needed equipment cannot be obtained locally at reasonable prices. It might also deal with the right of service providers and users to attach the requisite communications equipment to the public switched network. An agreement on standards for telecommunications equipment installed on customer premises is at an advanced stage of negotiations in the GATT. This agreement, generally referred to as the Interconnect Agreement, is being negotiated under the Standards Code of the GATT. The sectoral annotation could build on this agreement.

Exception Section. Issues pertaining to basic telecommunications services that are not covered by these annotations would be covered as exceptions.

Sectoral Annotation on Aviation Services

Because the aviation sector bears many similarities to the telecommunications sector, there is a certain logic in taking up this sector next. It differs from other sectors, however, in that trade in aviation is controlled by a comprehensive system of bilateral agreements. (See Kasper, 1988.) This system is well entrenched, and is considered satisfactory by most elements of the industry and by national authorities responsible for aviation.

If we accept the current system of bilateral aviation agreements as a given, what contribution could a General Agreement on Trade in Services make to international aviation? More specifically is there a role for a sectoral annotation on aviation services? These two questions need to be addressed separately. The principles and rules of the general agreement can contribute to the development of a more market-oriented system by influencing the evolution of bilateral aviation agreements as such agreements are renegotiated. Further down the road it could help spur an effort to develop a more competitive framework for air transport services.

In the near term, the principles and rules of the general agreement could be used to reduce regulatory barriers that now distort whatever competition is allowed by the existing agreements. From industry complaints, one would have to conclude that the bilateral agreements have not been very successful in dealing with many of the anticompetitive practices of national airlines in their home country or the restrictive regulations that limit the access of foreign air carriers to local passengers and freight. Foreign airlines that are granted landing rights thus often find that they are not allowed to compete with the national airline on an equal footing. The principal issues concern the quality of ground handling services provided by the national airline to foreign carriers, arrangements at airports for processing passengers and freight, regulations concerning the local marketing of international passenger service and international air freight services, and regulations requiring government officials to fly on a national airline and to ship government freight on a national airline.

Ground handling in many countries is performed by a local monopoly that is owned by the national airline. It should not be surprising that this leads to conflicts of interest in the services provided to competing foreign airlines. The range of complaints registered by airlines is quite wide and includes complaints about discriminatory treatment in customs clearance, air traffic control, data collected by airport authorities, location of passenger processing and ticketing facilities, docking arrangements, and other details.

With respect to marketing, many countries exercise strict regulatory controls over the minimum prices that can be charged for various services, and it is often argued that the regulations are less strictly enforced vis-à-vis the national airline than with respect to foreign airlines. This enables the national airline to undercut the regulated prices offered by foreign airlines, who are in a difficult position to follow suit without incurring the wrath of domestic regulators.

The Fly National restrictions imposed on official travel and government freight are no different from the government purchasing practices covered by the GATT Government Procurement Code negotiated during the Tokyo Round of multilateral trade negotiations.

Descriptive Section. This section of the annotation on airline services would describe the current organization of international aviation, the role of bilateral agreements on landing rights, the scope of the Chicago Convention (which sets out some common ground rules for international aviation) and the roles of the two principal international organizations in aviation, the International Civil Aviation Organization (ICAO), and the Internal Air Transport Association (IATA). ICAO is an intergovernmental organization that establishes common standards and procedures for international aviation. The membership of IATA is made up of airlines, and its purpose is to develop cooperative arrangements in such areas as ticketing, baggage handling, air schedules, and airport procedures.

This section should describe the various activities airlines have to be able to perform in order to provide international passenger and air freight services, and the various areas of regulatory policy that can affect the ability of airlines to carry out those functions on an equivalent competitive basis. It would also describe the various policy objectives that motivate government regulations that affect the operation of airlines. Finally, differences in the market structure and regulation of passenger service and air freight services could be addressed.

Interpretive Section. The interpretive section would focus on the application of the principles and procedures of the General Agreement on Trade in Services to ground handling, marketing, and other operational issues involved in running an airline.

Sectoral Exceptions. The exceptions section would spell out with some precision the extent to which the system of bilateral agreements should be exempted from the principles and rules of the general agreement.

Sectoral Annotation on Maritime Transport

One part of the international shipping industry is relatively free of barriers and open to international competition, while the other part of the industry is affected by a wide range of anticompetitive practices and protectionist measures. International maritime transport of bulk commodities is relatively free of restrictions. International maritime transport of nonbulk commodities, provided by shipping lines serving specific routes on a regularly scheduled basis, is restricted both by anticompetitive practices sanctioned by many governments and by government measures that favor domestic shipping companies. Shipping within national borders, between any two points within an individual country, tends to be restricted to domestic shipping companies under the cabotage laws.[2]

The major factor in international liner shipping, and the source of greatest international debate, has been the conference system. Most governments allow shipping firms that serve particular routes to form shipping conferences that are permitted to negotiate agreed rates and schedules and can agree to split the cargo among their members. In other words, normal antitrust laws are not applied to such conferences. While ships outside the conference can steam into port and pick up cargo, the conference has so much power vis-à-vis local shippers that they are usually reluctant to use nonconference carriers, even if the nonconference carriers offer cheaper rates.

The second major institutional influence in international shipping is the United Nations Conference on Trade and Development (UNCTAD) Liner Code, negotiated in the mid-1970s at the insistence of the developing countries. The UNCTAD Liner Code allows two countries connected by a shipping route to reserve 80 percent of the freight carried between them for their own merchant fleets, split evenly, 40 percent for each country's fleet. This leaves 20 percent of the cargo for shipping companies from third countries, carriers called cross-traders in the terminology used by the industry.[3]

In order to reduce the spread of bilateralism in shipping in the aftermath of the UNCTAD Liner Code, the United States negotiated an understanding with most of the other developed countries, who some time ago formed an organization called the Consultative Shipping Group (CSG). Parties to the U.S.-CSG agreement agree not to invoke their right under the UNCTAD Liner Code to reserve 40 percent of the cargo carried in bilateral traffic, thus leaving at least 60 percent of the cargo open to each other. The U.S. and CSG countries also agreed to discourage other countries from reserving their 40 percent of the cargo. The U.S.-

CSG agreement also addresses the long-standing concern of the United States about the anticompetitive aspects of the closed conference system by establishing the right of excluded shipping companies to challenge exclusionary practices by the conference in the national courts.

Governments also protect their national shipping industries through a variety of measures, including requirements that government cargo or cargo benefiting from government subsidies be carried by ships owned by nationals. Most countries heavily subsidize the construction and operation of the national merchant fleet and reserve all shipping within a country's borders to the national fleet.

Increasingly, the competitive advantage in shipping goes to companies that can handle freight all the way from any inland point of origin to any inland points of destination; access to land transportation facilities therefore can also be a crucial factor in determining the competitive position of a shipping company.

The principal objectives of a sectoral annotation on maritime transport should be to build on the U.S.-CSG agreement and provide a framework for an exchange of meaningful market access commitments. The annotations would have to take the conference system and the UNCTAD Liner Code as givens but could provide for as much market-oriented competition as possible within the existing system.

Descriptive Section. The descriptive section of the annotations on maritime transport would be divided into two parts. The first would deal with general issues, and the second would deal with the institutional environment, market structure, and trade problems associated with scheduled liner shipping. The first part would describe the various facilities shipping companies need for transferring cargo to and from inland points and for marketing their services, and the trade barriers created by laws and regulations that create unequal access to such facilities. This part could also generally describe the various types of measures used by governments to protect their shipping industry, including restrictions placed on the shipment of government-owned or subsidized cargo and domestic cabotage laws.

The second part of the descriptive section would describe the conference system and the UNCTAD Liner Code. It would address the anticompetitive practices that have traditionally created concerns about competitive access to cargo, and the extent to which national government regulations and existing international agreements deal with such practices.

Interpretive Section. The interpretive section, like the descriptive section, would be divided into two parts, one part dealing with regulations affecting access to shore facilities and marketing activities, and the other part dealing with the operation of the liner conference system and the UNCTAD Liner Code. Among the principles and rules of the general agreement that could be given added precision for shipping are those dealing with transparency, national treatment, and the establishment of local facilities.

Sectoral Rulemaking Section. The sectoral rulemaking section would have to include supplementary principles designed to curb the most restrictive and anticompetitive aspects of the closed conference system and the UNCTAD Liner Code.

Sectoral Exceptions. The section dealing with exceptions would need to spell out the extent to which the conference system and the UNCTAD Liner Code require deviations from the principles and rules of the General Agreement on Trade in Services.

Sectoral Annotation on Insurance Services

International trade in insurance is affected by virtually every protective device that governments have invented to restrict international trade in services. The insurance industry is probably the services industry that most closely fits the generic discipline that might be contained in the General Agreement on Trade in Services. It is also one of the most protected sectors in many countries, and the sector that could most benefit from negotiations aimed at the liberalization of trade in services.[4]

Since the primary purpose of insurance is to cover risk, and this requires the spreading of the larger and peak risks as widely as possible, there is an inevitable international dimension to insurance. This is particularly the case with respect to reinsurance and international transport insurance. At the other end of the spectrum, life insurance is often viewed as a pool of national savings, and policies to restrict the participation of foreign companies in such cases are motivated by a desire to keep such savings at home.

Yet, despite the inherent advantage in spreading risk over a global market, the insurance industry is protected in many countries by every protectionist device conceivable. The barriers include restrictions on entry, restrictions on lines of insurance that an admitted firm can offer, restrictions on the right of residents to purchase insurance abroad, restrictions on the sourcing of compulsory insurance (motor vehicle insurance), controls on the use of foreign exchange to purchase insurance abroad, employment restrictions on foreign firms, compulsory reinsurance with a national company, excessive deposit and paid-in-capital requirements that apply only to foreign firms, restrictions on the number of offices a foreign firm can set up, restrictions on the regional areas that a foreign firm can serve, restrictions on the type of clients a foreign insurance company can serve, discriminatory taxes imposed on foreign firms, and restrictions on the ability of foreign firms to insure government cargo or facilities.

In structuring the annotation on insurance, it might be useful to distinguish between four separate segments of the global insurance industry.

1. Reinsurance and international transport insurance, which are the most inherently international segments of the insurance industry. Insurance in this area would be subject to the greatest international discipline, and buyers would be given considerable freedom on where they purchase such insurance.

2. Insurance purchased by large business enterprises against property, casualty, and liability risks. This segment of the industry is not as inherently international as the first but nevertheless can benefit extensively from international trade. Business enterprises that are large enough to be able to buy insurance abroad would be guaranteed considerable freedom to do so. Governments often cannot prevent large businesses from buying certain types of insurance abroad anyway.

3. Fire, auto, and general liability insurance purchased by individuals. Such insurance is usually purchased locally from insurance companies that have established themselves in the national market under applicable national regulations. Foreign insurance companies have to establish themselves in the importing country and invest in local facilities in order to service this segment of the market. The international rules in this area would provide for a greater degree of national discretion in the nature of domestic regulations, though foreign insurance companies would be guaranteed the right to participate in the local market on the basis of negotiated conditions.

4. Life insurance, which many developing countries consider a major domestic source of savings. This is an activity they wish to control in order to direct the savings into high-priority domestic investment projects. Life insurance is therefore likely to be the area of insurance that will be most difficult to open up internationally.

Descriptive Section. This section will need to list the various segments of the industry, including export/import insurance, fire insurance, auto insurance, general liability insurance, reinsurance, life insurance, and insurance brokerage services. It will describe the various activities associated with insurance, including testing laboratories, loss appraisal and claims adjustment, insurance inspection and investigation, loss prevention services, risk management and consulting, and creation and management of self-insurance pooling arrangements.

Interpretive Section. All the principles and rules are likely to find important areas of application in the insurance sector. The national treatment principle, for example, will need to be defined with greater precision with respect to the processing of license applications, the design and enforcement of standards with respect to financial soundness, requirements imposed on the investment and valuation of reserves, tax treatment, and the presence required to service insurance contracts. The equivalent competitive opportunity principle will need to be given precision in order to establish a standard of market access where a country restricts the total number of domestic and foreign insurers. The due process principle might be given greater precision with respect to the processing of licenses by regulatory authorities, and the transparency principle might be given precision by enumerating the type of administrative actions that will be covered by this principle.

Sectoral Rulemaking Section. The sectoral rulemaking section would establish added principles and rules with respect to deposit and capital adequacy requirements imposed on foreign insurance companies. It is reasonable for governments to ask foreign firms to maintain a capital base and an adequate level of deposits inside a foreign market to assure policyholders that their claims will be serviced. The question is: What is a reasonable level to achieve this worthy regulatory objective? This is clearly an area where additional standards of fairness are needed, since the national treatment principle is difficult to apply in this area. The sectoral rulemaking section might also relate the national treatment principle to the activities of local insurance agents, loss investigators, and claims adjusters, the processing of claims, the role of testing laboratories, loss prevention programs, and risk management.

Sectoral Annotation on Professional Services

An annotation on professional services could cover a wide range of professional activities, including accounting, law, economic consulting, advertising, medicine, educational consulting, engineering, architecture, hotel management, and many more. The annotation could be quite broad, covering all professional services that can be sold across national borders, or it could cover a narrower range of professions in greater depth. As in the other sectors, the annotation should only provide a framework for the subsequent exchange of binding, substantive commitments.

Some will undoubtedly raise the question whether it is possible to deal with all professional services in one agreement. Given the similarity in the issues, it probably will be of some advantage to deal with all the professions in one agreement, while segmenting each of the four sections of the annotation into separate subsections for the individual professions.

International trade in professional services takes place both through the sale of professional services by individual practitioners to residents of other countries and through the sale of professional services by international firms specializing in particular areas of professional activity. International trade in professional services also takes place inside multinational corporations, which typically share a common international pool of professional experts. In both international professional firms and multinational corporations, there is obviously a great deal of intermingling of professional services provided by nonresident professionals and by local, resident professionals. This intermingling makes it difficult to identify pure trade of professional services across national borders, and services produced locally by international firms.

The typical international firm in professional services is made up of national professional practices staffed largely by local nationals who have completed their professional training in their own country and have satisfied the professional qualifications established by local accreditation authorities. International firms also seek to establish uniform standards of professional performance and to develop international name recognition. Each firm also provides some opportunity for international movement by its professional staff, both to broaden the expertise of its professional staff and to augment the expertise available to individual practices.

A short discussion of professional services as different and complex as law, accounting, and advertising cannot do justice to the issues that must be addressed. More detailed information can be found in a compendium published by the University of Chicago Legal Forum.[5] Additional information can be found in Noyelle (1988) in this series.

Descriptive Section. After covering the range of professional services addressed by the annotation on professional services, this section would describe the various means by which such trade takes place, including cross-border transmission of information, temporary travel by individual professionals, and services provided by international professional firms. This section would also need to describe the various things professionals and international firms have to be able to do to engage effectively in international trade in professional services. At the same time, it would be necessary to discuss the principal areas of government regulation and the major policy objectives that motivate such regulations.

Interpretive Section. This section would need to relate the national treatment principle to the principal operational problems faced by foreign professionals and professional firms as a result of government regulations, including such issues as taxation, accreditation of qualified foreign professionals, and the right of foreign professional firms to establish commercial linkages with local professionals, including partnership arrangements and the sharing of fees. This section could also relate the general principles and rules dealing with the movement of information, people, money, and goods to such issues as international data flows, visa regulations, foreign exchange controls on remittances, and customs rules on such material accessories as computer tapes, architectural blueprints, advertising copy, and portable computers.

Sectoral Rulemaking Section. This section could establish the principle that local partners of an international firm have a right to use the internationally recognized name of the firm. Another delicate area concerns the accreditation of qualified foreign professionals. Obviously, a foreign professional unfamiliar with local laws or building codes should not be accredited automatically. On the other hand, it might be useful to establish the principle that such professionals should be given credit for relevant professional education and experience in their home country or in third countries.

Sectoral Annotation on Banking Services

For purposes of analyzing the potential scope of sectoral agreements that might be negotiated for international trade in banking services, it is useful to divide international banking into three segments: offshore banking, foreign retail banking, and foreign sales of fee-based services by banks.

Offshore Banking Activities. In the offshore banking market, the foreign client comes to the bank. Banks and their business customers operate in the global offshore market with relatively few government constraints. In order to participate in this market, however, both the bank and its customer have to be large enterprises.

Offshore banking comes closest to a pure trade model, since it involves cross-border sales of services without any local establishment. In fact, it comes close to a model of free trade based on a single international market. The competitive pressures of this international market are so strong that many governments have found it in their interest to relax regulations and tax provisions that affect the offshore banking activities carried out within their national borders. Other countries, including the Nordic countries and Australia, have found it in their interest to relax restrictions on the establishment of foreign banks in order to attract banking activities that had migrated to the international offshore banking market.

Foreign Retail Banking. Foreign retail banking is conducted through branches and subsidiaries located abroad, (though the parent bank could provide a wide range of support services from the home office). Foreign retail banking is the furthest removed from cross-border trade, since most of the actual banking work is done on location abroad.

Foreign retail banking is most often cited as an example of international trade in services that cannot be conducted without major foreign investment. Any trade agreements in services will not achieve much liberalization for foreign retail banking unless such agreements cover foreign investment.

Fee-based Banking Services. Fee-based services cover a wide range of financial support services that banks sell for a fee; in other words these are services that are not provided free in conjunction with deposit or loan activity. Among fee-based services are global cash management for a multinational enterprise, data processing of a firm's payroll, investment advisory services, traveler's checks, credit cards, and mail order shopping services. Some of these services are produced in centralized data processing facilities or by investment analysts located in the home office, and therefore involve cross-border trade; others are produced in branches located abroad.

Fee-based services provided by banks have been widely discussed in the press but are still poorly understood. Many fee-based services provided by banks to international customers are produced at the home office or in regional financial centers like London, Tokyo, and Singapore. It is not clear, however, to what extent the ability of a bank to sell such services to clients in a particular country depends on the establishment of retail banking activities in that country.

Coverage of a Banking Agreement. One of the more difficult questions that will have to be addressed in the negotiation of a General Agreement on Trade in Services is the extent to which such an agreement should apply to any of the three segments of the international banking industry. The agreement on services negotiated between the United States and Israel, for example, covered the activities of representative offices of foreign banks, but not agencies, branches, and subsidiaries. The agreement thus implicitly covers offshore banking and fee-based services that can be produced at home or in third countries and sold through local agents in the importing country. By the same token, the agreement excludes foreign retail banking.

In the book written for the AEI series on trade in services, Ingo Walter (1988) provides a comprehensive survey of the international banking industry and of the wide range of restrictions imposed by governments on foreign banking activity. He also discusses how international agreements on trade in services could facilitate the liberalization and expansion of international banking. A detailed discussion of the application of trade concepts to international banking is found in Feketekuty (1981d), "International Trade in Banking Services: The Negotiating Agenda," which is part of a collection titled *The International Framework for Money and Banking*.

Illustrative Sectoral Annotation

The crucial question that has to be answered first with respect to an annotation on banking services is the coverage of such an agreement. Should it encompass all three banking segments—offshore banking, fee-based banking services, and foreign retail banking—or only the first two, insofar as they involve cross-border sales? There is likely to be considerable resistance to any trade agreement on banking, but particularly one that covers the operation of retail banks abroad. The suggestions below cover all three segments, although an agreement might not cover all three areas.

Descriptive Section. For each of the three segments of the market, the descriptive section would provide a detailed description of the services covered by the annotation, the functional, operational activities banks need to carry out in order to provide financial services to foreign customers, and the various types of government regulations that have a bearing on the ability of the banks to carry out the enumerated operational activities. The descriptive section would also review the major regulatory objectives that commonly motivate government regulations that affect banking activities.

Interpretive Section. The interpretive section would focus on the principal concerns that have been expressed by the banking community with respect to their ability to operate internationally.

With respect to offshore banking, for example, the interpretive section could apply the effective market access principle and national treatment principle to the operation of representative offices abroad and the scope of local marketing efforts. It could also apply provisions dealing with the movement of money and personnel to specific issues in offshore banking, such as the application of foreign exchange controls to repayments of loans and travel arrangements for bank officials.

With respect to international sales of fee-based services, this section could apply the principles and rules of the general agreement to such issues as nonestablishment, access to communications facilities, appointment of local agents, access to the credit histories of potential credit card holders, and the ability to collect bills that are due.

With respect to the operation of foreign retail banks abroad, the interpretive section might relate the application of the general principles and rules to the full range of operational problems faced by foreign retail banks, including access to local sources of funds, use of central bank rediscount facilities, scope of lending activities, employment of personnel, discriminatory tax treatment, and the application of foreign exchange restrictions.

The interpretive section of the annotation on banking would thus provide a checklist of the type of commitments that governments would need to make in order to allow banks to operate in a reasonably efficient and equitable manner in another country. Since a number of governments will not want to give up their ability to control foreign banks, the interpretive section could also contain recommendations concerning the type of policy instruments preferred for controlling foreign banking activity.

CONCLUSIONS

The general principles, rules, and procedures of a General Agreement on Trade in Services will have to be augmented by sectoral annotations that spell out with some precision how the general provisions are to be interpreted in the unique environment of each sector. The analytical work on barriers and regulations described in Chapter 10 and the sectoral annotations described in this chapter will thus form the foundation for the general exchange of binding commitments covering all areas of services.

NOTES

1. Other useful material can be found in Feketekuty and Aronson (1984b), Sauvant (1986), Jussawalla (1987), and Rada (1987). Bruce, Cunard, and Director (1985) contains a comprehensive review of the telecommunications regime in the major countries, including recent reforms and the likely course of future regulatory reform. References to further readings can be found in Snow and Jussawalla (1986) and Feketekuty and Aronson (1986).
2. For a comprehensive description of the industry, see White (1988). Other useful sources are Office of Technology Assessment (1983), Schrier, Nadel, and Rifas (1985), and Böhme (1978).
3. For a comprehensive description of the problems created by closed conferences and the UNCTAD Liner Code, provided in testimony before the House Merchant Marine Committee of the U.S. Congress, see Feketekuty (1981b). The restrictive effects of both the closed conferences and the UNCTAD Liner Code create a more serious distortion of free trade in liner shipping than the list of restrictive U.S. measures exhaustively documented by White (1988).
4. For further material on barriers to trade in insurance services see Carter and Dickinson (1979), Hindley (1982), and Baker (1987).

5. See the following articles contained in *Barriers to International Trade in Services*, the 1986 issue of the University of Chicago *Legal Forum*: on legal services, Cone; on negotiations on professional services, Barton; on barriers to trade in professional services, Bhagwati; for an overview of trade in professional services, Feketekuty; on trade in business services, Noyelle and Dutka; and on accounting services, Rossi.

12
NEGOTIATING STRATEGIES FOR BINDING AND REDUCING BARRIERS TO TRADE IN SERVICES

Adoption of a general framework of principles and rules and sectoral annotations that could be negotiated in the Uruguay Round of multilateral trade negotiations would establish basic ground rules for subsequent negotiations aimed at the reduction of barriers to trade but would not commit the signatory governments to reduce specific barriers to trade in services. Such substantive commitments will have to be negotiated over a period of years. Indeed, the dismantling of barriers to services is likely to require many future rounds of negotiations under the umbrella provided by a General Agreement on Trade in Services.

This chapter addresses (a) how negotiations aimed at the liberalization of barriers to trade might be organized, (b) the time sequence in which the general agreement, the sectoral annotations, and the substantive commitments might be negotiated, and (c) the relationship that might exist between them. It also addresses how general trade negotiations carried out on an unconditional most-favored-nation (MFN) basis could relate to negotiations of higher level commitments on regulations that would be carried out on a conditional most-favored-nation basis.

REVIEW OF THE BASIC FRAMEWORK

Signatories of a General Agreement on Trade in Services would be obligated to notify other countries of substantial changes in their regulations that would affect foreign suppliers of services. They would have to give foreign suppliers an opportunity to consult with regulatory officials on the impact such regulations would have on their business. Signatory governments would be obligated to consult with another signatory government when regulation adversely affects the commercial interests of a foreign supplier of services. If such consultations failed to resolve the problem involved, the countries involved would agree to participate in a conciliation or dispute settlement procedure.

Signatories of the general agreement would also be committed to participate in substantive negotiations aimed at binding the level of protection and eliminating barriers to trade. The substantive commitments that would result from negotiations carried out under the general agreement would be bound in national schedules attached to it. The countries involved would agree not to take any actions that would erode the value of such commitments in terms of the commercial opportunities it would provide to commercial enterprises from signatory countries.

While the provisions of the general agreement would not directly commit governments to change specific policy measures affecting trade in services, it would commit governments to pursue the liberalization and expansion of international trade and investment in services and to facilitate the international movement of information, people, and money in support of that objective. By establishing these basic principles as long-term objectives, the general agreement would establish a firm philosophical foundation for the negotiations that would be carried out under the agreement.

In order to give the agreement some immediate applicability at the time of signature, the participating governments could agree to negotiate an initial exchange of substantive commitments prior to the actual signature of the agreement. A number of options are explored below. One would be to establish a standstill commitment that would freeze levels of protection at current levels and commit governments to accord other signatories national treatment with respect to all new regulatory measures that are enacted. A second option would be to establish a soft, best efforts commitment that would commit governments to do what they can within the limits of current laws to facilitate trade and investment in services and the movement of information, people, and money connected with trade in services. A third option would be to organize an initial exchange of negotiated commitments.

In order to prepare for negotiations aimed at the progressive liberalization of barriers to trade in services, governments would agree to participate in a review of national regulations that create barriers to trade in services. Each country would identify regulations in effect in other countries that pose obstacles to trade in services. Such notifications would be compiled into a list available to all member countries, and the affected government would be given an opportunity to defend the measures involved in terms of the regulatory objectives served by such measures. In the course of the examination of the notified measures, other countries would have an opportunity to explore whether the regulatory objectives might be achieved through alternative approaches that would create fewer trade distortions.

NEGOTIATING SUBSTANTIVE COMMITMENTS ON AN MFN BASIS

As discussed in Chapter 8, barriers to trade in services can take the form of 1) regulations that restrict the sale or consumption of services produced by foreign enterprises, 2) regulations that restrict the ability of foreign producers of services to establish or to invest in local facilities and to operate such facilities, 3) regulations that impede the movement of information generated by foreign producers of services, 4) regulations that limit the movement of people employed by foreign enterprises producing services, 5) regulatory barriers to the movement of money or other financial assets, and 6) measures that make it difficult to import or export goods associated with trade in services. In some cases the regulations explicitly discriminate against foreign producers. In other cases, the regulations are not discriminatory but are nevertheless so restrictive that foreign suppliers are unable to obtain meaningful market access. This tends to be the case, in particular, in services subject to tight licensing provisions.

Some barriers may apply only to narrowly defined categories of services (e.g., foreign insurance companies may be prohibited from selling compulsory auto insurance, insuring telephone poles, or insuring buildings in towns of less than 10,000 inhabitants). Other barriers may apply to all services within a broadly defined sector (e.g., all foreign insurance companies may be required to maintain prohibitive deposits in non-interest-earning accounts). Still other barriers may apply to all foreign providers of services (e.g., immigration rules may not allow businesses selling services to obtain commercial visas on the basis of the treaty-trader principle), or to all foreign business activities (e.g., foreign investment restrictions).

There are large differences among countries with respect to the regulations that restrict trade. While in one country investment restrictions may create the most severe barriers to foreign trade, in another country regulations that restrict all forms of competition may pose the most difficult barrier. Negotiations aimed at any one type of policy instrument may therefore result in very different degrees of liberalization in different countries.

These observations about the nature and scope of government regulations that potentially restrict trade in services lead to important conclusions about the organization of negotiations. Negotiations aimed at the progressive liberalization of barriers to trade in services will have to focus on policy instruments that restrict trade as much as on the specific areas of services that might be affected by such restrictive regulations. In order to achieve reciprocal, and therefore negotiable, liberalization of barriers, however, the negotiations will have to address simultaneously a broad range of policy instruments that serve to restrict trade in particular services in different countries.

For the sake of analytical clarity and negotiating efficiency, one could break the process of negotiating the progressive liberalization of barriers to trade in services into three parts. One task facing negotiators will be to identify the policy instruments each country intends to use to achieve trade policy objectives as against domestic regulatory objectives and the policy instruments it is willing to subject *ab initio* to international disciplines designed to assure market access by foreign enterprises.[1] A second task will be to "bind" the degree of protection provided with respect to specific service activities. A third task will be to negotiate a reduction or the elimination of specific discriminatory or restrictive measures.

These three aspects of the negotiating process could be organized into sequential steps, or they could be carried out simultaneously and packaged together with the adoption of the framework agreement. The options involved are explored in greater detail later in this chapter.

The "Exceptions" Approach versus the "Request and Offer" Approach

A key strategic decision facing negotiators will be to decide whether they should adopt an "exceptions" approach or a "request and offer" approach to the negotiation of an initial list of policy instruments and service activities that would be subjected to international discipline. Under an exceptions approach, governments would agree to accept disciplines such as national treatment for all policy instruments and service activities except those enumerated in an exceptions list. Under a request and offer approach governments would agree to accept the disciplines only with respect to specified policy instruments and service activities. In other words, under an exception approach the negotiations would focus on the policy instruments and service activities that would not be covered by the agreed disciplines, while under a request and offer approach the negotiations would focus on the policy instruments and service activities that would be covered.

To some extent, this is an argument over whether it is better to describe a bottle as half full or as half empty. The negotiating dynamics under the two approaches could be quite different, however, and the choice between the two approaches could lead to quite different results. There is wide disagreement, however, about how governments would behave under the two approaches. Those who argue in favor of an exceptions approach believe that adoption of such an approach would lead to a more substantial result, that is, a much wider range of services and policy instruments would initially be subjected to international commitments.

The argument in favor of an exceptions approach revolves around externalities in the negotiating process.[2] Under a request and offer approach, an exporting country must request the application of international disciplines to specific services and policy instruments, but it will do so only if it expects to derive enough benefit from such treatment to warrant "paying" for it through a reciprocal concession. If each of many countries would derive a little benefit, but no one country could expect to derive enough of a benefit to "pay" for it, no request will be made and therefore no offer will be forthcoming.

Under an exceptions approach, services that are not very important to any exporting country would nevertheless automatically be covered by any general commitments to the agreed disciplines unless the importing country felt strongly that it needed to protect that industry. A country, it is argued, would not take an exception unless it was willing to "pay" for it by allowing its trading partners to take additional exceptions. The exceptions approach also leads to the establishment of disciplines in services that are not very important items of trade today but could become important items of trade in the future.

In general, these arguments in favor of an exceptions approach to trade negotiations in services are the same ones that lead to the adoption of a formula/exceptions approach to past tariff negotiations in the GATT.

Those who favor a request and offer approach to the negotiations argue that governments will be afraid to make open-ended commitments since the number of regulations that could be affected by such commitments is very large and it will be difficult for a government to analyze the potential impact of national treatment and market access commitments for all such regulations in the course of the initial negotiating round. In the face of such uncertainty, it is argued, governments will overreact and establish exceptions in many areas where no protection currently exists. Establishment of exceptions where there are no barriers currently could have the perverse result of increasing the uncertainty for business in these areas.

Governments that want to maximize the degree of market liberalization in services will have to weigh the potential advantages against the risks. On the other hand, those governments that are reluctant to go very far in liberalizing markets will certainly insist that negotiations follow a request and offer approach. On balance, this probably tilts the scales in favor of a request and offer approach.

The choice between the two negotiating approaches, however, need not be an either/or proposition. Some elements of the negotiations could follow the exceptions approach, while other elements of the negotiations could be based on the request and offer approach. The negotiations of national treatment, for example, could be based on an exceptions approach, while negotiations on investment and immigration issues could be based on a request and offer approach.

Binding Current Levels of Protection

An early objective of negotiations on trade in services will be to bind the maximum allowable protection. It will be difficult, however, to establish objective, quantifiable ceilings on the maximum allowable protection in services. Under the GATT regime for goods, binding commitments based on tariffs and quotas can be measured with considerable quantitative precision. In services, many restrictive measures take the form of highly complex regulations that are not easily reduced to a single number.

These difficulties argue in favor of the adoption of relatively simple and transparent means for protecting domestic service industries, and this should be a key objective of negotiations aimed at the establishment of maximum ceilings for the protection that is provided. Whatever the difficulties, negotiations aimed at the reduction of barriers will be meaningless unless governments develop the means for establishing meaningful limits on allowable levels of protection.

Negotiating the Reduction of Barriers

As discussed above, negotiations aimed at the reduction of barriers will have to focus both on specific service activities and on the policy instruments that adversely affect the ability of foreign enterprises to sell such services. Any negotiated commitments may apply to the application of a policy instrument to specified services, or they may encompass all services affected by that policy instrument. In other words, commitments to reduce the restrictiveness of investment, taxation, immigration, information transfer, or other regulatory policies could cover specific services, all services that fall into a particular industry, or all tradeable services.

How the reduction of barriers is negotiated will depend, in part, on whether the initial set of commitments are negotiated on an "exceptions" basis or a "request and offer" basis. If the initial commitments are established on an exceptions basis, then subsequent negotiations will naturally be aimed at narrowing or eliminating the initial list of exceptions. If the initial commitments are negotiated on a request and offer basis, then subsequent negotiation will be aimed at expanding the range of services and policy instruments covered by national treatment and open market access commitments.

One issue that will need to be resolved is whether negotiations aimed at the reduction of barriers to trade in services should be organized on a sector-by-sector basis or on a comprehensive basis covering many different sectors. The principal argument in favor of organizing negotiations along sectoral lines is that each service sector tends to have a unique regulatory and institutional structure and that policy issues also tend to be defined in sectoral terms.

The principal argument against organizing negotiations along sectoral lines is that any negotiation limited to a particular sector will be dominated by the regulators in that sector, and in such a negotiation the economic benefits of liberalization would receive very little weight as compared with the concern of the regulators to preserve the current regulatory structure. A negotiation organized purely along sectoral lines would also limit the possibility for negotiating mutually acceptable reductions in barriers since it may be very difficult to persuade a country that lacks competitive strength in any given sector to liberalize its policies in that sector in exchange for the removal of barriers in that same sector by a country that has a highly competitive industry. In short, a sectoral negotiation limits the possibility of mutually advantageous trade-offs.

In the first instance, any negotiations aimed at the reduction of barriers to trade in services should be organized on as broad a basis as possible, covering many different sectors. Negotiations organized on purely sectoral lines should generally be pursued only after the possibilities for liberalization on a comprehensive basis are exhausted. There is one major exception to this rule of thumb, and that involves negotiations carried out among governments that have committed themselves to deregulate a particular sector in services.

NEGOTIATING REGULATORY COMMITMENTS ON A CONDITIONAL MFN BASIS

In certain services, real liberalization of international trade is possible only among countries that permit unlimited domestic competition. Countries that would be prepared to agree, for example, to ensure unlimited competition in a particular industry could decide to grant each other open access to their respective markets. Such agreements would be negotiated on a conditional most-favored-nation basis. As noted in the last chapter, however, governments that enter into such agreements would be required to extend such agreements to other countries, provided such countries are prepared to accept the substantive obligations of the agreement, including commitments of the nature and scope of domestic regulations in that sector.

The possibilities for negotiating higher level agreements involving binding commitments on regulatory policies are explored below for a number of key sectors.

Telecommunications and Data Processing

The wide divergence in regulatory policies, and the differences in the pace at which different countries are adjusting their policies to changes in telecommunications technology, make it highly probable that countries that have moved further than others in deregulating the telecommunications sector will want to negotiate agreements among themselves, providing expanded opportunities for international competition in telecommunications services. The companion volume by Aronson and Cowhey (1988) on telecommunications services contains many interesting ideas on the scope and content of such agreements.

Aviation

In the companion volume on aviation, Dan Kasper (1988) describes economic forces that are likely to lead to a gradual breakdown of the current system of bilateral agreements in aviation. He describes in detail an agreement that might be negotiated among a number of like-minded countries for open, multilateral competition among airlines. An agreement along the lines proposed by Kasper could well be accommodated within the framework of a general agreement as proposed in Chapter 10 and sectoral annotations on aviation as proposed in Chapter 11.

Maritime Transport

The degree of liberalization that can be achieved within the existing institutional and regulatory framework for international shipping is probably quite limited. In order to achieve a breakthrough, it will be necessary to negotiate a new regulatory framework that will subject the operation of the conference system to strict international disciplines. In addition, such an agreement would have to encompass the right to invest in shore facilities and in local land transport facilities. Without such a major overhaul among like-minded countries, the resistance to liberalization will be difficult to overcome.

Insurance

A regulatory agreement on insurance among like-minded countries could establish common fiduciary standards for insurance companies admitted to the countries covered by the agreement, and mutual recognition of the fiduciary supervision exercised by each country's regulatory authorities. Such an agreement could open the way for the elimination of special deposit requirements on foreign insurers, and the open sale of insurance across national borders without local establishment.

Professional Services

It is highly likely that major breakthroughs in the liberalization of barriers to the international movement of professionals will come only in the context of agreements negotiated among smaller groups of like-minded countries. Such agreements will probably have to be negotiated by those most directly involved in the accreditation of professionals, and the respective professional associations. A model of what such agreements could look like is provided by the inter-recognition agreement negotiated by the National Association of Architectural Review Boards in the United States with their counterparts in the United Kingdom. Similar agreement are under negotiation with a number of other countries including Australia and Canada.

Banking

In his volume on international banking, Ingo Walter (1988) describes the contents of a sectoral agreement that might be negotiated on international trade in banking services. It would provide (a) freedom to establish branches, agencies, subsidiaries, or other facilities, (b) regulatory symmetry with respect to domestic and foreign competitors, which would include the right to manage local currency issues, (c) freedom to import critical resources, including travel and resettlement of professional staff, access to telecommunications, and the ability to process data locally or abroad, (d) symmetry with respect to the application of foreign exchange controls, and (e) equality of access to domestic client groups.

ALTERNATIVE SCENARIOS FOR NEGOTIATING BARRIERS TO TRADE IN SERVICES

A number of negotiating scenarios either have been proposed by some countries or should be considered as logical alternatives. Five such scenarios are described below. Each of these negotiating strategies or scenarios has different strengths and weaknesses in terms of the criteria described above. Each would help advance the achievement of some of the objectives and retard others.

Scenario 1: Evolutionary. The general agreement would establish a framework for bilateral, plurilateral, and multilateral negotiations among signatory countries on any sector in services they wish to address in such negotiations.[3] Basically the agreement would encourage groups of countries that shared common objectives or a common regulatory philosophy to get together and negotiate agreements that would be open to other countries that have signed the general agreement to join. Signature of the general agreement would initiate an evolutionary process whereby agreements negotiated among small groups of like-minded countries are gradually expanded to cover all the countries that have signed the general agreement.[4]

Scenario 2: Sectoral. The framework of principles and procedures contained in the general agreement would provide a common reference point for subsequent sectoral negotiations.

All substantive commitments would be negotiated in the context of such sectoral negotiations, and in the case of any conflicts between the principles of the general agreement and the terms of a sectoral agreement, the provisions of the sectoral agreement would prevail.[5]

Scenario 3: Sequential. The negotiation of the general agreement would be followed by the negotiation of annotations for the key sectors, which would be followed by a general exchange of legally binding commitments on a request and offer basis. Each step would require a consensus among all the countries that decide to join the general agreement. The negotiation of higher level agreements among like-minded countries would not take place until the possibilities for liberalization on an MFN basis had been exhausted. The general agreement would include a standstill commitment on the introduction of new restrictions and a conciliation procedure for the resolution of disputes. The sectoral annotations would be developed in conjunction with the identification and examination of regulations that are seen by businesses as barriers to trade in services.[6]

Scenario 4: Grandfather. The general agreement would commit governments to substantive commitments on market access, national treatment, and foreign investments, but it would grandfather all existing laws and regulations. Such laws and regulations that create barriers to trade would be reduced through subsequent negotiations. These negotiations would encompass all countries that signed the general agreement, though any subset of those countries would be free to go ahead with an agreement on their own if a general consensus among all countries proved too difficult to achieve.[7]

Scenario 5: Exceptions. The general agreement would commit governments to substantive commitments on market access, national treatment, and foreign investment except to the extent that such countries notified specific regulations as barriers to trade and investment. This would be followed by negotiations aimed at the removal of barriers that were notified at the time the general agreement was adopted. Under this scenario, the negotiation of sectoral annotations as well as a subsequent general exchange of commitments among signatory countries could be seen as steps in the process of reducing the number of barriers.[8]

CRITERIA FOR EVALUATING ALTERNATIVE NEGOTIATING SCENARIOS

The decisions that are made on these organizational issues will influence the outcome of the negotiations. The decision to include many substantive commitments in the framework agreement, for example, might reduce the number of countries willing to sign the agreement. Since such commitments could not be very precisely defined, countries might insist on a long list of national exceptions, or they could interpret the commitment so broadly as to create many subsequent disagreements over the scope and interpretation of the commitment.

The decision to obligate all signatory countries to participate in the negotiation of sectoral annotations or a subsequent general exchange of substantive commitments would be likely to slow down the pace of the negotiations and reduce the overall depth of liberalization, while it would ensure that a wider group of countries participate in the liberalization process and that the resulting agreements can be implemented on an unconditional most-favored-nation basis.

A decision to carry out all substantive negotiations on a sectoral basis would inevitably leave some sectors behind, and it would also reduce the overall liberalization achieved since it would increase the influence of sectoral regulators who can be expected to resist commitments that require changes in their regulations. On the other hand, the absence of a sectoral focus would result in agreements that cannot be fully implemented because their implementation requires domestic regulatory reforms that can be achieved only with the participation of the regulatory authorities involved.

The various negotiating scenarios thus need to be evaluated in terms of their effect on the achievement of various operational objectives one might establish for the negotiations. Six such objectives readily come to mind. As will become apparent, however, it is impossible to frame a negotiating approach that will facilitate the achievement of each of these six objectives simultaneously. As is often true in life, difficult trade-offs must be confronted.

The six operational objectives that can be used as criteria for evaluating alternative negotiating strategies or scenarios are as follows:

1. ***Early results.*** Everyone involved in the process—the services industry, the government, and the press—will lose patience with the process if it takes too long to achieve concrete results.

2. ***Significant liberalization.*** The success or failure of the negotiations will ultimately be judged on the extent to which they have advanced the liberalization of trade in services, their principal objective.

3. ***Broad liberalization across sectors.*** Any ambitious trade liberalization agreement has to cover a large number of sectors both to gain domestic political support and to muster the necessary international consensus among a significant number of countries. There has to be something in an agreement for a broad range of economic interests if it is to succeed. This is a simple matter of political arithmetic. It is also good economic policy.

4. ***Clarity and precision of binding legal commitments.*** A lack of precision and clarity in legal commitments leads to future disputes and a loss of credibility for the agreement. While the art and politics of negotiations frequently require a certain degree of ambiguity in trade agreements, excessive ambiguity is bound to discredit the agreement and create more friction and rancor than would have existed without the agreement.

5. ***Resolution of disputes.*** An agreement should facilitate the resolution of commercial disputes over trade in services. A framework agreement cannot establish detailed rules covering the full range of regulatory issues that can arise, but it should be

able to establish principles and procedures that make it easier to resolve disputes.

6. *Nondiscriminatory treatment of countries.* While it will be necessary to modify the unconditional most-favored-nation principle of the GATT to build international cooperation in the face of widely different domestic regulatory systems, discrimination among countries should be kept to a minimum. Excessive discrimination among countries undermines the common sense of purpose among members of an agreement and leads to ill will.

These six objectives inevitably conflict. For example, in order to assure early results it may be necessary to sacrifice precision in commitments, magnitude of liberalization, the number of sectors covered by any liberalization, or the number of countries included in the agreement. In order to obtain precision in commitments it may be necessary to narrow the focus of the negotiation on a sectoral basis, sacrificing the scope of any liberalization.

BASIC GROUND RULES FOR ORGANIZING THE NEGOTIATIONS

While there is no ideal strategy that is inherently superior, it is possible to establish some basic ground rules for developing a strategy that is balanced in terms of its impact on the six operational negotiating objectives enumerated above.

Ground Rule 1. Any negotiating approach should maintain a constant balance between the general principles contained in the framework agreement and sectoral realities. Much of the work in connection with the negotiations will have to be carried out on a sectoral basis by sectoral experts. But such sectoral results should always be a part of broader negotiations and subjected to the general principles of the framework agreement. Any purely sectoral discussion is likely to turn into an effort to justify and reinforce sectoral regulations that tend to be restrictive and interventionist. Any negotiation carried out on a purely sectoral basis is also likely to miss liberalizing opportunities by not making such sectoral results a part of a broader package. On the other hand, any discussion carried out by generalists operating under general trade principles is likely to be significantly removed from the real world and therefore unlikely to be taken seriously in the end and will not provide the necessary precision and clarity that are desirable for binding legal commitments incurred by governments.

Ground Rule 2. Governments should not enter into binding legal commitments unless they have been able to develop a clear understanding of the issues involved and are able to spell out the binding legal commitment with some clarity. If it becomes desirable to achieve some early substantive results, best efforts commitments are likely to be better than binding legal commitments based on imprecise information about the impact of such commitments on existing policies and regulations and unrealistic expectations by foreign suppliers about the nature of the commitments.

Ground Rule 3. Governments should bend over backward to preserve the broad multilateral character of the agreement and include as many countries as possible in the negotiations as long as possible. Negotiations among smaller groups of countries that want to make faster and more far-reaching progress should be treated as the exception rather than the rule. Conversely, countries that are not prepared to participate in agreements that result in substantial liberalization of trade and a reduction in domestic regulations should not be encouraged to sign the framework agreement.

Ground Rule 4. Governments should organize the negotiations in such a way that they can achieve some substantive results reasonably early in the negotiating process in order to convince people that this is a worthwhile effort that will yield practical results. Since it will not be possible to establish precise understandings on many subjects in a short period of time, such early substantive results either will have to be limited in terms of the services covered or will have to take the form of a best efforts commitment rather than a legally binding obligation.

Ground Rule 5. Governments should recognize the evolutionary character of an effort to build a comprehensive trade regime for services. There has to be considerable room for experimentation and for the negotiation of practical solutions to problems.

CONCLUSIONS

In order to make real substantive progress toward the liberalization of trade in services, governments will have to address a long list of sensitive issues in a new and untried context. Officials from a wide range of government departments who have not spent much time speaking to one another will have to cooperate, overcoming basic instincts of bureaucratic turf. The negotiations will have to deal with complex domestic regulations, without becoming enmeshed in a debate over regulatory philosophy or haggling over detailed regulations.

Will it work? Ultimately all the principles, rules, and procedures are merely tools. The negotiations will succeed in making substantive progress toward a greater liberalization of services if everyone involved—trade officials, regulatory officials, business and labor leaders—sees the broader opportunity for mutual economic gain and comes to share the sense of excitement provided by a new challenge.

NOTES

1. The term *international disciplines* is used here to cover a broad range of commitments, including national treatment of service products (which would cover cross-border trade in services), national treatment of service providers (which would cover the production of services by foreign enterprises inside the importing country, including the right to invest in production facilities), market access commitments (which would establish market

access rights where domestic regulations limit overall competition in a particular service product, and commitments with respect to cross-border flows of information, money, goods, or people tied to trade in services).
2. These externalities exist under any request and offer approach. They are magnified when the negotiating results are covered by the most-favored-nation principle, under which commitments negotiated between any two governments are automatically extended to all other governments.
3. Plurilateral negotiations are negotiations that would be conducted by some but not all countries that have signed the general agreement. Multilateral negotiations are negotiations that would be conducted among all countries that have signed the general agreement.
4. An approach along these lines has been proposed by Switzerland in the multilateral trade negotiations on services currently under way in Geneva. Another variation has been proposed informally by Joseph Greenwald, a former senior U.S. diplomat with extensive experience on trade negotiations. Greenwald suggests that the development of substantive rules could take place through a common law approach, in which the resolution of bilateral disputes gradually leads to a body of generally accepted norms.
5. This scenario is similar in some ways to suggestions made by John Jackson in a monograph to be published by the American Enterprise Institute in 1988.
6. This scenario would be the most logically consistent approach to the negotiations, and would emerge naturally from the structure of agreements proposed in Chapters 10 and 11. In some ways the pattern of this scenario is similar to the process that has been followed under the bilateral agreement on trade in services negotiated between the United States and Israel. The negotiation of a framework agreement has been followed by the discussion of sectoral annotations as a prelude to the establishment of legally binding commitments.
7. This scenario is closely patterned after the bilateral agreement on trade in services between Canada and the United States. It also is a close approximation of the scenario implied by the negotiating proposal tabled by the United States in the multilateral trade negotiations in Geneva. The European Community has proposed a variation on this proposal that also bears a strong resemblance on to the second and third scenarios described above. According

to the proposal by the European Community, adoption of the framework agreement would be accompanied by (a) an agreed list of policy objectives for each services sector; (b) an agreed illustrative list of regulations that would be considered an appropriate means for achieving such objectives; (c) an agreed list of inappropriate types of regulation that would become subject to liberalization through negotiations carried out on an MFN basis. Any regulations that violated the nondiscrimination and national treatment principles would be considered inappropriate on an a priori basis, and therefore subject to negotiations. Negotiations aimed at the liberalization of measures deemed inappropriate would be carried out periodically in an effort to move toward comparable market access in all countries in each sector. In addition, the framework agreement would contain a standstill commitment with respect to new regulations similar or comparable to those already identified as inappropriate.

8. This approach closely parallels the approach that OECD countries took in the negotiation of the Invisibles Code.

APPENDIX: THE HISTORY OF A CAMPAIGN: HOW SERVICES BECAME A TRADE ISSUE

How do you sell a new concept such as trade negotiations on services to the world community? This book has documented all the reasons it makes sense to negotiate multilateral trade agreements in services. However compelling the arguments for trade negotiations on services, the international consensus to include trade in services in the Uruguay Round of multilateral trade negotiations did not emerge spontaneously and was forged only with considerable difficulty. Undoubtedly the time was ripe for a new approach to services, and if the growing role of trade in services in the world economy were not so apparent all around us, no amount of planning and cajoling would have persuaded ministers from around the world to embark on global negotiations on an entirely new issue. At the same time if it had not been for the foresight and determined leadership of a small group of individuals, it would not have happened in 1986 and it might not have emerged in a trade framework.

This appendix traces the history of the events that led from an idea in the early 1970s to a decision in 1986 by ministers from around the world to launch multilateral trade negotiations on services as part of the Uruguay round of multilateral trade negotiations.[1] This is a remarkably short time if one considers that before 1973 there had been no public discussion of trade in services, no one had thought about the issue in a systematic manner, most people thought that services were not tradeable, and it would have been difficult to find a trade official who thought that services had anything to do with trade policy.

APPENDIX

THE BIRTH OF A CONCEPT

One of the first people to recognize the new importance of trade in services in a rapidly integrating world economy was Hugh Corbet, an Australian who had written on international economic issues for the *Times* in the mid-1960s. As a writer on international economic issues, Corbet had become increasingly aware that the "informed" public understood very little about trade policy. Moreover, neither the academic community nor government policymakers seemed equipped or inclined to fill this gap in public knowledge, which in practice meant a lack of public support for "good" trade policy. Corbet therefore decided in 1968 to establish the Trade Policy Research Center in London, which commissions articles and books on trade policy geared to the intelligent layman and sponsors conferences and seminars on trade policy.

As Corbet thought about the trade policy issues the center should address, it occurred to him that services were playing an increasingly important role in the world economy. Indeed, it would have been difficult for an economic observer in London during the 1960s not to be aware of the rapid growth of international services. During these years, London was one of the principal centers in the world for international services such as insurance, banking, publishing, theater, and shipping. What is more, an earlier study of nontariff barriers to trade in goods and how they might be tackled in GATT negotiations gave Corbet the idea that a similar study of barriers to trade in services might provide the basis for similar negotiations in services (Corbet, 1977). He therefore commissioned Brian Griffiths, an economist at the London School of Economics, to undertake a study of international flows of services and restrictions on transactions in the services sector. The resulting book, *Invisible Barriers to Invisible Trade*, was published by the Trade Policy Research Center in 1975. It became the starting point for much of the subsequent work in the field, and the Trade Policy Research Center has played a key role in the development of international thinking on trade and investment in services since that time.

First Official Recognition of Trade in Services

In the meantime, in September 1972, a group of eminent individuals from key industrial countries, under the chairmanship of Jean Rey, the former president of the Commission of the European Community, issued a report on the long-term trade issues facing the world economy. The *Report by the High Level Group on Trade and Related Problems* provided the intellectual underpinnings for the Tokyo Round of multilateral trade negotiations. It contained a short chapter on trade in services and was the first published document of any kind to discuss trade in services as "trade in services."

The Rey group was the brainchild of Emile van Lennep, the secretary general of the Organization of Economic Cooperation of Development, an intergovernmental organization that seeks to improve economic cooperation among industrial countries through the analysis of common policy challenges. By learning from each other, policymakers from different countries are able to develop a better understanding of economic problems and, where appropriate, to establish a coordinated approach to required solutions. Every year, the ministers from the member countries meet in May to review economic trends and to evaluate the major challenges facing the world economy.

In 1971 many trade policy officials in the key industrial countries had come to the conclusion that a new effort was needed to liberalize trade. Van Lennep therefore convened a group of eminent individuals to analyze trade and related problems in a longer term perspective, i.e., to define the problems and assess their relative urgency, consider how they might be dealt with, and set out options for their solution.

The decision to include a chapter on trade in services was largely due to several individuals associated with the preparation of the report. One was Bill Eberle, a prominent American businessman; another was Bertil Ohlin, a well-known Swedish economist. A third was Sir Richard Powell, who had been extensively briefed by a study group put together by the Trade Policy Research Center. Drawing on their own experiences and those of their associates, they shared the view that services were of growing importance to world trade and that barriers to services would need to be addressed more systematically by governments.

Another person who played a key role in adding services to the report of the Rey group was Harald Malmgren, a brilliant American trade policy thinker and friend of Hugh Corbet who had been hired by van Lennep to draft the papers used by the high level group in its work.

The report issued by the high level group noted that while

> a large number of activities in the services sector do not give rise to international transactions ... there are important areas in which international exchanges have risen steeply, in fact in the same proportion as trade in goods or to an even greater extent.... The services sector, like the industrial sector, is experiencing a measure of internationalization and interpenetration. For some countries trade in services is at least as important as, and in some cases more important than, merchandise trade (OECD, 1973: p. 63).

The report also noted that

> the Group has not made a detailed examination of questions concerning international trade in services. It considers however that, from the point of view of international economic relations, this sector poses problems similar in nature to those met with in merchandise trade. Given that services are a sector which seems likely to expand rapidly in countries' economies, the main need is to avoid any tendencies to protectionism and to aim at achieving a more thorough liberalization (OECD, 1973).

The report concluded, "The Group considers that action should be taken by the developed countries to ensure liberalization and non-discrimination in the services sector."

Even though the report succinctly established the rationale for launching negotiations aimed at the liberalization of trade in services, the Rey group stopped short of recommending that the GATT address trade in services. Instead, the group recommended that the OECD work out further steps to be taken in areas such as tourism and transport. Curiously, the last sentence on services was addressed to the treatment of developing countries: "As in the case of goods, consideration might be given to allowing developing countries a limited time to adapt themselves before undertaking the full commitments" (OECD, 1973). This sentence seems to point to future negotiations on trade in services outside the OECD framework, without saying so explicitly.

The U.S. Congress Mandates Negotiations on Trade in Services

The next major step toward the incorporation of services in trade policy took place in the U.S. Congress. Without an explicit delegation of authority by the Congress, a U.S. president can do very little in the trade policy area. Before it could therefore participate in the new Tokyo Round of multilateral trade negotiations, the administration needed to obtain legislation authorizing U.S. participation. It is always ironic that the United States, which usually takes the lead in developing an international consensus on the launching of multilateral trade negotiations, usually finds itself without the necessary authority to participate in such negotiations at the time they are launched.

Congressional consideration of legislation to authorize U.S. participation in multilateral trade negotiations inevitably becomes a broader debate over the conduct of U.S. trade policy. Every economic interest group is given the opportunity to make its case for special consideration not only in the coming multilateral trade negotiations but also in the conduct of day-to-day trade policy. One of the new issues to emerge from congressional consideration of the Trade Act of 1974 was trade in services. It is not entirely clear which company first came up with the idea of using the trade bill to advance the international commercial interests of the services industries, though the recollections seem to point to Pan American Airways.

Pan American had run into some difficulties in persuading a number of countries that it was as qualified to carry the international mail as the national airline, and it seemed to Pan

American that national regulations preventing them from carrying the mail were no different from barriers to trade in goods. Pan American had also run into restrictive regulations on aircraft repairs, which it believed could be dealt with in the context of trade negotiations.

It was an executive at another company, however, who saw the full potential of expanding the definition of international trade to cover international trade in services. Ron Shelp had only recently been appointed vice president in charge of international relations at the American International Group (AIG), the American insurance company with the largest international business. Shelp had previously been with the International Department of the U.S. Chamber of Commerce, where he worked on international trade issues. He was therefore familiar with international trade concepts, and with the assistance provided by the U.S. government to merchandise exporters in the form of export promotion activities and negotiations aimed at the reduction of foreign trade barriers. Shelp reasoned that if services could be included under the definition of trade, the government would give U.S. exporters of services the same kind of assistance.

With the full support of the president and CEO of his company, Hank Greenberg, Shelp organized a full-fledged campaign to extend many of the provisions of the trade act to services. Representatives from a number of service industries joined the campaign and offered public testimony in hearings organized by the Senate Finance Committee. Persuasive testimony was offered by representatives of the Air Transport Association, the American Institute of Marine Underwriters, the American Institute of Merchant Shipping, and the National Constructors Association. It is an ironic twist of history that all of these organizations, with the exception of the insurance industry, are now either opposed to or at best reluctant supporters of multilateral trade negotiations in services.

The Trade Act of 1974 included a number of key provisions on trade in services. The most important of these provisions is probably found in Section 102, which gave the president authority to negotiate on nontariff barriers to trade. Paragraph g(3) of Section 102 says simply that "the term 'international trade' includes trade in both goods and services." By simply expanding the definition of international trade, the Congress thus directed the president to concern himself not only with barriers to trade in goods, but also with barriers to trade in services.

Section 121, which dealt with the reform of the GATT, directed the president to seek "the extension of GATT articles to conditions of trade not presently covered in order to move toward more fair trade practices." While services were not explicitly mentioned, the language of the text, read in conjunction with the other provisions, clearly implied such coverage.

Section 135 of the bill directed the president to establish an Advisory Committee for Trade Negotiations to provide overall policy advice for the negotiations, and the language of paragraph b(1) makes it clear that the committee should include "representatives of . . . service industries."

Section 163 of the Trade Act dealt with the annual report which the president must submit to the Congress on the administration of trade policy. Section 163a directed the president to include information on "the results of action taken to obtain the removal of foreign trade restrictions (including discriminatory restrictions against U.S. exports) and the removal of foreign practices which discriminate against U.S. service industries (including transportation and tourism)."

Section 301 directs the president to retaliate against foreign practices that burden the commerce of the United States, and at the end of paragraph a the Senate Finance Committee had added, "For purposes of this subsection, the term 'commerce' includes services associated with international trade."

THE EFFORT TO NEGOTIATE ON TRADE IN SERVICES IN THE TOKYO ROUND

The Tokyo Round of multilateral trade negotiations was launched in September 1973, on the basis of an agenda approved by trade ministers at a ministerial meeting held in Tokyo. By the time the Congress passed the legislation authorizing U.S. participation (January 3, 1975), the negotiations had already been under way for more than a year. The agreed agenda for the negotiations was extremely ambitious even without the inclusion of trade in services, and services was a totally unfamiliar subject for most trade policy officials, including officials in the United States.

Development of a U.S. Government Strategy

The first step taken by the government was to ask one of the young professionals who had recently joined the Office of the Special Trade Representative to prepare a policy paper for consideration by the interagency policy committee. The professional assigned to the task was Bruce Wilson, who is now the assistant U.S. trade representative for industry and services. Wilson reached a number of key conclusions:

> International trade in services has become an important element of almost every country's balance of payments. Consequently, it is necessary that such trade be carried on in a manner that is fair and equitable to each party involved. The aim of multilateral negotiations on trade problems is to create a world trading system which is just to all who participate in that system. For that reason, it may be no longer appropriate for the participants to focus exclusively on international trade in goods without giving proper attention to the problems still encountered in international trade in services.... Although the GATT is not presently structured to address problems of international trade of services, the President may seek to reform the GATT to include such problems should he deem it necessary (Wilson, 1975, p. 3).

Interagency discussion of the issue on the basis of Wilson's paper led to a decision to establish a White House Interagency Task Force on Services and the MTN to identify the problems faced by U.S. service industries in international commerce and to develop recommendations for addressing them. To support the work of the task force, the Commerce Department commissioned a comprehensive study of trade in services by Wolf and Company, a private consulting firm (Wolf and Company, 1976).

The task force concluded that trade in services posed far too many complex issues to permit a comprehensive negotiation with so little preparation. The U.S. administration, however, could not ignore the legislative mandate without possibly jeopardizing congressional approval of the final results of the negotiations. Moreover, Frederick Dent, who had become the special trade representative in 1975, was determined to negotiate an agreement that would receive the support of all U.S. industries and economic groups, including the services industries. Dent also took a special interest in services. The task force report, issued in December 1976, therefore recommended that issues related to trade in services should be raised in the multilateral trade negotiations on a "carefully selected" basis. More specifically, the report proposed that the special trade representative should be requested to explore the feasibility of

1. Introducing selected and specific trade-related service industry problems into discussion of codes pertaining to subsidies and to government procurement practices
2. Discussing a limited number of barriers pertaining to services trade with selected countries in the bilateral phase of the MTN
3. Introducing service industries in the broader context of improving the GATT (U.S. Department of Commerce, 1976, p. 62)

Tokyo Round Negotiating Results in Services

On the basis of this strategy, the United States succeeded in inserting references to services in three nontariff agreements. The three references to services established relatively modest, indirect obligations on the treatment of services and they applied to services only insofar as they affected trade in goods. Nevertheless, a precedent was set for addressing services issues in trade agreements.

One of the three nontariff codes with a reference to services was the Government Procurement Code, which established agreed bidding procedures for purchases made by government in order to assure that foreign suppliers would not be disadvantaged. The provisions of the Government Procurement Code were extended to services such as transportation and insurance, insofar as such services were required to sell internationally traded goods to governments.

The second nontariff code that contains a provision dealing with services is the Standards Code, which establishes some basic rules and procedures for the adoption of government standards on internationally traded goods, in order to assure that such standards do not discriminate against foreign goods. The Standards Code includes provisions dealing with the recognition of test results provided by foreign testing laboratories. Such testing, of course, is a service and use of such test results in other countries constitutes trade in services.

The third nontariff code that contains language on services is the Subsidies Code, which limits the use of government subsidies with respect to internationally traded goods. Under the Subsidies Code, services used to export goods are not allowed to be subsidized.

In addition to these provisions, the United States obtained an informal commitment from the other industrial countries to undertake a comprehensive study of trade in services in the Trade Committee of the Organization for Economic Cooperation and Development. The objective of the study was to determine if it was possible to identify trade issues in services that would lend themselves to negotiation in future trade agreements.

Ultimately, the Tokyo Round achieved some results because business leaders such as Shelp and Greenberg from AIG and Harry Freeman from American Express were not willing to let the administration forget about services. Bob Strauss appointed Greenberg to the Presidential Advisory Committee for Trade Negotiations, which provided high-level private sector advice to U.S. negotiators, and once on the committee, Greenberg kept reminding Strauss of the legislative mandate on services. At the same time Shelp persuaded the U.S. Chamber of Commerce to organize a services committee, which could monitor the government's response to the legislation and exert pressure on the administration to take the legislation seriously.

DEVELOPMENT OF A STRATEGY TO BUILD SUPPORT FOR NEGOTIATION

With the decision to launch a comprehensive study of trade in services in the OECD, the work on trade in services entered a new stage. It was now possible to approach the subject in terms of serious, long-term effort to lay the groundwork for future negotiations. Since I represented the United States in the OECD Trade Committee, it fell to me to organize the campaign, and soon thereafter I was given full responsibility for all facets of U.S. trade policy in services.

At about the same time, a change in administration led to the appointment of William E. Brock as the new U.S. trade representative. Brock had developed a keen interest in services previously as a member of the Banking Committee of the U.S. Senate, and he brought dynamic political leadership to the effort to integrate services into the domestic and international trade policy framework.

It had become quite apparent that building an international consensus in support of multilateral trade negotiations represented a major challenge. First, except for the excellent study carried out by Wolf and Company in 1975–76 and the 1975 study prepared by Brian Griffiths for the Trade Policy Research Center in London, information about trade in services and barriers to such trade was totally inadequate. Moreover, very few businessmen, including those in the services sector, looked at international services activities in trade terms. In fact, most people, including most economists, thought that one of the principal distinctions between services and goods was that services were not tradeable and that economic activity in the services sector was therefore insulated from global economic pressures.

Trade officials had little knowledge about services and the policy responsibility was scattered among dozens of departments, ministries, and regulatory agencies in the national government, and in lower levels of government. The industries benefiting from existing systems of protection and the regulatory agencies that administer that protection are well entrenched and politically powerful, and the protective measures are not easy to identify because they are embedded in domestic regulations. How are you to know what is a trade barrier and what is a purely domestic regulatory measure? Giving trade officials a role in the administration of domestic regulatory policies in services was bound to be highly controversial, and it was easy to understand why the average trade official would want to shirk the resulting bureaucratic wars.

In order to break through the widespread public ignorance and sectoral resistance it was necessary to develop a comprehensive strategy that would address both directly. A strategy was needed that would change public perceptions of the nature and role of services in the international economy and would institutionalize a role for trade policy officials in services. Accordingly I developed such a strategy in cooperation with a loose international coalition of about a dozen key business executives and government officials. The strategy included a comprehensive program of studies and conferences, a pubic information campaign, full integration of services into the trade policy machinery, active use of bilateral trade channels to resolve bilateral disputes in services, full utilization of all existing international institutions and mechanisms in the trade area, and a long-term program to improve government statistics on trade in services.[2]

The aim of the program of studies and conferences was not only to supplement the fairly limited resources available to trade officials to gather information, but to develop a core of government officials, business leaders, and academicians knowledgeable about trade in services, involved in the work on trade in services, and committed to the effort to build a consensus in support of multilateral negotiations.

The public information program was designed to create public awareness of trade in services to overcome the wide public view that such trade did not exist, and to educate the trade policy community about the issues in trade in services and how they might be tackled in trade negotiations. In each country, a certain number of business executives, academicians, and former trade policy officials play an important role in developing a national consensus on trade policy, and this collection of individuals had to become informed on the substantive issues in trade in services in order to change the policies of the countries involved.

The effort to integrate services into the trade policy machinery and trade policy process in the United States was designed both to provide some immediate benefits for U.S. exporters of services and to engage trade officials in other governments on issues dealing with trade in services. Dealing with current issues on a bilateral basis provided an immediate rationale for building the governmental machinery that was needed to support multilateral trade negotiations on services. It also forced governments to sort out the responsibilities of dozens of bureaucratic fiefdoms in each government.

Building Up Information and Knowledge on Services

With the completion of the Tokyo Round, the relationship between the U.S. government and the American business community entered a new cooperative phase. Up to this time, the business community felt it was fighting an uphill battle trying to persuade a reluctant government to adopt a more activist trade policy in services. The government on its part was sympathetic to the cause but felt that its resources and the time available were inadequate to achieve major breakthroughs in the Tokyo Round. Once the Tokyo Round was completed, however, the government was willing to dedicate itself to the more long-term task of building the domestic and international consensus necessary to pursue successful negotiations. In turn, the business community recognized that it had to shoulder part of the responsibility for developing the information and analysis needed to prepare for the negotiations and for building wider support in the business community at home and abroad for negotiations on services.

Ron Shelp continued to play a key part in this effort in multiple roles. For some time, Shelp had been attending meetings of the OECD insurance committee, and this had given him unique insights into the OECD process and how it could be used to build governmental consensus. As chairman of the services committee of the Chamber of Commerce, he was able to help the government in collecting information on barriers to trade in services, and later, as chairman of the Industry Sector Advisory Committee on Services, he worked closely in crafting a trade strategy for services. Shelp also wrote a pathbreaking book on trade in services titled *Beyond Industrialization*, and publication of that book helped to broaden public understanding of the issue.

In addition to Shelp, Harry Freeman and Joan Spero from the American Express Company assumed leading roles in organizing conferences, developing press material, lobbying in Congress, and building support in the business community at home and abroad. Freeman and Spero used their participation in bilateral business meetings with business leaders from other countries to develop statements of business support for negotiations on trade in services. Together with other business leaders, they helped to support conferences on trade in services in the United States and abroad. They also used their membership in a variety of business organizations and public policy research institutes to persuade these organizations to launch research studies on trade in services. When the time came to establish a senior advisory committee to the U.S. trade representative on services trade policy, Freeman persuaded James D. Robinson, the chairman and CEO of the American Express Company, to become its chairman.

Through the efforts of Shelp, Freeman, and others a long list of organizations and institutions became involved in carrying out studies of trade in services, in sponsoring seminars and conferences, and in passing resolutions in support of trade negotiations in services. The list of organizations includes the U.S. Council for International Business, the Council of Foreign Relations, the National Foreign Trade Council, the Committee for Economic Development, the Conference Board, the Center for Strategic and

International Studies, and the American Enterprise Institute. With the help of the German Marshall Fund, I organized a research conference that brought together international economists and economists who specialized in specific areas of services.

The government also had more specific needs for information in order to support the establishment of policy objectives and priorities for future negotiations on trade in services and to provide the necessary raw material for studies in the OECD and the GATT. The government could have chosen to collect this information through official surveys, but the bureaucratic requirements proved too cumbersome and time consuming. U.S. trade officials therefore turned to the U.S. Chamber of Commerce and its services committee to help organize a survey of barriers faced by U.S. service industries in selling services abroad. The data collected from that survey, organized by industry and type of barrier, provided the first comprehensive overview of the barriers faced by businesses engaged in international trade in services. This document, which has come to be referred to as the U.S. trade representative's inventory, remains one of the most detailed sources of information about barriers in this area. (See Office of the U.S. Trade Representative, 1979.)

In addition to the information about barriers to trade, trade policy officials needed information about the market structure in each industry, both in the United States and abroad. In order to provide this information, analysts at the Commerce Department, under the able leadership of Brandt Free, provided sectoral profiles of the key industries. (See, for example, U.S. Department of Commerce, 1982 and 1984.)

On the basis of these profiles and the information contained in the USTR Inventory of Barriers to Trade in Services, USTR policy analysts developed sectoral policy papers for each major services industry. These papers summarized the key international trade issues in each industry and presented some initial ideas on how future trade negotiations might address those issues. They became the basis for interagency policy discussions and served to establish initial negotiating objectives for each sector that could be discussed with the private sector. These sectoral papers were subsequently included in the *U.S. National Study on Trade in Services* submitted to the GATT in 1983 (Office of the U.S. Trade Representative, 1983).

Internationally, Hugh Corbet and the Trade Policy Research Center continued to play a leading role in organizing conferences and sponsoring studies. In fact, conferences organized by the Trade Policy Research Center in places like Ditchley Park outside Oxford, Bellagio in northern Italy, and Wiston House near Steyning (south of London) provided focal points for the international coalition-building efforts. The meetings provided a unique opportunity to compare notes on the evolution of thinking in various countries, to coordinate plans for conferences and seminars, and to develop an informal consensus on the future direction of work in the OECD, in the GATT, and elsewhere.

Studies sponsored by the Trade Policy Research Center also provided a growing body of literature on trade in services that could be used as background material by governments when preparing their position on issues discussed in the OECD and the GATT. The Trade Policy Research Center also publishes a quarterly journal, *The World Economy*, and that publication gave researchers an opportunity to publish articles on trade in services at a time when more mainstream journals did not believe trade in services was a suitable subject for their publication.

In addition to the Trade Policy Research Center, the International Chamber of Commerce played a key role in developing an international consensus in the business community in support of multilateral trade negotiations aimed at the liberalization of trade in services. Hans Svedberg, a Swedish businessman, became head of a services working group in the International Chamber of Commerce, and this group produced a clear and forceful statement in support of the negotiations in 1981. Another key participant in the work of the international chamber was Bill Eberle, who headed the Trade Committee of the chamber.

More recently, many different organizations have organized international conferences, seminars, and discussions, including the World Bank, the Center for the Study of International Negotiations in Geneva, the Center for Transnational Corporations in New York, the Atwater Institute in Montreal, Promethée in Paris, and the Services World Forum, a private support group headquartered in Geneva.

Developing a Public Information Program

It is difficult to launch negotiations on a difficult and complex issue such as trade in services without some degree of support from the educated public—the one-tenth of 1 percent of the population that participates in serious discussions of public policy issues. In addition, every government draws to some extent on an informal network of trade policy specialists in developing its position on trade policy issues, and it is therefore important that such individuals develop a reasonable understanding of the issues related to negotiations on trade in services. Both the Office of the U.S. Trade Representative and the Department of Commerce spent considerable effort in developing background materials that could be provided to the press for articles on trade in services and more in-depth papers that could be shared with trade specialists around the world who expressed an interest in trade in services and wanted access to available policy papers, analytical studies, and data.

For a number of years, the services section of the Office of the U.S. Trade Representative also circulated a mimeographed newsletter to individuals around the world who were working on policy issues related to trade in services. Eventually, other organizations such as the Coalition of Service Industries in the United States, the Liberalization of Trade in Services Committee (LOTIS) in the United Kingdom, and Progres in Geneva took over the task of circulating informative newsletters that kept everyone with an interest in trade in services posted on conferences, books, key events, and progress made in various negotiations.

Ironically, countries such as Brazil and India that were opposed to launching multilateral negotiations on trade in services helped considerably in spreading information about trade in services. Their opposition to U.S. efforts in various meetings to advance international discussions and negotiations on trade in services created the drama needed to make news. While some success had been achieved earlier in persuading various newspapers and magazines to write background stories on trade in services and the preparation of negotiations, that coverage was nothing compared with the worldwide treatment of the confrontations over services in the GATT. Such news stories inevitably led to increased requests by the press for additional materials, which in turn led to more articles.

Integrating Services into the Trade Policy Machinery

Services cover a large number of sectors, each with its own domestic regulatory structure, international agreements, and problems. In order to demonstrate that negotiations covering all of these sectors would be a feasible undertaking, it became necessary to develop a group of trade policy professionals who could become experts in the different service industries. Accordingly, both the Office of the U.S. Trade Representative (USTR) and the Office of the Department of Commerce established separate units for services, each staffed with professionals assigned to specific industries.

Both the USTR and the Department of Commerce also took steps to bring the services industries fully into the private sector advisory process, thus giving the services industries the same status in that process as the goods-producing industries. The USTR established a Services Policy Advisory Committee, made up largely of chief executive officers of major firms in each of the major services industries. At the same time, the USTR and Commerce jointly established a working level Industry Sector Advisory Committee on Services, largely made up of industry representatives at the vice-president level.

The establishment of separate units with responsibility for trade in services made it possible to take other steps to integrate services into U.S. trade policy programs. The Commerce Department, for example, has a variety of programs to support U.S. exports. The Export-Import Bank helps finance exports. The

USTR conducts bilateral consultations and negotiations with trade officials from other countries on a regular basis. By extending each of these programs to services, the government was able to give the service industries some immediate commercial benefits.

Using bilateral trade channels to solve trade problems in services had a number of benefits aside from the immediate commercial benefits. It helped to demonstrate to foreign governments that there were real trade problems in services and that the United States would use its commercial leverage to deal with those problems bilaterally even if it proved impossible to launch multilateral negotiations. Such bilateral problem-solving efforts also helped to educate foreign trade policy officials about services issues and made it necessary for foreign governments to establish internal mechanisms for resolving bureaucratic conflicts between trade ministries and ministries responsible for regulating individual service industries. In effect, it was possible to use the bilateral trade policy process to induce foreign governments to integrate services into their own trade policy machinery. Bilateral negotiations thus helped pave the way for the future multilateral negotiations.

In more recent years, the negotiation of bilateral free trade area agreements with Israel and Canada provided an opportunity to develop agreements on trade in services that could provide models for the multilateral negotiations. It also enabled trade officials in the countries involved to give their business communities and regulatory agencies in services an operational reason for addressing the many issues that will have to be covered in the multilateral negotiations. In other words, these negotiations served as dress rehearsals for the multilateral negotiations, and enabled the officials involved to work out many of the problems associated with organizing and implementing agreement on trade in services.

APPENDIX

THE OECD STUDY OF TRADE IN SERVICES

The OECD study on trade in services went through several phases, and each phase was characterized by a debate over different, though related issues, and foreshadowed the debates that later took place in the preparation of negotiations on trade in services in the GATT. The debate in the first phase was over the desirability of conducting a comprehensive study of trade in services. There was obviously widespread skepticism whether there was such a thing as trade in services. The debate in the second phase was over what aspect of trade in services should be studied. The debate in the third phase revolved around the question whether the factual information collected in the course of the study should be analyzed on an industry-by-industry basis, or whether it would be possible and meaningful to analyze the information on an aggregate, cross-sectoral basis. The debate in the fourth phase concerned whether it was possible to relate the issues that had been identified to existing trade concepts. The debate in the last phase was over the possibility of developing meaningful rules and principles for trade in services. Each of these phases took about a year.

Discussion of Rationale and Scope of Study

The debate over the desirability of conducting a study of trade in services in the Trade Committee of the OECD, as against the Invisibles Committee that had dealt with services in the past, took place in 1978–79. Everyone understood, of course, that the primary reason for agreeing on the study was the need of the United States to be able to demonstrate to the Congress that it had taken steps toward preparing comprehensive negotiations on trade in services. Nevertheless, it was obviously necessary to establish an objective rationale for the study, which would enable trade officials to justify their action to their colleagues in the other ministries. In preparing its case for such a study, the U.S. delegation to the Trade Committee was considerably helped by a background paper that had been prepared on the subject by Ron Shelp (1979), who was familiar with the OECD and who had thought the most about the subject.

The Trade Committee agreed in the course of 1979 to undertake a study of trade in services, and this led to a debate over what information to collect. Some members of the Trade Committee argued that the study should be based on a collection of statistics on trade in services. Others argued that the study should focus on government regulations in each services industry in member countries. Still others argued that the study should examine existing international agreements and arrangements on services. The United States argued that the study should focus on barriers to trade in services.

The positive reason for the U.S. proposal to focus on trade barriers in services was that a study of trade barriers in services would most directly and effectively demonstrate the need for negotiations on trade in services. The negative reason was that every other approach had major drawbacks. Government data on trade in services were very poor, and a focus on such data could have quickly convinced everyone that nothing could be done until governments had prepared better data, an effort that has only just begun and could take another five to ten years to yield results. A study of government regulations on services would have proved so overwhelming that the committee would quickly have gotten lost in a sea of information they did not understand. A study of existing agreements and arrangements would be useless unless you could evaluate such agreements and arrangements vis-à-vis an unfulfilled public policy objective related to trade in services.

In responding to the U.S. proposal for a study of barriers to trade in services, other delegations asked how such information could be obtained, and for which industries relevant information could be made available. Some proposed that the committee embark on a case study involving a particular sector. The United States responded that the information could be obtained by asking the representatives of businesses involved in trade in services about the barriers they face and that such an exercise should cover the full range of services. Most members of the

Trade Committee expressed great skepticism about the feasibility of such an approach.

To overcome the skepticism expressed by other members of the Trade Committee regarding the feasibility of obtaining information on barriers to trade in services, the United States decided to demonstrate to the committee that it could be done. By drawing on information collected by the Wolf and Company study in 1975, the United States compiled an initial inventory of trade barriers to services and proposed to undertake a more comprehensive survey that would provide more up-to-date information. Since the United States agreed to do the work, the committee ultimately agreed to pursue the approach it had proposed.

Analysis of Information on Barriers to Trade in Services

U.S. trade officials turned to the U.S. Chamber of Commerce and its services committee to help organize a survey of barriers faced by U.S. service industries in selling services abroad. The data collected from that survey, organized by industry and type of barrier, provided the first comprehensive overview of the barriers faced by businesses engaged in international trade in services. The USTR inventory remains one of the most detailed sources of information about barriers in this area (Office of the U.S. Trade Representative, 1979).

The USTR inventory had its weaknesses. Some of the information about foreign laws and regulations provided by businesses was outdated. In other cases, the businessmen had misunderstood the scope and application of foreign laws and regulations. Later editions of the inventory were subjected to a more intense scrutiny by U.S. embassies in the countries involved, and most of the factual errors were eliminated. The purpose of the inventory, however, was not to accuse foreign governments of wrongdoing in individual areas but to get an insight into the range of barriers faced by business. The survey defined barriers as discriminatory measures or laws that served as an impediment to the sale of services by foreign suppliers. Eventually, other countries undertook to collect information about barriers to trade in services from their own businesses, and this information supplemented the information made available to the OECD Secretariat by the United States.

With the question of the study's focus settled, the discussions in the Trade Committee turned to the method of analyzing the data. Many members of the committee argued that the information about barriers should be analyzed on a sectoral basis, since the institutional, regulatory, and market structure in each services industry is quite different. The United States argued that the barriers should be analyzed in terms of the type of barriers encountered by exporters of services, regardless of industry. The reason for this approach was that it would help demonstrate the applicability of trade negotiating techniques and trade concepts in services, and that it was possible to achieve broad-based liberalization of trade in services through comprehensive negotiations that simultaneously covered all sectors. The U.S. concern was that an analysis focused on sectors would quickly reduce the scope of the study to one or two sectors, that it would emphasize all the sectoral regulatory issues that will make negotiations difficult, and that it would ultimately reduce the scope for liberalization. After considerable debate, the committee agreed to follow a dual approach to the analysis of trade barriers.

As information from the USTR–Chamber of Commerce survey of barriers to trade in services became available, the USTR used its in-house computer processing facilities to organize the information on barriers by type of barrier, by industry, and by country. This information provided much of the raw material for Secretariat papers analyzing major types of barriers.

The next question was how papers on the individual sectors should be prepared. Since the OECD has a number of committees that have responsibility for specific services industries, it was felt that those committees should be asked to provide the Trade Committee with background papers on those sectors, while the Trade Directorate agreed to prepare papers on sectors not covered by sectoral committees in the OECD. The first such sectoral paper prepared by the Secretariat, with the help of trade officials from the member governments, covered the construction and engineering sector. Interestingly enough, many delegates discovered to their surprise that their national industry was a large exporter of construction services, and this helped generate greater enthusiasm for the whole trade in services effort.

Development of a Conceptual Framework for Trade in Services

The papers prepared by the Secretariat on various types of barriers led to a discussion in the next phase of the OECD work of the applicability of trade concepts and techniques. After considerable debate the committee came to accept the transferability of many of the trade concepts and principles to services. This led to a decision to draft a document that would discuss the key concepts and principles that could serve as the foundation for a future trade regime for services. This document, "Elements of a Conceptual Framework for Trade in Services" (OECD, 1987), was published by the OECD in 1987.

With the achievement of substantial consensus in the committee on the conceptual framework that might be used to negotiate on trade in services, it was agreed that the applicability of the conceptual framework to trade in individual service industries should be tested, in cooperation with the sectoral committees of the OECD. That process is still under way. The next step in the OECD work is likely to focus on the development of possible sectoral interpretations or annotations of the general trade concepts and principles contained in the conceptual framework.

THE GATT DEBATE

At the same time that the United States persuaded the OECD Trade Committee to launch a study of trade in services, U.S. representatives continued to pursue the discussion of issues related to trade in services in the GATT. For example, the United

States used the opportunity provided by a GATT exercise to update the inventory of nontariff barriers to include an illustrative notification of barriers to trade in services. The United States also tabled proposals for a work program on trade in services in the Consultative Group of 18, an informal advisory body of senior trade officials that meets periodically to advise the director general of the GATT on trade policy issues that should be addressed by the GATT. U.S. representatives to the GATT also circulated a number of background papers.

The Debate over Services at the 1982 GATT Ministerial

Discussion of trade in services in the GATT reached a more intense level in 1981 with the preparation of a meeting of GATT trade ministers. In 1981 OECD ministers had concluded that there were a number of trade issues, including barriers to trade in services, that should be examined as possible topics for another round of multilateral trade negotiations. This led to a discussion in the GATT of a possible meeting of trade ministers to decide on a work program in preparation for a future round of multilateral trade negotiations. GATT member countries agreed in November 1981 to hold such a meeting in November 1982 and to prepare a draft work program for the consideration of ministers.

As a result of the work undertaken in the OECD Trade Committee most developed countries had come to the conclusion by 1981 that they had an economic interest in trade in services, and that the issue should be examined in the GATT as a possible topic for future multilateral negotiations. Developing countries, however, strongly resisted the discussion of trade in services in the GATT, and this set the stage for a confrontation at the ministerial meeting. After a fairly contentious meeting, the U.S. trade representative, Bill Brock, succeeded in hammering out a compromise agreement. It was agreed that interested countries could prepare national studies of trade in services and that the GATT could arrange for an exchange of views based on such studies. Even though this outcome fell short of the original U.S. objective of establishing a GATT committee or working party on trade in services, the legitimacy of work on trade in services in a GATT context had been established.

In spring 1983, the United States and other developed countries decided it would be desirable to organize an informal discussion in the GATT of the information that should be included in national studies. This request inevitably led to procedural struggles with Brazil and India over the use of GATT facilities to arrange such meetings, the attendance of members of the GATT secretariat, and the preparation of minutes and other documents. These struggles continued through most of 1983 and 1984, first in connection with the coordination of the national studies and next in connection with the exchange of views on the national studies.

The United States was the first country to submit a national study on trade in services at the end of 1983. Other countries followed.

The Debate Leading to the Decision to Launch Negotiations on Trade in Services

The ministerial communiqué on the GATT work program provided for a review of the work at the end of 1984, with the objective of deciding on the topics that might be ripe for inclusion in a new round of multilateral trade negotiations. The GATT council took up the issue at its meeting in November 1984 but could not reach a consensus on the terms for the establishment of a preparatory committee that could lay the groundwork for a new round of multilateral negotiations. The failure to reach a consensus on the agenda of a new round of multilateral trade negotiations was largely due to disagreements over the inclusion of trade in services. It was all the more noteworthy that the council agreed on the establishment of a committee to examine whether services should be included in a new round of negotiations.

The committee promptly elected Ambassador Jaramillo, the Colombian ambassador to the GATT, as chairman. Ambassador Jaramillo had previously been chairman of the more informal sessions organized to exchange information on the national studies. He now played an indispensable role in facilitating a dialogue between developed countries and developing countries on trade in services. The meetings proved invaluable in persuading a substantial group of developing countries to support the inclusion of services, thus isolating such hardliners as Brazil and India, and paving the way for a consensus by the trade ministers. Besides Ambassador Jaramillo, the key players in this process were Richard Self, the U.S. representative on the committee, and John Richardson, the representative of the European Community.

In preparation for the meeting of ministers at Punta del Este, a group of mostly small and medium-sized developed and developing countries, acting under the leadership of the Swiss and Colombian ambassadors to the GATT, developed a draft text of a mandate for the negotiations. That draft text ultimately became the key working document at the ministerial. As in the 1982 GATT ministerial, the debate over trade in services was one of the principal issues facing ministers at their meeting in Punta del Este. Clayton Yeutter, who had replaced Bill Brock as the U.S. trade representative in 1986, was as determined as Brock to include services in the negotiations, and was prepared to allow the meeting to fail if acceptable terms could not be worked out for including services in the negotiations. In the end, agreement was achieved on a mandate acceptable to everyone, and the Uruguay Declaration was approved by the ministers as the basis for launching the Uruguay Round of multilateral trade negotiations.[3]

NOTES

1. For other sources on the history of U.S. and international efforts to build support for multilateral negotiations, see Margaret Sims

and Richard Rivers (1987), Ron Shelp (1979), and Christopher Madison (1981).
2. I described the elements of the strategy in some detail in testimony provided before a committee of the U.S. Senate in 1980 and before a committee of the House of Representatives in 1982. See Feketekuty (1980b) and Feketekuty (1982a). Major elements of the strategy were also incorporated in a government policy statement on trade in services adopted in 1981; see Office of the U.S. Trade Representative (1981). For a contemporary news account, see Madison (1981).
3. The final debates that took place in hammering out the final text are more fully discussed in Chapter 10.

REFERENCES

Alexander, Arthur J., and Hong Tan. 1984. "Barriers to U.S. Service Trade in Japan." Santa Monica, Calif.: Rand Corporation.

Aronson, Jonathan D. 1984. "Computer, Data Processing, and Communication Services." In Robert M. Stern (ed.), *Trade and Investment in Service Industries: U.S.-Canadian Bilateral and Multilateral Perspectives*. Toronto: University of Toronto Press, for the Ontario Economic Council.

Aronson, Jonathan D., and Peter F. Cowhey. 1984. *Trade in Services: A Case for Open Markets*. Washington, D.C.: American Enterprise Institute for Public Policy Research.

———. 1988. *When Countries Talk: International Trade in Telecommunications Services*. Cambridge, Mass.: Ballinger.

Ascher, Bernard, and Obie G. Whichard. 1987. "Improving Services Trade Data." In Orio Giarini (ed.), *The Emerging Service Economy*. Oxford: Pergamon Press for the Services World Forum, Geneva.

Baker, Antony M. 1987. "Liberalization of Trade in Services—The World Insurance Industry." In Orio Giarini (ed.), *The Emerging Service Economy*. Oxford: Pergamon Press for the Services World Forum, Geneva.

Balassa, Carol. Forthcoming. "Negotiation of Services in the U.S.-Israel Free Trade Area." *Journal of World Trade Law*.

Baldwin, Robert E. 1971. "Determinants of the Commodity Structure of United States Trade." *American Economic Review* 61 (May): 126–146.

Barton, John H. 1986. "Negotiating Patterns for Liberalizing International Trade in Professional Services." In *Barriers to International Trade in Professional Services*. Chicago: University of Chicago Legal Forum.

Basche, James R. 1986. "Eliminating Barriers to International Trade and Investment in Services." *The Conference Board Research Bulletin*.

REFERENCES

Baumol, William J. 1985. "Productivity Policy and the Service Sector." In Robert P. Inman (ed.), *Managing the Service Economy: Prospects and Problems*. Cambridge, England: Cambridge University Press.

Bell, Daniel. 1967. "Notes on the Industrial Society." *Public Interest* (Spring).

Benz, Steven F. 1985. "Trade Liberalization and the Global Service Economy." *Journal of World Trade Law 19*, no. 2 (March-April).

Bhagwati, Jagdish N. 1984a. "Splintering and Disembodiment of Services and Developing Nations." *The World Economy* 7: 133–144.

———. 1984b. "Why Are Services Cheaper in the Poor Countries?" *Economic Journal*.

———. 1985. "International Trade in Services and Its Relevance for Economic Development." Reprinted in Orio Giarini (ed.), *The Emerging Service Economy*. London: Pergamon Press for the Services World Forum, Geneva.

———. 1986. "Economic Perspectives on Trade in Professional Services." In *Barriers to International Trade in Professional Services*. Chicago: University of Chicago Legal Forum.

———. 1987. "Services, Trade Talks and the Developing Countries." Paper prepared for the World Bank and the Thailand Development Research Institute, mimeo.

Black, Fischer. 1985. "The Future for Financial Services." In Robert P. Inman (ed.), *Managing the Service Economy: Prospects and Problems*. Cambridge, England: Cambridge University Press.

Böhme, Hans. 1978. "Restraints on Competition in World Shipping." Thames Essay 15. London: Trade Policy Research Center.

Bressand, Albert. 1983. "Mastering the Worldeconomy." *Foreign Affairs* (Spring).

Bressand, Albert, and Catherine Distler. 1985. *Le Prochaine Monde*. Paris: Seuil, Collection Odyssée.

Brock, E. William. 1982. "A Simple Plan for Negotiating Trade in Services." *The World Economy* 5: 229–240.

Bruce, Robert; Jeffrey P. Cunard, and Mark D. Director. 1985. *From Telecommunications to Electronic Services*. London: Butterworth for International Institute of Communications.

Business Roundtable. 1985. "International Information Flow: A Plan for Action." A Statement by the Business Roundtable, January. Washington, D.C.

REFERENCES

Carter, Robert L., and Gerard M. Dickinson. 1979. "Barriers to Trade in Insurance." Thames Essay 19. London: Trade Policy Research Center.

Chamber of Commerce of the United States. 1980. "Report 1978–1980." International Service Industry Committee.

Clark, Mel. 1983. "The General Agreement on Tariffs and Trade (GATT) and Services." Report prepared for the Canadian Government Trade in Services Project, mimeo.

Coffield, Shirley A. 1982. "International Services Trade: Issues and the GATT." American Society for International Law.

Collins, Eileen, and Lucretia Dewey Tanner (eds.). 1984. *American Jobs and the Changing Industrial Base.* Cambridge, Mass.: Ballinger.

Cone, Sydney M., III. 1986. "Government Trade Policy and the Professional Regulation of Foreign Lawyers." In *Barriers to International Trade in Professional Services.* Chicago: University of Chicago Legal Forum.

Cooper, Richard N. 1987. "Survey of Issues and Critical Review of the Conference on International Trade in Services." Paper delivered at the Pacific Trade and Development Conference, Wellington, New Zealand, January, mimeo. Harvard University.

Corbet, Hugh. 1977. "Prospects for Negotiations on Barriers to International Trade in Services." *Pacific Community* (April): 454–470.

Deardorff, Alan V. 1985. "Comparative Advantage and International Trade and Investment in Services." In Robert Stern (ed.), *Trade and Investment in Services: Canada/U.S. Perspectives.* Toronto: University of Toronto Press, for the Ontario Economic Council.

Diebold, William, and Helena Stalson. 1982. "Negotiating Issues in International Service Transactions," mimeo.

Dizard, Wilson P., and Lesley D. Turner. 1987. "Telecommunications and the U.S.-Canada Free Trade Talks." Paper published by the International Communications Project of the Center for Strategic and International Studies, Washington, D.C., mimeo.

Economic Consulting Services, Inc. 1981. "The International Operation of U.S. Service Industries: Current Data Collection and Analysis." Report prepared for the Office of the U.S. Trade Representative and the Department of Commerce, mimeo.

Ewing, A. F. 1985. "Why Freer Trade in Services Is in the Interest of Developing Countries." *Journal of World Trade Law* 19, no. 2 (April-May).

Feketekuty, Geza. 1980a. "Statement on Transborder Data Flows and Trade in Services," before the Subcommittee on Government

Information and Individual Rights, Committee on Government Operations, U.S. House of Representatives, April 21.

———. 1980b. "Statement on Trade in Services," before the Committee on Commerce, Leisure, and Transportation, U.S. Senate, Ninety-sixth Congress, Second Session, September 24.

———. 1981a. "Statement on Transborder Data Flows and Trade in Services," before the Subcommittee on Government Information and Individual Rights, Committee on Government Operations, U.S. House of Representatives, March 31.

———. 1981b. "Statement on Trade in Shipping Services and the UNCTAD Liner Code," before the Subcommittee on Merchant Marine, Committee on Merchant Marine and Fisheries, U.S. House of Representatives, April 2.

———. 1981c. "Statement on Trade in Telecommunications Equipment and Services," before the Subcommittee on Telecommunications, Consumer Protection, and Finance, Committee on Energy and Commerce, U.S. House of Representatives, April 29.

———. 1981d. "International Trade in Banking Services: The Negotiating Agenda." In Gary Hufbauer (ed.), *The International Framework for Money and Banking*. Washington, D.C.: Georgetown University Law Center.

———. 1982a. "Statement on U.S. Trade Policy in Services," before the Subcommittee on Commerce, Transportation, and Tourism, Committee on Energy and Commerce, U.S. House of Representatives, March 11.

———. 1982b. "Statement on Effect of Deregulation of Telecommunications on Trade and Services," before the Committee on Commerce, Science, and Transportation, U.S. Senate, June 14.

———. 1983. "Statement on Proposed Legislation on Trade in Services," before the Subcommittee on Commerce, Transportation, and Tourism, Committee on Energy and Commerce, U.S. House of Representatives, March 15.

———. 1985a. "Negotiating Strategies for Liberalizing Trade and Investment in Services." In Robert M. Stern (ed.), *Trade and Investment in Services: Canada/U.S. Perspectives*. Toronto: University of Toronto Press, for the Ontario Economic Council.

———. 1985b. Comments on Rodney Grey, "Negotiating about Trade and Investment in Services." In Robert M. Stern (ed.), *Trade and Investment in Services: Canada/U.S. Perspectives*. Toronto: University of Toronto Press, for the Ontario Economic Council.

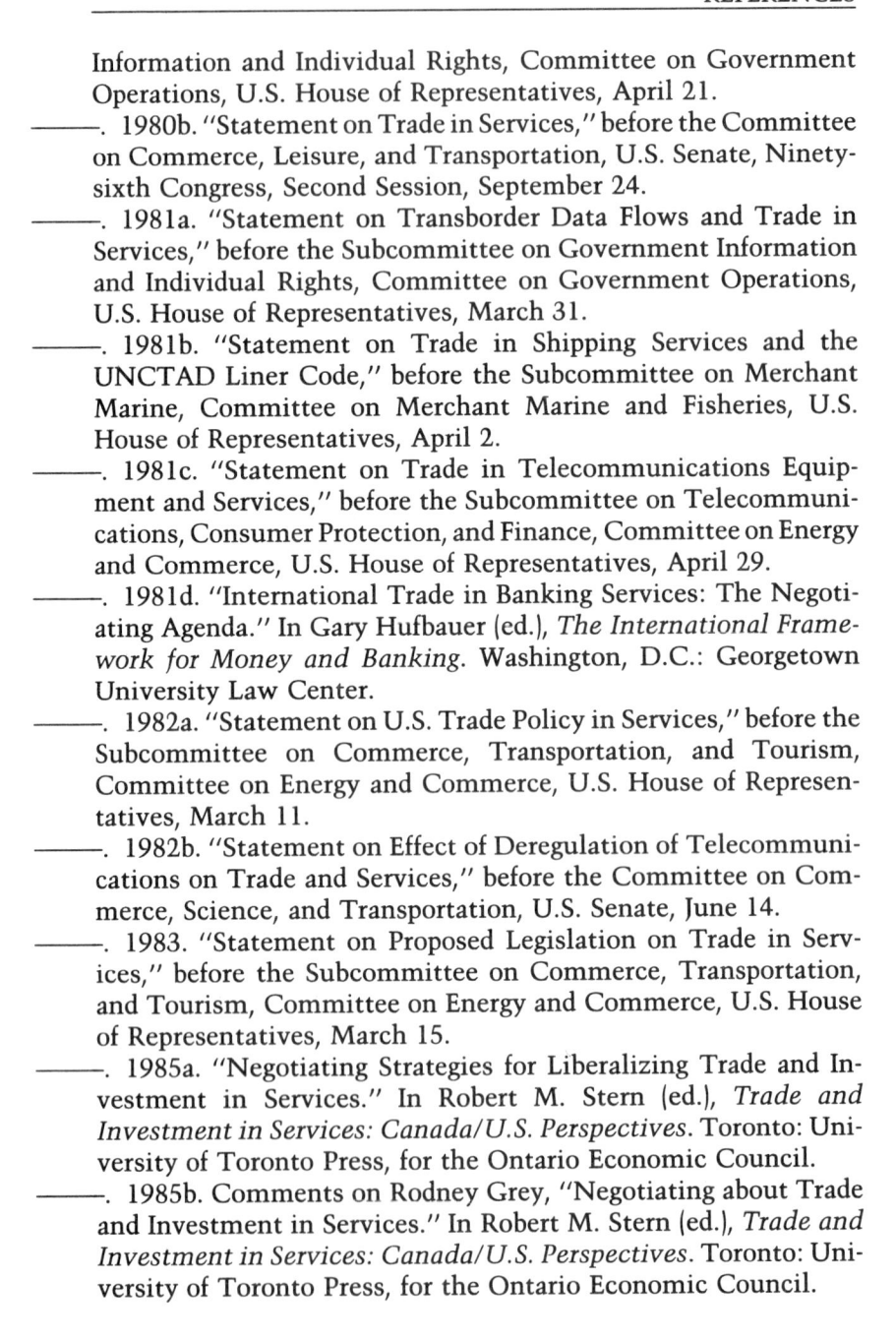

———. 1985c. "Impact on Informatics and Communications and Their Free Flow," *The Washington Round: World Telecommunications Forum*. Geneva: International Telecommunications Union, pp. 293-305.

———. 1986. "Trade in Professional Services: An Overview." In *Barriers to International Trade in Professional Services*. Chicago: University of Chicago Legal Forum.

———. 1987a. "About Trade in Tourism Services." In Orio Giarini (ed.), *The Emerging Service Economy*. Oxford: Pergamon Press for the Services World Forum, Geneva.

———. 1987b. "Trade Policy Objectives in Telecommunications." Paper published by the International Telecommunications Union in connection with the Legal Symposium of Telecom 87, a conference organized by the International Telecommunications Union in Geneva, Switzerland, October.

Feketekuty, Geza, and Jonathan Aronson. 1984a. "Meeting the Challenges of the World Information Economy." *The World Economy* 7: 63–86.

———. 1984b. "Restrictions on Trade in Communications and Information Services." *The Information Society* 2, no. 3–4.

Feketekuty, Geza, and Kathryn Hauser. 1985. "Information Technology and Trade in Services." *Economic Impact*. Washington, D.C.: United States Information Agency.

Feketekuty, Geza, and Larry B. Krause. 1986. "Services and High Technology Goods in the New GATT Round." Paper prepared for a meeting of the Pacific Economic Cooperation Conference in Seoul, Korea.

Forester, Tom (ed.). 1985. *The Information Technology Revolution*. Cambridge, Mass.: MIT Press.

Freeman, Harry. 1987. "The Importance of Services." In Edward R. Fried and Philip H. Tresize (eds.), *Building a Canadian-American Free Trade Area*. Washington, D.C.: Brookings Institution.

Fuchs, Victor R. 1985. "An Agenda for Research on the Service Sector." In Robert P. Inman (ed.), *Managing the Service Economy: Prospects and Problems*. Cambridge, England: Cambridge University Press.

Gavin, Brigid. 1985. "A GATT for International Banking?" *Journal of World Trade Law* 19, no. 2 (March-April).

Gershuny, Jonathan I. 1987. "The Future of Service Employment." In Orio Giarini (ed.), *The Emerging Service Economy*. Oxford: Pergamon Press for the Services World Forum, Geneva.

REFERENCES

Gershuny, J., and I. Miles. 1983. *The New Service Economy.* London: Frances Pinter.

Giarini, Orio (ed.). 1987. *The Emerging Service Economy.* Oxford: Pergamon Press for the Services World Forum, Geneva.

Gibbs, Murray. 1985. "Continuing the International Debate on Services." *Journal of World Trade Law* (May-June).

Golt, Sidney. 1982. "Toward Freer Trade in Services?" *The Banker* (May).

Gray, H. Peter. 1983. "A Negotiating Strategy for Trade in Services." *Journal of World Trade Law* (Sept.-Oct.).

Grey, Rodney C. 1985. "Negotiating about Trade and Investment in Services." In Robert M. Stern (ed.), *Trade and Investment in Services: Canada/U.S. Perspectives.* Toronto: University of Toronto Press, for the Ontario Economic Council.

———. 1986. "A Not-So-Simple Plan for Negotiating on Trade in Services," mimeo. Grey, Clark, Shih and Associates of Ottawa, Canada, and Malingren, Kingston and Golt, Washington, D.C. and London, England.

Griffiths, Brian. 1975. *Invisible Barriers to Invisible Trade.* London: Macmillan for the Trade Policy Research Center.

Grossman, Gene M., and Carl Shapiro. 1985. "Normative Issues Raised by International Trade in Technology Services." In Robert M. Stern (ed.), *Trade and Investment in Services: Canada/U.S. Perspectives.* Toronto: University of Toronto Press, for the Ontario Economic Council.

Hart, Jeffrey A. 1987. "The Employment Impact of International Trade in Services," mimeo; forthcoming in volume to be published by the National Academy of Sciences.

Heckscher, Eli. 1919. "The Effect of Foreign Trade on the Distribution of Income." *Ekonomisk Tidskrift.* Reprinted in *Readings in the Theory of International Trade.* Philadelphia: Blakiston, 1950.

Heilbroner, Robert L. 1961. *The Worldly Philosophers.* New York: Simon and Schuster.

Herman, B., and B. van Holst. 1981. "Toward a Theory of International Trade in Services." Netherlands Economic Institute, mimeo.

———. 1985. "International Trade in Services: Some Theoretical and Practical Problems." Netherlands Economic Institute, mimeo.

Hindley, Brian. 1982. "Economic Analysis and Insurance Policy in the Third World." Thames Essay 32. London: Trade Policy Research Center.

REFERENCES

———. 1987. "Introducing Services into the GATT." Trade Policy Research Center, London, mimeo.

Hindley, Brian, and Alisdair Smith. 1984. "Comparative Advantage and Trade in Services." *The World Economy* 7: 369–390.

Holmstrom, Bengt. 1985. "The Provision of Services in a Market Economy." In Robert P. Inman (ed.), *Managing the Service Economy: Prospects and Problems*. Cambridge, England: Cambridge University Press.

Hufbauer, Gary C. 1970. "The Impact of National Characteristics and Technology on the Commodity Composition of Trade in Manufactured Goods." In Raymond Vernon (ed.), *The Technology Factor in International Trade*. New York: Columbia University Press for the National Bureau of Economic Research.

Inman, Robert P. (ed.). 1985a. *Managing the Service Economy: Prospects and Problems*. Cambridge, England: Cambridge University Press.

———. 1985b. "Introduction and Overview." In Robert P. Inman (ed.), *Managing the Service Economy: Prospects and Problems*. Cambridge, England: Cambridge University Press.

Jackson, John H. 1987. "Potential Umbrella MTN Agreement on Services." American Enterprise Institute, Washington, D.C., mimeo; publication forthcoming.

Jones, Ronald W. 1985. Comments on Alan V. Deardorff, "Comparative Advantage and International Trade and Investment in Services." In Robert M. Stern (ed.), *Trade and Investment in Services: Canada/U.S. Perspectives*. Toronto: University of Toronto Press, for the Ontario Economic Council.

Jussawalla, Meheroo. 1987. "The Information Revolution and Its Impact on the World Economy." Paper prepared for the international seminar, Toward an International Service and Information Economy: A New Challenge for the Third World, sponsored by the Friedrich Ebert Foundation, mimeo; publication forthcoming.

Kakabadse, Mario A. 1987. "International Trade in Services: Prospects for Liberalization in the 1990's." Atlantic Paper 64. New York: Croom Helm, for the Atlantic Institute for International Affairs.

Kendrick, John W. 1985. "Measurement of Output and Productivity in the Service Sector." In Robert P. Inman (ed.), *Managing the Service Economy: Prospects and Problems*. Cambridge, England: Cambridge University Press.

REFERENCES

Keynes, John Maynard. 1935. *The General Theory of Employment, Interest, and Money*. New York: Harcourt, Brace and Company (1958 reprint).

Kindleberger, Charles P. 1961. *Foreign Trade and the National Economy*. New Haven, Conn.: Yale University Press.

Koekkoek, K. A., and J. B. J. M. de Leeuw. "A Note on the Applicability of the GATT to the International Trade in Services." University of Rotterdam and the Netherlands Bank, mimeo.

Kravis, Irving. 1983. "Services in the Domestic Economy and World Transactions." Working Paper 1124. Cambridge, Mass.: National Bureau of Economic Research.

———. 1985. "Services in World Transactions." In Robert P. Inman (ed.), *Managing the Service Economy: Prospects and Problems*. Cambridge, England: Cambridge University Press.

Krommenacker, Raymond J. 1979. "Trade Related Services and GATT." *Journal of World Trade Law 13*, no. 6 (Nov.-Dec.).

———. 1984. *World-Traded Services: The Challenge for the Eighties*. Dedham, Mass.: Artech House.

Krommenacker, Raymond J., and Jean Rémy Roulet. 1987. "Bibliography, Research Programmes and Institutions Related to Services." In Orio Giarini (ed.), *The Emerging Service Economy*. Oxford: Pergamon Press for the Services World Forum, Geneva.

Krugman, Paul R. (ed.). 1986. *Strategic Trade Policy and the New International Economics*. Cambridge, Mass.: MIT Press.

Lanvin, Bruno. 1987. "International Trade in Services, Information Services and Development: Some Issues." UNCTAD, Discussion Paper 23. Geneva, mimeo.

Lary, Hal B. 1968. *Imports of Manufactures from the Less Developed Countries*. New York: Columbia University Press for the National Bureau of Economic Research.

Lederer, Evelyn Parrish, Walter Lederer, and Robert L. Sammons. 1982. "International Services Transactions of the United States: Proposals for Improvement in Data Collection." Report prepared for the Office of the U.S. Trade Representative and the Department of Commerce, mimeo.

Leveson, Irving. 1980. "Productivity in Services: Issues for Analysis." Paper presented at the Conference on Productivity Research of the American Productivity Center, Houston, April 21–24.

———. 1985. "Services in the U.S. Economy." In Robert P. Inman (ed.) *Managing the Service Economy: Prospects and Problems*. Cambridge, England: Cambridge University Press.

REFERENCES

Machlup, Fritz. 1962. *The Production and Distribution of Knowledge in the United States.* Princeton, N.J.: Princeton University Press.

Madison, Christopher. 1981. "Now It's the Services Industry's Turn to Press for Removing Trade Barriers." *National Journal,* October 31.

Malmgren, Harald B. 1985. "Negotiating International Rules for Trade in Services." *The World Economy 8:* 11–26.

McCulloch, Rachel. 1985. Comments on Gene M. Grossman and Carl Shapiro, "Normative Issues Raised by International Trade in Technology Services." In Robert M. Stern (ed.), *Trade and Investment in Services: Canada/U.S. Perspectives.* Toronto: University of Toronto Press, for the Ontario Economic Council.

Modwell, Suman Kumar, K. N. Mehrotra, and Sushil Kumar. 1986. *Trade in Services.* New Delhi: Indian Institute of Foreign Trade.

Naisbitt, John. 1982. *Megatrends.* New York: Warner Books.

Nayyar, Deepak. 1986. "International Trade in Services: Implications for Developing Countries." Exim Bank Commencement Day Annual Lecture, Exim Bank of India, Bombay.

Newlin, Barbara. 1985. *Answers on Line.* Berkeley, Calif.: Osborne/McGraw-Hill.

Noyelle, Thierry J., and Anna B. Dutka. 1986. "The Economics of the World Market for Business Services: Implications for Negotiations." In *Barriers to International Trade in Professional Services.* Chicago: University of Chicago Legal Forum.

Nukazawa, Kazuo. 1980. *Japan's Emerging Service Economy.* New York: Rockefeller Foundation.

———. 1981. "International Trade in Services: A Japanese Perspective—Problems and Implications for U.S.-Japanese Relations." Paper presented at a meeting of the Council of Foreign Relations, June 2, mimeo.

Nusbaumer, Jacques. 1987. *Services in the Global Market.* Boston: Kluwer.

Office of Technology Assessment. United States Congress. 1983. *An Assessment of Maritime Trade and Technology.*

———. 1987. *International Competition in Services.*

Office of the U.S. Trade Representative. 1979. "Inventory: Selected Impediments to Trade in Services by Industry and Type of Action." June, mimeo.

———. 1981. "U.S. Government Work Program on Trade in Services." Policy paper approved by the Trade Policy Committee on April 3 and issued in a USTR press release.

REFERENCES

———. 1983. *U.S. National Study on Trade in Services*, submitted to the GATT, December.

———. 1984. *Annual Report of the President of the United States on the Trade Agreement Program: 1983.*

———. 1985. *Annual Report of the President of the United States on the Trade Agreement Program: 1984–85.*

———. 1986. *National Trade Estimate: 1986 Report on Foreign Trade Barriers.*

Ohlin, Bertil. 1933. *Interregional and International Trade.* Cambridge, Mass.: Harvard University Press.

Organization for Economic Cooperation and Development. 1972. "Report by the High Level Group on Trade and Related Problems." Paris.

———. 1973. *Code of Liberalization of Current Invisible Operations.*

———. 1979. *The Usage of International Data Networks in Europe.* Study prepared by Logica Limited, London, for the Information, Computer, Communications Policy Committee. Paris.

———. 1980. *Policy Implications of Data Network Developments in the OECD Area.* Papers presented at a working session of the Information, Computer, Communications Policy Committee. Paris.

———. 1983. "Transborder Data Flows in International Enterprises." DSTI/ICCP/82.23, a report issued by the Information, Computer, Communications Policy Subcommittee of the Industry, Science and Technology Committee.

———. 1987. *Elements of a Conceptual Framework for Trade in Services.* Paris.

Oulton, Nicholas. 1984. *International Trade in Services and the Comparative Advantage of E. C. Countries.* Trade Policy Research Center, London.

Peat, Marwick, Mitchell and Company. 1986. "A Typology of Barriers to Trade in Services." A report prepared for the European Community, mimeo.

Pipe, Russ. 1987. "The Ultimate Bypass." *Datamation,* August 1.

Porat, Marc. 1977. *Information Economy: Definition and Measurement.* Washington, D.C.: U.S. Department of Commerce, Office of Telecommunications.

Price Waterhouse. 1983. "Business Views on International Trade in Services: The Results of a Survey of Fortune's Directory of Service Companies." December, mimeo.

REFERENCES

———. 1985. "North-South Issues in Trade in Services." *The World Economy* 8: 27–42.
Sapir, André, and Ernst Lutz. 1980. "Trade in Non-Factor Services: Past Trends and Current Issues." World Bank, Staff Working Paper 410.
Sauvant, Karl P. 1986. *International Transactions in Services: The Politics of Transborder Data Flows*. The Atwater Series on the World Information Economy, no. 1. Boulder, Colo.: Westview Press.
Saxonhouse, Gary R. 1985. "Services in the Japanese Economy." In Robert P. Inman (ed.), *Managing the Service Economy: Prospects and Problems*. Cambridge, England: Cambridge University Press.
Schott, Jeffrey J., and Jacqueline Mazza. 1986. "Trade in Services and Developing Countries." *Journal of World Trade Law* 20: 253–272.
Schrier, Elliot, Ernest Nadel, and Bertram Rifas. 1985. "Outlook for the Liberalization of Maritime Transport." Thames Essay 44. London: Trade Policy Research Center.
Schwamm, Henri, and Patrizio Merciai. 1985. "The Multinational and Services." Report issued by Institute for Research and Information on Multinational, Geneva, mimeo.
Scitovsky, Tibor. 1942. "A Reconsideration of the Theory of Tariffs." *Review of Economic Studies*. Reprinted in *Readings in the Theory of International Trade*. Philadelphia: Blakiston, 1950.
Shelp, Ronald Kent. 1976. "The Proliferation of Foreign Insurance Laws: Reform or Regression?" *Law and Policy in International Business* 8, no. 3.
———. 1979. "Service Industry Aspects of Legislation to Implement the Multilateral Trade Negotiations." Statement before Subcommittee on International Trade, Senate Finance Committee, July 10.
———. 1981. *Beyond Industrialization*. New York: Praeger.
———. 1986. "Trade in Services." *Foreign Policy* 65 (Winter).
Sims, Margaret, and Richard R. Rivers. 1987. "The International Trade in Services Agenda: Origins, Evolution and Agenda." Paper prepared for the Institute for Research and Public Policy, Victoria, British Columbia, Canada.
Smith, Adam. 1776. *The Wealth of Nations*. Reprinted. New York: Random House, 1937.
Snape, Richard H. 1987. "Prospects for Liberalizing Services Trade." Paper to be published in the proceedings of the Pacific Trade and Development Conference on Trade and Investment in Services in the Pacific, Wellington, New Zealand, January.

———. 1985. "Business Views on Public Policy and Internat in Services: The Results of a Survey of Fortune's I Service Companies." February, mimeo.

Rada, Juan F. 1987. "Information Technology and Service Giarini (ed.), *The Emerging Service Economy*. Oxford Press for the Services World Forum, Geneva.

Ribe, Halvor, and Friedrich Schneider. 1986. "Are Regulatio International Trade in Financial Services?" Kiel Institu Economics, Working Paper 47.

Ricardo, David. 1817. *Principles of Political Economy*.

Richardson, John. 1987. "A Sub-Sectoral Approach to Serv Theory." In Orio Giarini (ed.), *The Emerging Service* Oxford: Pergamon Press for the Services World Forur

Richter, Christine. 1987. "Tourism Services." In Orio Giari *Emerging Service Economy*. Oxford: Pergamon Pro Services World Forum, Geneva.

Riddle, Dorothy. 1986. *Service-led Growth: The Role of Sector in World Development*. New York: Praeger.

———. 1987. "The Role of the Service Sector in Econom: ment: Similarities and Differences by Development C: Orio Giarini (ed.), *The Emerging Service Economy*. C gamon Press for the Services World Forum, Geneva.

Robinson, James D., III. 1979. "America's 'Invisible' Trade— by Invisible Barriers." *National Journal*, September 9

Robinson, Peter. 1987. "An International Policy Framewor in Services and Data Services: The Current Debate in In Organizations." Paper prepared for the internation: Toward an International Service and Information E New Challenge for the Third World, sponsored by th Ebert Foundation, mimeo; publication forthcoming.

Rossi, Frank. 1986. "Government Impediments and Profes: straints on the Operations of International Accountin, tions." In *Barriers to International Trade in Profession* Chicago: University of Chicago Legal Forum.

Rubin, Michael Rogers. 1986. "US Information Economy *Transnational Data and Communication Report* (Jur

Sampson, Gary P., and Richard H. Snape. 1985. "Identifyin; in Trade in Services." *The World Economy* 8: 171–18

Sapir, André. 1982. "Trade in Services: Policy Issues for th *Columbia Journal of World Business* (Fall).

REFERENCES

Snow, Marcellus S., and Meheroo Jussawalla. 1986. *Telecommunication Economics and International Regulatory Policy: An Annotated Bibliography*. New York: Greenwood Press.

Stalson, Helena. 1984. "Effects of Foreign Government Policies on U.S. International Competitiveness in Services." Council of Foreign Relations, New York, mimeo.

———. 1985a. "U.S. Trade Policy and International Service Transactions." In Robert P. Inman (ed.), *Managing the Service Economy: Prospects and Problems*. Cambridge, England: Cambridge University Press.

———. 1985b. *U.S. Service Exports and Foreign Barriers: An Agenda for Negotiations*. Washington, D.C.: National Planning Association.

Stanback, Thomas M., Peter J. Bearse, Thierry J. Noyelle, and Robert A. Karasek. 1981. *Services: The New Economy*. Totowa, N.J.: Allanheld, Osmun for Conservation of Human Resources, Columbia University.

Stern, Robert M. (ed.), 1985a. *Trade and Investment in Services: Canada/U.S. Perspectives*. Toronto: University of Toronto Press, for the Ontario Economic Council.

———. 1985b. "Global Dimensions and Determinants of International Trade and Investment in Services." In Robert M. Stern (ed.), *Trade and Investment in Services: Canada/U.S. Perspectives*. Toronto: University of Toronto Press, for the Ontario Economic Council.

———. 1985c. "Introduction and Overview." In Robert M. Stern (ed.), *Trade and Investment in Services: Canada/U.S. Perspectives*. Toronto: University of Toronto Press, for the Ontario Economic Council.

Stern, Robert M., and Bernard M. Hoekman. 1986a. "Conceptual Issues Relating to Services in the International Economy." Seminar Discussion Paper 188, Research Seminar in International Economics, University of Michigan, mimeo.

———. 1986b. "GATT Negotiations on Services: Analytical Issues and Data Needs." Seminar Discussion Paper 189, Research Seminar in International Economics, University of Michigan, mimeo.

Stigler, George. 1956. *Trends in Employment in the Service Industries*. Princeton, N.J.: Princeton University Press.

Summers, Robert. 1985. "Services in the International Economy." In Robert P. Inman (ed.), *Managing the Service Economy: Prospects and Problems*. Cambridge, England: Cambridge University Press.

Toffler, Alvin. 1970. *Future Shock*. New York: Random House.

REFERENCES

———. 1980. *The Third Wave.* New York: William Morrow and Company.

U.S. Department of Commerce. 1976. *U.S. Service Industries in World Markets: Current Problems and Future Policy Development.*

———. 1982. *Service Industries.*

———. 1984a. *A Competitive Assessment of the U.S. Data Processing Services Industry.*

———. 1984b. *U.S. International Trade and Investment in Services: Data Needs and Availability.* Bureau of Economic Analysis Staff Paper 41.

———. 1985. *U.S. Direct Investment Abroad: 1982 Benchmark Survey Data.*

U.S. Department of the Treasury. 1979. *Report to Congress on Foreign Government Treatment of U.S. Commercial Banking Organizations.*

U.S. International Trade Commission. 1982. *The Relationship of Exports in Selected Service Industries to U.S. Merchandise Exports.* USITC Publication 1290.

Verner, Liipfert, Bernhard, and McPherson. 1982. "Report to the United States Trade Representative on the Treatment of Services under United States Trade Law and Reciprocity in United States Regulation of Service Sector Industries." Report prepared for the USTR by Alan Wolff and John Greenwald of Verner, Liipfert, Bernhard, and McPherson.

Walter, Ingo. 1985. "Barriers to Trade in Banking and Financial Services." Thames Essay 41. London: Trade Policy Research Center.

White, Lawrence J. 1988. *International Trade in Ocean Shipping Services: The United States and the World.* Cambridge, Mass.: Ballinger.

Wilcox, Clair. 1949. *A Charter for World Trade.* New York: Macmillan.

Wilson, Bruce. 1975. "Services, the Trade Act of 1974, and MTN: Preliminary Briefing Material." Background paper prepared for the Office of the Special Trade Representative, Washington, D.C., January 31.

Wolf and Company. 1976. "Study of Service Industries and Their Relation to Domestic and International Trade." Report submitted to the Department of Commerce.

Yochelson, John N., and Gordon Cloney (eds.). 1982. "Services and U.S. Trade Policy: A White Paper of the Panel on Services and U.S.

Trade Policy." Center for Strategic and International Studies, Georgetown University, Washington, D.C.

Name Index

Aronson, Jonathan D., 255, 273 n.1, 284
Ascher, Bernard, 36 n.6

Baker, Antony, M., 273 n.4
Balassa, Carol, 180
Barton, John H., 274 n.5
Bastiat, Frederic, 93–94
Bearse, Peter J., 45, 63
Bell, Daniel, 58 n.1, 62
Bhagwati, Jagdish N., 35 n.4, 36 n.5, 124 n.1, 125 n.4, 167, 274 n.5
Böhme, Hans, 145 n.1, 273, n.2
Bressand, Albert, 58 n.1
Brock, William E., 305, 321
Bruce, Robert, 273 n.1

Carter, Robert L., 145 n.1, 273 n.4
Clark, Mel, 239 n.3
Cone, Sydney M. III, 274 n.5
Corbet, Hugh, 296, 298
Cowhey, Peter F., 255, 284
Cunard, Jeffrey P., 273 n.1

Deardorff, Alan V., 94, 125 n.4, 125 n.5, 126 n.8
Dent, Frederick, 305
Dickinson, Gerard M., 145 n.1, 276 n.4
Director, Mark D., 275 n.1
Distler, Catherine, 58 n.1
Dutka, Anna B., 274 n.5

Eberle, Bill, 297

Feketekuty, Geza, 174 n.2, 250, 255, 271, 273 n.1, 273 n.3, 274 n.5, 322 n.2
Freeman, Harry, 308

Greenberg, Hank, 300, 304
Greenwald, Joseph, 293 n.4
Griffiths, Brian, 296, 305

Heckscher, Eli, 68, 98
Heilbroner, Robert L., 94
Herman, B., 94
Hindley, Brian, 94, 103, 125 n.4, 126 n.8, 274 n.4
Hufbauer, Gary C., 99
Holst, B. van, 94

Inman, Robert P., 63

Jackson, John H., 239 n.6, 293 n.5
Jones, Ronald W., 125 n.5
Jussawalla, Meheroo, 273 n.1

Karasek, Robert A., 45, 63
Kasper, Dan, 258, 284
Keynes, John Maynard, 59
Krugman, Paul R., 124 n.2

Lary, Hal B., 99
Lederer, Evelyn Parrish, 36 n.6
Lederer, Walter, 36 n.6
Leontief, Wassily, 99

McMillan, 124 n.1
Madison, Christopher, 322 n.1, 322 n.2
Malmgren, Harald B., 298

Nadel, Ernest, 273 n.2
Naisbitt, John, 24 n.2, 62
Noyelle, Thierry J., 24 n.3, 45, 63, 267, 274 n.5

339

Name Index

Ohlin, Bertil, 68, 98, 297
Oulton, Nicholas, 94, 122, 123

Polo, Marco, 37
Porat, Marc, 58 n.1, 58 n.2, 62
Powell, Richard, 297

Rada, Juan F., 273 n.1
Rey, Jean, 297
Ricardo, David, 68, 91, 92, 125 n.3
Richardson, John, 94, 125 n.4, 321
Rifas, Bertram, 273 n.2
Rivers, Richard R., 322 n.1
Robinson, James D., 308
Rossi, Frank, 25 n.3, 274 n.5

Sammons, Robert L., 36 n.6
Sampson, Gary P., 36 n.5, 89 n.5, 89 n.7, 94, 125 n.4
Sapir, André, 122, 123
Sauvant, Karl P., 273 n.1
Schrier, Elliot, 273 n.2
Self, Richard, 321

Shelp, Ronald Kent, 300, 304, 305, 308, 315, 322 n.1
Sims, Margaret, 321 n.1
Smith, Adam, 59, 60–61, 91, 92, 93–94, 129
Smith, Alisdair, 94, 125 n.1, 126 n.8
Snape, Richard H., 36 n.5, 89 n.5, 89 n.7, 94, 125 n.4
Snow, Marcellus S., 273 n.1
Spero, Joan, 308
Stanback, Thomas M., 24 n.2, 45, 50, 63
Stern, Robert M., 125 n.5
Stigler, George, 50
Strauss, Bob, 304, 305
Svedberg, Hans, 312

van Lennep, Emile, 297, 298

Walter, Ingo, 145 n.1, 271, 285
Whichard, Obie G., 36 n.6
White, Lawrence J., 272 n.2, 272 n.3
Wilcox, Clair, 174 n.1
Wilson, Bruce, 302

Yeutter, Clayton, 321

Subject Index

Advertising, and business services, 50
Airlines and aviation industry
  barriers to trade in services in, 144
  conditional most favored nation (MFN) status and, 284
  General Agreement on Trade in Services and, 226, 258–260, 299, 300
American International Group (AIG), 300

Balance of payments
  currency control programs and, 130
  trade in services definitions and, 76–77, 84
  trade policy and, 167
Banking
  conditional most favored nation (MFN) status and, 285–286
  data processing and information services and, 253
  descriptive model of international trade in services and, 28, 70
  fee-based, 269
  General Agreement on Trade in Services and, 270–273, 285–286
  government regulation of, 34, 110
  international trade in services and, 19–20, 56
  local agents in, 13
  multinational corporations in, 22
  offshore activities of, 269
  purchase of imports and, 10
  representative offices for export sales and, 15–16
  retail, 270
  trade in services definitions and, 83–84

U.S./Canadian Free Trade Agreement on, 186
Barriers to trade in services, 129–145
  added costs from, 131–132
  bureaucratic tendencies and, 141–142
  definition of, 131–135
  discriminatory practices under government policies and, 138, 141
  domestic regulation and, 162–163
  future concerns about, 143
  General Agreement on Trade in Services and, 207, 209–214, 316
  government-owned firms and, 139
  information flows and, 134
  insurance regulation in Japan example of, 142–143
  licensing of lawyers and, 143
  negotiating strategies for binding and reducing, 275–292
  ownership by foreign firms and, 138
  point of erection of, 135–137
  public monopolies and, 143–144
  as a quantitative limit, 132–133
  reciprocity principle in trade policy and, 153
  services purchased abroad and, 135–136
  services purchased at home and, 136–137
  sources of information on, 130–131
  suppliers of services and, 133, 137–138
  surveys for information on, 137–141
  tourism industry and, 249–250
  trade policy and, 131
  transborder data flows and, 140

341

Subject Index

types of transactions or activities under government control and, 129
Uruguay Declaration on, 195
work permits and immigration rules and, 140–141
Bilateral agreements
trade policy negotiation of, 156–158
U.S./Israeli Declaration of Trade in Services and, 176–183
Blue-collar workers
manufacturing purchase of imports and, 8
production of services and, 66
U.S./Canadian Free Trade Agreement on, 185
B-1 visa, and trade in services, 81
Border controls, as barriers to trade in services, 135, 136
Bureaucracy, and barriers to trade in services, 141–142
Business enterprises
decision to buy services abroad and, 16–17
global economic integration and, 40–41
imported services purchased by, 8–12
insurance industry and, 263–265
international trade in service inputs in, 10–12
trade in services definitions and, 78–79
see also Multinational corporations
Business services
centralization of, 48–52, 54, 55
emergence of, 48–52
employment effects of, 51–52
external sources for, 51
financial institutions and, 50
future advances in, 55–56
government regulations and, 52
growth of, 41–42
information revolution and world economy and, 46–48
internationalization of, 52–54
international trade in, 54
local sources for, 50
manufacturing companies as suppliers of, 49–50
networks and, 47–48
organizational trends in, 50–51

specialized service inputs in, 49
vendors of, 53–54
Buyers of services
competition among, 108–109
exported services and, 12–16
imported services and, 5–12
options for decision making in, 16–17

Canadian/U.S. Free Trade Agreement, 183–186
lessons learned from, 185–186
provisions of, 184–185
Capital and theory of comparative advantage, 103
Cash, insurance, and freight (CIF) method of valuation, 69, 85–86
Centralization
business purchase of imports and, 10–11
business services and, 48–52, 54, 55
consumer services and, 55
data processing services and, 52–53, 271
financial institutions and, 110–111
limitations of, 21–22
manufacturing enterprises and, 49
Columbia University, 63
Communication and communication services
barriers to trade in services and, 144
business purchase of imports and, 10
business services and, 49
cash, insurance, and freight (CIF) method of valuing, 69, 85–86
costs and capacity increases in, 46
global economic integration and, 40
international trade in services and, 71
monopolies in, 108–110, 144
trade in services definitions and, 85–86
as transport system of world information economy, 45–46
see also Telecommunications
Comparative advantage, *see* Theory of comparative advantage
Competition
barriers to trade in services and, 139
buyers and, 108–109

Subject Index

centralization of financial services and, 110–111
domestic services regulation and, 161–162
foreign suppliers and, 107–108
gains from trade in services and, 116
government-owned enterprises and, 139
infant industries and, 117–118
liberalization of trade policy and, 201, 202
maritime transport under General Agreement on Trade in Services and, 260–262
market principle, and trade policy and, 152–153
public service monopolies and, 164
regulatory approach to international delivery of services and, 171
telecommunications and, 252–254
theory of comparative advantage and, 106–107, 122–123
trade in services and, 105–111
transportation and, 122–123
Competitiveness
business services and, 54
economic development and, 119
international trade in business service inputs and, 11, 23
losses from trade in services and, 116–117
manufacturing and service inputs and, 57
Computers
business services and, 46–48, 50, 51
international trade in, 56
Conditional most favored nation (MFN) status
General Agreement on Trade in Services and, 283–286
trade policy and, 154, 222
Congress
international trade in services and, 71, 170
negotiations on trade in services and, 299–301
trade policy and, 156, 191, 198

Conservation of Human Resources Project, Columbia University, 63
Construction, and export sales, 16
Consultation principle, and trade policy, 155–156
Consulting, and export sales, 16
Consultive Shipping Group (CSG), 261–262
Consumers, imported services purchased by, 5–8
Consumer services
future advances in, 55–56
growth of, 41–42
international trade and, 55
Consumption
interpretation of patterns of, 64–65
theory of comparative advantage and, 96
Contractors, and foreign purchase of exports, 13–14
Cooperatives with local businesses, and exports, 14
Cost of services
barriers to trade in services and, 131–132
capacity of communication technology and, 46
economic development and, 121
global economic integration and, 40
specialization and, 39
Costs and benefits of trade in services, 112–114
Culture and cultural factors
trade in services, 82–83, 114
trade policy negotiations and, 160

Data collection
invisibility of trade in services and, 31–32
service jobs and issues in, 63–64, 69–70
Data flows
General Agreement on Trade in Services and, 232–233, 252–257
trade policy and, 167–168
Data processing services
business purchase of imports and, 10
centralization of, 52–53, 270

343

conditional most favored nation (MFN) status and, 284
General Agreement on Trade in Services and, 252–257
representative offices for export sales in, 16
trade in business services in world economy and, 46–48
see also information and information services
Declaration of Trade in Services, Israeli/U.S., 176–183
contents of, 177–179
issues addressed during negotiations of, 179–181
sectoral annotations under, 182–183
Declaration on International Data Flows (OECD), 168, 233
Department of Commerce, 36 n.7, 45, 62, 89 n.6, 302–303, 309, 311
Department of the Treasury, 145 n.1, 186
Deregulation of telecommunications, 57, 109–110
Developing countries
economic development and, 119–120
protectionist policies and, 121–122
trade negotiations and role of, 204–205
Dispute settlement principle
General Agreement on Trade in Services and, 228–230
trade policy and, 156
Domestic production of services
trade gap and, 65–66
trade regulation and, 161–163
Due process, in U.S./Israeli Declaration of Trade in Services, 178

Economic Consulting Services, Inc., 36 n.6
Economic development, 119–122
multinational firms and, 120–121
protectionist policies and, 121–122
Economic factors
cost of services and, 23
global integration and, 39–41
international trade in services and, 18–23
service jobs and, 41–45, 66–67

theory of comparative advantage and, 98
trade deficit and, 65–66
see also International economy
Economic growth
global economic integration and, 40–41
government policy and, 71
information creation, processing, and distribution and, 38
international trade in services and, 41–42, 57, 71
Economic theory, and trade policy goals, 151–152
Economies of scale
competition and, 109–110, 123
local businesses franchises and exports and, 14
theory of comparative advantage and, 97–98
Education, consumer purchase of imports in, 6
Electronic shopping services, 56
Employment
business services and, 51–52
data collection interpretation issues for, 64–65
manufacturing purchase of imports and, 8
percentage distribution of service jobs in, 42, 45 (table)
service jobs in U.S. economy by sector and, 42, 43–44 (table)
trade deficit and, 65–66
Engineering, export sales in, 16
Entertainment
consumer purchase of imports in, 6
international trade in, 56
Eurodollar markets
government regulation of, 34
information revolution and, 47
theory of comparative advantage and, 103
Export of services
descriptive model of international trade in services and, 28, 98–100
examples of, 3–4
General Agreement on Trade in Services on, 213

Subject Index

government policy on, 97
home market of supplier and, 15–16
international financial services and, 19–20
invisibility of trade in services and, 30–31
local agents, contractors, and licensees and, 13–14
local production and distribution facilities and, 12–13
market principle, and trade policy and, 152–153
partnerships or cooperative arrangements with local businesses and, 14
sales to foreign customers in, 12–16
trade in services definitions and, 76–77, 81, 87

Fair trade provisions, General Agreement on Trade in Services, 226–228
Farming, productivity of, 61–62
Federal government, *see* Government
Fee-based banking services, 269
Finance
theory of comparative advantage and, 103–104
trade in services definitions and, 83–84
trade policy and, 167
Financial services
business purchase of imports and, 10
business services supplied by, 50
centralization of, 110–111
consumer purchase of imports and, 6
descriptive model of international trade in services and, 28–30
Eurodollar market and, 34
foreign exchange control systems and, 31, 33
global economic integration and, 39–40
government regulation of, 110
international trade in services and, 19–20, 68–69
invisibility of trade in services and, 31, 33
theory of comparative advantage and, 103–104
trade in services definitions and, 83–84

Foreign exchange control systems
barriers to trade in services and, 129, 130, 132–133, 139
General Agreement on Trade in Services and, 231–232
information revolution and, 47
invisibility of trade in services and, 31, 33
services purchased abroad and, 135–136
trade policy and, 165
Fortune (magazine), 51
Franchising companies, and exports, 14
Free on board (FOB) method of valuing trade, 86
Free trade, 91–92
Free Trade Agreement, U.S./Canadian, 183–186
lessons learned from, 185–186
provisions of, 184–185
Friendship, Commerce, and Navigation (FCN) Agreements
immigration and, 166
U.S./Israeli Declaration of Trade in Services as, 179

General Agreement on tariffs and trade (GATT), 150
balance of payments and, 167
Congress and, 156
General Agreement on Trade in Services framework under, 207–209
General Agreement on Trade in Services relationship to, 236–238
market principle and, 152
most favored nation (MFN) principle and, 153–154
multilateral trade negotiations under 158–159
national treatment principle in, 88, 154, 216–218
orderly adjustment principle and, 154–155
Organization for Economic Cooperation and Development (OECD) and, 191–192
reciprocity principle and, 153
Standards Code of, 219, 230, 304

345

Subject Index

Subsidies Code of, 304
telecommunications and, 253–255
Uruguay Declaration in, 193–199, 237, 241
Uruguay Round in, xiv, 89 n.8, 159, 167, 191, 192, 237
Tokyo Round in, 159, 191, 219, 299, 301, 305
General Agreement on Trade in Services (GATS)
analytical work and negotiations under, 272–273
aviation services under, 258–261
banking services under, 269–271
barriers to trade under, 209–214
basic framework of, 205–236, 275–277
conditional most favored nation (MFN) basis for, 283–286
dispute settlement under, 228–230
domestic regulation and, 218–220
"exceptions" approach versus "request and offer" approach to, 279–281
exceptions under, 225–226
fair trade provisions of, 226–228
foreign investment under, 234–235
General Agreement on Tariffs and Trade (GATT) framework for, 207–209
General Agreement on Tariffs and Trade (GATT) relationship to, 236–238
individual sectors under, 241–274
insurance services under, 263–266
international flows of information, people, and money and, 231–232
local governments and, 235–236
maritime transport under, 260–263
monopolies under, 224–225
most favored nation (MFN) basis for, 277–283
national treatment principle and, 216–218
negotiating strategies for, 277–294
negotiation rules for, 214–215
professional services under, 267–269
protection levels under, 281
reciprocity and most favored nation (MFN) treatment under, 221–224

sectoral annotations under, 243–249, 271–273
telecommunications and data processing under, 252–258
tourism services and, 249–252
trade policy and, 247–249
Glass Stiegel Act, 186
Goods, trade in, 84–85
Government
data collection on trade in services by, 31–32, 63–64, 95
industrial targeting policies of, 99, 100
invisibility of trade in services across borders and, 30–31
telecommunications monopolies of, 40
trade in services definitions and, 77–78
Government-owned enterprises, and barriers to trade in services, 139
Government regulation, 27
barriers to trade in services and, 129
business services and, 52
competition and, 110
democratic freedoms and, 32–33
Eurodollar markets and, 34
global economic integration and, 40–41
imports and, 23, 34, 129, 130
information services and, 147–148
insurance industry and, 142–143
international trade in services and, 56–57, 69, 70–71
invisibility of trade in services and, 32
Japanese examples of, 142–143, 147–148
public policy issues of, 23
purchases of services in foreign countries and, 33–34
telecommunications and, 254
theory of comparative advantage and, 97
trade policy related to, 169–173
transactions or activities covered by, 129
Gross National Product (GNP)
information services and, 62
percentage distribution of employment by industry and, 42, 45 (table)
Growth, see Economic growth

Historical perspective on trade in services, 38–39
Home markets, and export sales, 15–16
Hotel chains, 14

Immigration
 barriers to trade in services and rules on, 140–141
 invisibility of trade in services and government regulation of, 33
 trade in services definitions and, 81–82
 trade policy and, 166–167
Import of services
 banking and, 10
 business enterprises and purchase of, 8–12
 buyers of, 5–12
 centralized production of service inputs and, 10–11
 consumers and purchase of, 5–8
 descriptive model of international trade in services and, 28, 98–100
 examples of, 4
 government regulation of, 23, 34, 129, 130
 international trade in business service inputs and, 10–12
 international travel and, 6, 7
 invisibility of trade in services and, 30–31
 local production of service inputs and, 9–10
 manufacturing and service inputs and, 8–9
 multinational corporation and, 10–11
 national income and, 7–8
 national reputation for excellence and, 11–12
 public policy issues in, 23
 retail businesses and, 9
 specialization and suppliers and, 9
 trade deficit and, 65–66
 trade in services definitions and, 76–77, 85–86
Income, *see* National income
Industrial targeting policies, 99, 100
Infant industries, 116–119
Information and information services
 barriers to trade in services and restrictions on, 134, 140
 capacity of communication technology and cost of, 46
 communication system as world transport system for, 45–46
 descriptive model of international trade in services and, 28–30
 economic growth and creation of, 38, 62
 employment in U.S. economy and, 42, 43–44 (table)
 General Agreement on Trade in Services and, 231–232
 global economic integration and, 40–41
 Gross National Product (GNP) and, 42, 45 (table), 62
 growth of service jobs and, 41–42
 international trade in, 56, 69–70
 invisibility of trade in services in, 30–31
 Japanese regulation of, 147–148
 market internationalization and, 47
 networks and global activity in, 47–48, 253
 new job categories in, 42–44
 organization of manufacturing industries and, 47
 revolution in, 41–48
 trade in business services in world economy and, 46–48
 trade policy and, 167–168
 transborder data flows, and barriers to trade in services, 140
Insurance industry
 barriers to trade in services and, 132, 142–143
 conditional most favored nation (MFN) status and, 285
 data processing and information services and, 251
 General Agreement on Trade in Services on, 211, 263–266, 285
 government regulation of, 110
 international trade in, 56
 Japan Ministry of finance regulations of, 142–143
 local agents in, 13

347

multinational corporations in, 22
segments of, 263–265
U.S./Israeli Declaration of Trade in Services on, 182–183
International Air Transport Association (IATA), 259–260
International Chamber of Commerce (ICC), 71, 310
International Civil Aviation Organization (ICAO), 172, 260
International economy
  centralization of business services and, 48–52
  communications system as transport system of, 45–46
  consumer services and, 55–56
  global integration of, 39–41
  growth of service jobs and, 41–42
  historical perspective on, 38–39
  information revolution and, 41–48
  international trade in services and, 18–23, 68–69
  markets and information and, 47–48
  organization of manufacturing industries and, 47
  public policy issues and, 38
  role of information in, 42–45
  trade in business services and alterations in, 46–48
International Monetary Fund, 167, 233
International Standards Organization (ISO), 197
International Telecommunications Union (ITU), 172, 197, 200, 255, 256, 257
International trade in services
  barriers to, see Barriers to trade in services
  business services and, 52–54
  cash, insurance, and freight (CIF) method of valuing, 69, 85–86
  centralized production of service inputs and, 10–11
  consequences of invisibility of, 30–34, 94
  consumer services and, 55–56
  decision to buy services abroad and, 17
  descriptive model of, 28–30, 70, 98–100
  early theorists on 67–68
  economic growth and, 41–42, 57
  free on board (FOB) method of valuing, 86
  government regulation of, 56–57, 69, 70–71
  historical perspective on, 38–39
  importance of, 56–57
  information creation, processing, and distribution as new area in, 38, 69–70
  as interconnected national systems, 170
  international business and, 20–23
  international finance and, 19–20, 68–69
  international travel and, 20
  normative theories of, 96–98
  trade in goods and, 18–19
  travel and, 67–68
  world economy and, 18–23
International Trade Organization (ITO), 156, 237
Inventory of Barriers to Trade in Services (USTR), 130, 137, 138, 139, 140
Investment
  General Agreement on Trade in Services and, 234–235
  liberalization of trade policy and, 202
  theory of comparative advantage and, 104
  trade in services definitions and, 87–88
  trade policy and, 168–169
Investment houses, see Financial services
Israeli/U.S. Declaration of Trade in Services with, 176–183
  contents of, 177–179
  issues addressed during negotiations of, 179–181
  sectoral annotations under, 182–183

Japan
  information services regulation in, 147–148
  insurance industry regulation in, 142–143
Japan Ministry of Finance, 142–143

Subject Index

Labor
  economic development and, 121
  production of services and, 66, 113
Lawyers, and barriers to trade in services, 143
Legal services, consumer purchase of imports in, 6–7
Liability insurance, 265
Licenses
  barriers to trade in services and, 142–143
  foreign purchase of exports and, 13–14
  insurance industry and, 142
  lawyers and, 143
  national treatment principle and, 220
  U.S./Canadian Free Trade Agreement and, 185
Life insurance, 265
Liner Code, United Nations Conference on Trade and Development (UNCTAD), 262, 263–264
Local government, and General Agreement on Trade in Services, 235–236
Local production
  barriers to trade in services and, 133
  business purchase of imports and, 9–10
  business services and, 50, 51
  exporter sale of services to foreign customers and, 12–16
  investment and, 168
  local agents, contractors, and licensees for, 13–14
  multinational corporations and advantages to, 22
  partnerships or cooperatives for, 14

Management
  business services and, 51
  multinational corporations and centralization of, 21–22
Manufacturing industries
  business services supplied by, 49–50, 51–52
  centralization of, 49
  competitiveness of, 11, 23, 57
  information revolution and, 47
  purchase of imports as service inputs by, 8–9, 23–24

Maritime transport
  conditional most favored nation (MFN) status and, 284–285
  General Agreement on Trade in Services and, 260–263
Marketing, and business services, 50
Market principle, and trade policy, 152–153
Markets
  economic development and, 120
  export sales and home country of supplier and, 15–16
  historical perspective on trade in services and, 39
  infant industries and, 118
  information revolution and, 47
  theory of comparative advantage and, 105–106
  U.S./Israeli Declaration of Trade in Services on access to, 177
Medical services
  consumer purchase of imports in, 6
  export purchase by foreign customers and local production and distribution of, 13
Middle managers, and business services, 51
Monopolies
  barriers to trade in services and 143–144
  General Agreement on Trade in Services and, 224–225
  global economic integration and, 40
  telecommunications and, 40, 253–254
  theory of comparative advantage and, 108–110
  tourism industry and, 252
  trade in services and, 163–165, 171
  U.S./Israeli Declaration of Trade in Services on, 178
Most favored nation (MFN) principle
  conditional, 154, 222, 283–286
  General Agreement on Trade in Services and, 207, 221–223, 277–283
  multilateral trade negotiations and, 159
  trade policy and, 153–154
Multilateral trade negotiations
  developing countries and, 204–205

349

Subject Index

General Agreement on Tariffs and
 Trade (GATT) on, 158–159
liberalization of trade and, 200–202
sectoral approach to, 203–204
Multinational corporations
 business services and, 52–53
 centralized production of service
  inputs and, 10–11
 economic development and, 119–121
 gains from trade in services and,
  115–116
 global economic integration and, 40
 international trade in services and,
  20–23
 limitations of, 21–22
 professional services under General
  Agreement on Trade in Services and,
  267
 purchase of imports by, 10–11
 trade in services definitions and, 82–83

National Association of Architectural
 Review Boards, 285
National income
 consumer purchase of imported
  services and, 7–8
 theory of comparative advantage and,
  96–97
 trade in services definitions and,
  75–76, 76–77, 79
National sales offices, and foreign
 companies, 13–14
National treatment principle
 conditional most favored nation status
  and, 222
 General Agreement on Tariffs and
  Trade (GATT) and, 88, 216–218
 trade policy and, 154
 U.S./Canadian Free Trade Agreement
  and, 184
 U.S./Israeli Declaration of Trade in
  Services and, 177
National wealth, and economic gain
 calculation, 98
Navigation Act, 93
Networks
 global economic activity and, 47–48
 see also Information and information
  services

Nondiscrimination principle
 trade policy with, 153–154
U.S./Canadian Free Trade Agreement
 and, 185

Office of Technology Assessment (OTA),
 49–50, 58 n.1, 273 n.2
Office of the U.S. Trade Representative
 (USTR), 309, 310, 311, 322 n.2
 Inventory of Barriers to Trade in
  Services of, 130, 137, 138, 139, 140,
  316
 U.S./Israeli Declaration of Trade in
  Services and, 181
Offshore banking activities, 269
Orderly adjustment principle, and trade
 policy, 154–155
Organization for Economic Cooperation
 and Development (OECD), 52–53, 242,
 297–299
 Declaration on International Data
  Flows of, 168, 233
 General Agreement on Tariffs and
  Trade (GATT) and, 191–192
 study of trade in services of, 314–318
 trade in services negotiations and, 299,
  300, 303, 304, 308, 309

Pan American Airways, 299–300
Partnerships with local businesses, and
 exports, 14
Peat, Marwick, Mitchell, 131, 137
Personal computers, 56
Policy, see Public policy issues; Trade
 policy
Press, and trade in services, 82–83
Price Waterhouse, 131, 137, 138, 139
Privacy, and trade policy in services, 83
Product differentiation, and trade policy,
 99, 100
Productivity
 data collection issue for services and,
  63–64
 perception of service jobs and, 60–62
Professional services
 conditional most favored nation (MFN)
  status and, 285
 General Agreement on Trade in
  Services and, 267–269

350

Subject Index

Protectionist policies, and economic development, 121–122
Public opinion, and service workers, 59–60
Public policy issues
  descriptive theories of international trade and, 98–100
  economic development and, 121–122
  economic issues in, 38
  global economic integration and, 40–41
  government regulation of services and, 23–24
  normative theories of international trade and, 96–98
  trade deficit and, 65–66
  trade in services definitions and, 79–88
  see also Trade policy
Public service monopolies, *see* Monopolies
Public utility and trade in services definitions, 85–86
Public utility services, international agreements on, 163–164

Quality of life, and public policy issues, 24

Real estate industry, 22
Reciprocity principle
  General Agreement on Trade in Services and, 221–224
  trade policy and, 153
Regulatory policy, *see* Government regulation
Representative offices, and export sales, 15–16
Resident, definition of, 76
Retail banking, 270
Retail businesses
  consumer services and, 55
  information revolution and networks and, 47–48
  international trade in, 56
  local companies and exports and, 14
  multinational corporations in, 22
  purchase of imports and, 9
Rey Group, 297, 298

Sales offices, and foreign companies, 13–14
Scale economies, *see* Economies of scale
Service jobs
  Adam Smith on, 60–61
  categories of, 41–42
  consumption patterns and, 64–65
  data collection issues for, 63–64, 69–70
  domestic production and domestic consumption of, 65–66
  government policies on, 70–71
  growth of, 41–42
  information revolution and, 42–45, 62
  international flow of money and, 68–69
  new economy and, 42–44
  percentage distribution of employment in, 42, 45 (table)
  policy issues and, 59
  postindustrial economy and, 62–67
  productivity of, 60–62
  public perception of, 59–60
  stream of services used to produce, 66–67
  trade in, 67–70
  U.S. employment by sector in, 42, 43–44 (table)
  U.S. trade deficit and, 65–66
  see also Business services; Consumer services
Shipping, *see* Transportation and transportation services
Social costs and benefits of trade in services, 112–114
Specialization
  business services and, 49, 54
  cost of services and, 39
  decision to buy services abroad and, 17
  historical perspective on trade in services and, 39
  multinational corporations and, 22
  nonmarket costs of, 113
  purchase of imports and, 9
Standards Code, General Agreement on Tariffs and Trade (GATT), 219, 230, 304
State government, *see* Government

351

Subject Index

Statistics
 cash, insurance, and freight (CIF) method of valuing in, 69
 data collection issue for services and 63–64
 international trade in services and, 69–70, 95
 trade in services definitions and, 76–78
Stock brokerage
 information revolution and, 47
 multinational corporations in, 22
Subsidies
 exports and, 97
 General Agreement on Trade in Services on, 226–227
Subsidies Code, General Agreement on Tariffs and Trade (GATT), 304
Suppliers
 barriers to trade in services and, 133, 137–139
 cash, insurance, and freight (CIF) method of valuing, 69
 competition among, 107–108
 export sales and home country of, 15–16
 General Agreement on Trade in Services on, 215
 public service monopolies and, 164
 purchase of imports and, 9
 telecommunications and, 252–255
Support services
 business services and, 50
 descriptive model of international trade in services and, 29–30
 global economic integration and, 40
 international trade in services and, 18–19
 trade in services definitions and, 85–86
Sweden, banking regulation in, 34

Tariffs
 barriers to trade in services and, 129
 General Agreement on Trade in Services and, 207, 229, 281
 market principle and, 152
Taxation
 barriers to trade in services and, 131, 138

theory of comparative advantage and, 97
Technology leadership, and trade policy, 99, 100
Telecommunications
 competition and, 253–254
 conditional most favored nation (MFN) status and, 284
 deregulation of, 57, 109–110
 economies of scale and competition and, 109–110
 General Agreement on Trade in Services and, 253–258, 284
 global economic integration and, 40
 monopolies and, 253–254
 multinational corporations in, 22–23
 suppliers and, 254–255
 U.S./Israeli Declaration of Trade in Services on, 182–183
 see also Communication and communication services
Theory of comparative advantage, 96–97, 98–99
 application to trade in services of, 100–114
 competition among buyers and, 108–109
 competition among suppliers and, 105–108
 development of, 91–92
 empirical investigations of, 122–123
 investment in foreign facilities and, 104
 liberalization of trade policy and, 200
 questions addressed in, 101
 theoretical issues in, 102–105
 trade in goods and, 104–105
Tokyo Round, General Agreement on Tariffs and Trade (GATT), 159, 191, 219, 299, 301–305
Tourism
 barriers to trade in, 250
 consumer purchase of imports and, 6, 7
 General Agreement on Trade in Services and, 249–252
 international trade in services and, 20
 local agents in, 13
 monopolies and, 252

Subject Index

representative offices for export sales in, 16
U.S./Israeli Declaration of Trade in Services on, 182–183
see also Travel
Trade Act of 1974, 191, 198, 299, 300–301
Trade deficit, and services employment, 65–66
Trade in goods
 theory of comparative advantage and, 104–105
 trade in services and, 18–19
 Uruguay Declaration and, 197–199
Trade in services
 barriers to, *see* Barriers to trade in services
 competitiveness in, 116–117
 consequences of invisibilty of, 30–34
 culture and, 82–83, 114
 definitions of, 75–80
 developing countries and, 119–121
 dynamic gains from, 115–116
 dynamic losses from, 116–119
 economic development and, 119–122
 examples of, 3–5
 finance and, 83–84
 free on board (FOB) method of valuing, 86
 free trade arguments and, 91–92
 goods and, 84–85
 government trade statistics and, 77–78
 immigration and, 81–82
 infant industry principle in, 117–118
 international trade theory and, 91–124
 investment and, 87–88
 invisibility of, 94
 national income accounting and, 75–76, 76–77
 nonmarket social costs and benefits and, 112–114
 perceptions of range of, 1–2
 policy debate over definition of, 80–88
 protectionist policies and, 121–122
 public policy issues in, 23–24, 78, 79–80
 rationale for, 103
 shared public utility concepts and, 85–86
 theory of comparative advantage and, 100–114
 trade in goods and, 104–105
 use of term, 1–2
 see also International trade in services
Trade policy
 application to services of, 147–174
 barriers to trade in services and, 131
 bilateral discussions and negotiations of, 156–158
 consultation principle and, 155–156
 corporate culture and, 160
 dispute settlement principle and, 156
 domestic regulation and, 161–163
 economic theory and, 151–152
 existing trade policies and, 160–161
 extending framework to trade in services of, 160–169
 foreign investment and, 168–169
 General Agreement on Trade in Services and, 247–249
 goals and tools of, 149–160
 immigration and, 166–167
 information data flows and, 167–168
 institutions and, 156–159
 international flows of people, information, money, and goods and, 165–168
 legitimacy of domestic regulation principle and, 154
 market principles and, 152–153
 monetary flows and, 167
 most favored nation (MFN) principle and, 153–154, 159
 multilateral negotiations of, 158–159
 national treatment principle and, 154
 nondiscrimination principle and, 153–154
 orderly adjustment principle and, 154–155
 political economy of trade and, 155–156
 public service monopolies and, 163–165
 reciprocity principle and, 153
 regulatory policy related to, 169–173
 transparency principle and, 155
 see also Public policy issues

353

Subject Index

Trade Policy Research Center, 122, 310
Training, nonmarket benefits of, 112
Transborder data flows, and barriers to trade in services, 140
Transparency principle, and trade policy, 155
Transportation and transportation services
  barriers to trade in services and, 144
  business purchase of imports and, 10
  business services and, 49
  cash, insurance, and freight (CIF) method of valuing, 69, 85–86
  competition and, 108–109, 122–123
  data processing and information services and, 253
  deregulation of, 57
  descriptive model of international trade in services and, 28–30
  economies of scale and competition and, 109–110
  free on board (FOB) method of valuing, 86
  General Agreement on Trade in Services and, 226
  global economic integration and, 40
  historical perspective on trade in services and, 39
  insurance industry and, 264
  international trade in services and, 71
  maritime transport under General Agreement on Trade in Services and, 260–263, 284–285
  monopoly in, 108–110
  production of services and, 67
  representative offices for export sales in, 16
  trade in services definitions and, 85–86
  world economy and international trade in services and, 18
Travel
  barriers to trade in services and restrictions to, 134
  consumer purchase of imports and, 6, 7
  descriptive model of international trade in services and, 28–30
  global economic integration and, 39
  international trade in services and, 20
  production of services and, 67–68

representative offices for export sales in, 16
  see also Tourism
United Nations Conference on Trade and Development (UNCTAD) Liner Code, 261, 261–263
U.S./Canadian Free Trade Agreement, 183–186
  lessons learned from, 185–186
  provisions of, 184–18
U.S. Chamber of Commerce, 300
U.S./Israeli Declaration of Trade in Services with, 176–183
  contents of, 177–179
  issues addressed during negotiations of 179–181
  sectoral annotations under, 182–183
U.S. Trade Representative, see Office of the U.S. Trade Representative (USTR)
University of Chicago Legal Forum, 268
Uruguay Declaration, 193–199
  General Agreement on Trade in Services framework under, 205, 237, 241
  Negotiations on Trade in Services under, 193–194
  nontrade objectives of, 196–197
  objectives of trade negotiations in, 194–196
Uruguay Round, General Agreement on Tariffs and Trade (GATT), xiv, 89 n.8, 159, 167, 191, 192, 237, 295
USTR, see Office of the U.S. Trade Representative (USTR)

Vendors
  business services from, 53–54
  multinational corporations and, 21
  purchase of imports and, 9
Visas
  trade in services and, 81,
  trade policy and, 165, 173
  U.S./Canadian Free Trade Agreement on, 185

White-collar workers
  manufacturing purchase of imports and, 8
  production of services and, 66

354

U.S./Canadian Free Trade Agreement on, 185
Wolf and Company, 303, 305
Work permits, and barriers to trade in services, 140–141

World Bank, 122
World economy, *see* International economy

ABOUT THE AUTHOR

Geza Feketekuty, is counselor to the U.S. Trade Representative. Since 1976 he has been with the Office of the U.S. Trade Representative, where he develops and coordinates U.S. trade policy, including trade in services. He played a key role in coordinating U.S. participation in the Tokyo Round of Multilateral Trade Negotiations and in planning the next round of multilateral trade negotiations.

He was formerly senior staff economist for international finance and trade with the Council of Economic Advisers and an economist and budget examiner with the Office of Management and Budget. He has also been an instructor in economics at Princeton, a visiting professor at Cornell University, and an adjunct professor at the School of Advanced International Studies of Johns Hopkins University.

A graduate of Columbia University and Princeton, Mr. Feketekuty recently completed the Advanced Management Program at the Harvard Business School. From 1962 to 1966 he was editor in chief of *The American Economist*.